James Reason is a professor of psychology. In addition to extensive research in psychology, he has written several books and articles.

Klara Mycielska is a research psychologist and free-lance translator.

ABSENT-MINDED?

The Psychology of Mental Lapses
and Everyday Errors

James Reason
Klara Mycielska

A SPECTRUM BOOK

Prentice-Hall, Inc., Englewood Cliffs, N.J. 07632

Library of Congress Cataloging in Publication Data

Reason, J. T.
    Absent-minded? the psychology of mental lapses and everyday errors.

    A Spectrum Book
    Includes bibliographical references and index.
        1. Memory.   2. Attention.   3. Selectivity (Psychology)
4. Errors—Psychological aspects.   I. Mycielska, Klara.   III. Title.
BF371.R325   153.1'2   82-5424
ISBN 0-13-001743-4   AACR2
ISBN 0-13-001735-3 (pbk.)

10   9   8   7   6   5   4   3   2   1

ISBN 0-13-001743-4

ISBN 0-13-001735-3 {PBK.}

Editorial/production supervision by Suse L. Cioffi
Cover illustration by Jeannette Jacobs
Manufacturing buyer: Cathie Lenard

This Spectrum Book can be made available to businesses and organizations
at a special discount when ordered in large quantities.
For more information contact: Prentice-Hall, Inc., General Publishing Division,
Special Sales, Englewood Cliffs, NJ 07632.

PRENTICE-HALL INTERNATIONAL, INC. *(London)*
PRENTICE-HALL OF AUSTRALIA PTY. LIMITED *(Sydney)*
PRENTICE-HALL OF CANADA, INC. *(Toronto)*
PRENTICE-HALL OF INDIA PRIVATE LIMITED *(New Delhi)*
PRENTICE-HALL OF JAPAN, INC. *(Tokyo)*
PRENTICE-HALL OF SOUTHEAST ASIA PTE. *(Singapore)*
WHITEHALL BOOKS LIMITED *(Wellington, New Zealand)*

To Wanda Mycielska

CONTENTS

Acknowledgments   ix

chapter one   Slips of the Mind: Why Bother with Them?   1

chapter two   The Hallmarks of the
Absent-Minded Slip   16

chapter three   The Autopilots of Everyday Life   38

chapter four   Slips of Habit   62

chapter five   Recognition Failures   89

chapter six   Memory Blocks   112

chapter seven   Losing Track of Past Actions: Repetitions
and Omissions   134

chapter eight   Dismembered Demons: Blends and
Spoonerisms   158

chapter nine   The Freudian Slip Revisited   172 *chapter ten*   Catastrophic Lapses   85

chapter eleven   Attention and Control   218

appendix i   The Error Proneness Questionnaire   244

appendix ii   Tabulated Results from the Extended
                     Diary Study   256

                     Index 259

ACKNOWLEDGMENTS

We would like to thank all those whose comments, suggestions, and encouragement proved so valuable in the preparation of this book. Among these, we owe a particular debt to Donald and Margaret Broadbent, John Churcher, Alan Forbes, Sebastian Halliday, John Harris, Graham Hitch, Tony Marcel, Andrew Mayes, Neville Moray, Donald Norman, Patrick Rabbitt, and Tim Shallice. Very special thanks are due to Rea Reason who not only read each chapter carefully and constructively as it was written, but also pointed out the relevance of hypnosis to the theoretical ideas advanced in the book; to Deborah Lucas for collecting and providing the original research material on memory blocks discussed in Chapter 6, and for the transcripts of her interviews with actors included in Chapter 7; to Alan Fish for running the computer analyses of the data and for helping to make sense of them; to Laura Miles for typing the manuscript and for eliminating many stylistic inconsistencies in the process; and to Terry Evans and Peter Harforth for preparing the illustrations. We would also like to express our warm gratitude to all the many people who kept diaries, completed questionnaires, and sent us letters concerning their everyday slips and lapses. Without their interest, patience, and frank admissions of human falibility there would have been nothing to write. Finally, we gratefully acknowledge the support of the Social Science Research Council (Research Grant No. HR/6290) that funded the greater part of this work.

chapter one
SLIPS OF THE MIND: WHY BOTHER WITH THEM?

Struggling to open a friend's front door with your own key; stepping into the bathtub with your socks on; failing to recall the name of someone you have known for several years; squeezing shaving cream on to the toothbrush; putting oatmeal into the washing machine; trying to drive away without turning on the ignition; pouring a second kettle of water into a pot of freshly made tea; saying "Thank you" to a stamp machine ... the list goes on, but you will have already recognized the species. We have all experienced occasions when we suddenly become aware that our minds have been "absent" from the task in hand so that our words or actions no longer run according to plan. Similarly, we have all known times when our minds go blank, and we are unable to retrieve from memory something we know to be there, lurking just beyond the reach of consciousness. Our lives are strewn with such trivial and inconsequential lapses— what Freud has called "the refuse of the phenomenal world,"[1] or, in a more daunting phase, *the psychopathology of everyday life.*[2]

For the most part, these commonplace slips and lapses cause us little more than momentary embarrassment. They may occasionally

[1]Sigmund Freud, *Introductory Lectures on Psychoanalysis*, trans. Joan Riviere (London: George Allen & Unwin Ltd., 1922), p. 20. Used by permission of Liveright Publishing Corporation and George Allen & Unwin (Publishers) Ltd.
[2]Sigmund Freud, *The Psychopathology of Everyday Life*, trans. Alan Tyson (Middlesex, England: Penguin Books Ltd., 1975).

1

disconcert us but do not bother us unduly. So why bother with them? What is to be gained from rooting around in the contents of this psychological dustbin, particularly when some believe that Freud has already taken the choicest pickings?

Leaving aside the question of whether he left us anything worth finding, Freud himself provided an excellent reason for studying these apparent trivia. He wrote: "In scientific work it is more profitable to take up whatever lies before one whenever a path towards its exploration presents itself. And then, if one carries it through thoroughly, one . . . may find, even in the course of such humble labor, a road to the study of the great problems."[3] If for no better reason, absent-minded errors are worth studying because they are there, and because they occur quite literally under our noses. As Freud was the first to point out, these slips give every indication of being systematic rather than random in their origin. As such, they are amenable to meaningful classification and interpretation. They are, in short, "windows to the mind."

For Freud, the truly great problem was the unconscious mind—to which, he believed, a close study of slips of the tongue and bungled actions would give him privileged access. For contemporary psychologists, however, the priorities are somewhat different. Over the past twenty years or so, a major concern of psychology has been with the way the brain processes information and exercises its various control functions. In other words, the emphasis has shifted to the mechanics of such cognitive processes as perceiving, remembering, thinking, attending, and the like, and away from the underlying forces to which, Freud would argue, they are ultimately subservient. Such a change presents new "great problems" that can be approached usefully via a fresh examination of these everyday slips and lapses. In our case, there are two major issues, the one of practical and the other of theoretical significance.

THE ACCIDENT PROBLEM

The first of these great problems, and the one that initially prompted our interest in mental lapses, is that of accidents. A compelling reason for studying the normally banal slips of everyday life is

[3]Sigmund Freud, *Introductory Lectures on Psychoanalysis*, p. 21.

that they provide us with relatively accessible and painless examples of accidental behavior in general.

Catastrophic accidents are comparatively rare and, by definition, largely unpredictable events, hence they are difficult to study scientifically. In addition, there is the problem that when we are faced with a much publicized disaster like an aircraft accident, we have a natural inclination, particularly when some kind of human error is implicated, to believe that it could have occurred only as the result of some equally monumental blunder. Thus, there is a tendency for the consequences of an accident to color and even distort our perception of the events that led up to it. But a careful consideration of the reports of major accidents shows that this is not necessarily the case. Quite often, the contributing errors are relatively trifling things that in more forgiving circumstances would pass without significance.

One of the major conceptual problems in accident research is the confusion that exists between the erroneous act and its consequences. An accident has been described most succinctly as "an error with sad consequences."[4] In other words, an accident is defined not only by the occurrence of some chance or erroneous event but also by the fact that it produces damaging or injurious results. But unless we adopt the strict Freudian line that errors and also their foreseeable consequences are unconsciously motivated, we have no good reason to suppose any purely *psychological* connection between the error and its outcome. Should we inadvertently switch on the toaster when we meant to turn on the electric coffeepot, the result is mildly inconvenient, but no more than this. Should precisely the same *kind* of mistake occur on the flight deck of a large passenger aircraft or in the control room of a nuclear power plant, the results can be and sometimes are catastrophic. The difference lies not in the nature of the error, but the extent to which its circumstances of occurrence will penalize it. If, as we would wish to argue here, errors "with sad consequences" are simply a subset of the total human error population, and one that is distinguished by circumstantial rather than psychological considerations, then an accident researcher would be well advised to extend the scope of an investigation to include the full range of human errors, irrespective of their consequences.

[4]A.B. Cherns in *Society: Problems and Methods of Study*, ed. A.T. Welford (London: Routledge and Keegan Paul, 1962, p. 162).

Shown in Table 1.1 are the details of a number of private aircraft accidents in which pilot error was implicated. Examination of the errors indicated that they display many of the characteristics of absent-minded slips in that they involve the apparently unintentional execution of some well-established control actions (or their omission). The resemblance between these pilot errors and everyday absent-minded slips does not by itself constitute an explanation for these accidents, but it does suggest we could learn a good deal more about catastrophic errors from a closer scrutiny of the more mundane slips of daily life.

UNDERSTANDING COGNITIVE PROCESSES

The second major reason for studying mental lapses is for what they can tell us about the mental processes that control our words and actions, especially those that require very little in the way of conscious attention to form and guide them. A clear lead in this direction was given by linguists interested in the mechanisms underlying language production. For nearly a hundred years now, linguists and others have been recording, classifying, and analyzing slips of the tongue and pen. The rationale for this kind of investigation was well expressed by Bawden in 1900:

> Now just as little irregularities in the road enable one accustomed to it to make his way in the dark, so to the student of human nature little *inadvertencies of expression, aberrations in speech, lapses of thought, confusions of ideas, hitches* or *slips* in speaking or writing are sometimes most useful and unerring guides in the understanding of mental process. Neglected trifles are sometimes suggestive of most fruitful problems for research.[5]

Subsequent studies, particularly over the last ten years, have shown this view to be well founded.[6] By working backwards from small and

[5]H. Heath Bawden, "A study of lapses." *Psychological Review: Monograph Supplements* 3 (1900), 1–22, p. 5.
[6]V.A. Fromkin (ed.) *Speech Errors as Linguistic Evidence* (The Hague: Mouton, 1973). V.A. Fromkin (ed.) *Errors in Linguistic Performance* (New York: Academic Press, 1980, pp. 11–243).

Table 1.1 Details of Aircraft Accidents in Which the Errors Resembled Absent-Minded Behavior

Date & Place	Aircraft Type	Nature of Accident/Incident	Contributing Factors*
22/6/55 London Airport (CAP 133)	Dove (G-ALTM)	Crash following power failure.	Pilot shut down port engine instead of the starboard one that was developing trouble.
23/7/55 New Forest (CAP 136)	Dove (G-AKSK)	Crash following power failure.	Pilot mistakenly shut down port engine instead of the starboard engine that had developed a serious mechanical fault.
20/1/56 Blackbushe Airport (CAP 138)	Viscount (G-AMOM)	Crash shortly after take-off on training flight.	Error by training captain who operated No. 3 high pressure cock lever instead of No. 4 when simulating a failure of No. 4 engine during take-off. This resulted in loss of all power from both starboard engines at a critical point of take-off.
28/4/58 Tarbolton Ayrshire (CAP 154)	Viscount (G-AORC)	Aircraft flew into high ground.	Captain misread altimeter: read 4,500 as 14,500 ft. and perpetuated the error of 10,000 ft. until aircraft crashed 5 minutes later.
19/9/61 Cloghran, Co. Dublin (CAP 190)	Skymaster (G-ARJY)	Landing approach abandoned and satisfactory emergency landing made.	Incorrect management of fuel system by crew that resulted in partial loss of power and control.
27/4/63 Gloucester (CAP 203)	Varsity (G-APAZ)	Aircraft crashed during asymmetric approach and overshoot exercises with port propeller feathered.	Pilot selected starboard engine IDLE CUT-OFF switch to CUT OFF instead of the port engine switch to the RUN position when attempting to restart port engine.

5

Table 1.1 (*continued*)

Date & Place	Aircraft Type	Nature of Accident/Incident	Contributoring Factors*
2/2/64 Nairobi Airport (CAP 224)	Comet (G-APDL)	Aircraft touched down 9 miles from runway—climbed away and landed alright.	Altimeter incorrectly set resulting in instrument reading 3,000 ft. too high. Essential checks were not carried out satisfactorily.
1/9/66 Ljubljana, Yugoslavia (CAP 303)	Britannia (G-ANBB)	Aircraft crashed short of runway on landing approach.	Captain did not set altimeter to local airport barometric pressure in accordance with information passed by Air Traffic Control. Error was overlooked in check procedure.
10/1/67 Hamble (CAP 306)	Piper Apache (G-ASDH)	Port engine failed to respond when overshooting from a simulated single engine approach and hit obstructions.	Instructor probably omitted to return the mixture control lever of port engine to FULL-RICH-ON position when propeller was unfeathered during approach.
4/6/67 Stockport, Cheshire (CAP 302)	Argonaut (G-ALHG)	Aircraft crashed on landing approach.	Fuel starvation due to inadvertent fuel transfer in flight resulting in loss of power to both starboard engines.
23/12/67 Luton Airport (CAP 326)	HS 125 (G-AUGW)	Crash following practice engine failure after take-off.	Immediately following close of one thrust lever to simulate engine failure, the other engine was inadvertently shut down.

14/1/69 Italy (CAP 347)	BAC 1-11 (G-ASJJ)	Crash immediately after take-off.	Failure in No. 2 engine, crew closed throttle of No. 1 engine in error. Failed to recognize their mistake and also were not aware that thrust of No. 2 engine had been reduced after an inadvertent displacement of throttle control.
23/12/69 Over Surrey (CAAR 4/71)	Boeing (4X-ABB)	An air miss occurred.	Captain of Boeing failed to reset his altimeter at transition altitude.
20/3/70 Turnhouse Airport Edinburgh (CAAR 9/72)	HS 125 (G-AXPS)	Crash during simulated engine failure take-off.	Application of incorrect rudder following simulated engine failure. Suggested that pilot unconsciously set himself for "failure" of specific engine.
18/6/72 Newbury (CAAR 11/73)	Piper Twin Comanche (G-ASRN)	Crashed after power loss in one engine during initial climb.	Probably due to misalignment of engine fuel selector cock.
29/6/72 Blackpool Airport (CAAR 15/73)	Hausa (O-CASY)	Aircraft failed to leave runway during take-off.	Elevator gust lock had not been removed during preflight checks. Take-off was abandoned at too high a speed.

*The information in this table is taken from a number of Accident Investigation Branch, Civil Aviation Authority reports published by Her Majesty's Stationery Office, London. The report numbers are given in parentheses in the first column. The aircraft's registration letters are given in the second column.

often insignificant anomalies in verbal output, modern psycholinguists have discovered a great deal about the underlying structure
and organization of speech production. As one psycholinguist put it:

> Speech errors place strong constraints on theories of speech
> production, since an adequate model of normal speech must also
> allow for these errors, as does the actual speech production
> system. Conversely, an adequate explanation of speech errors
> must incorporate the general principles of normal speech pro-
> duction, in the sense that an explanation of the backfiring of an
> automobile engine must incorporate the general principles of
> internal combustion.[7]

Just as a careful analysis of slips of the tongue and pen can allow us to
make useful theoretical inferences about the language system, so also
can a study of their nonverbal counterparts, the slips of action, provide
important clues about the organization of human performance and
the role of consciousness in the guidance of action. Surprisingly,
psychologists (with some notable exceptions) have tended to neglect
these errors until quite recently. The reasons for this disregard are
many and complex. But perhaps the most important is the historical
fact that for approximately 40 years, from 1920 to around 1960,
psychology lacked the climate in which such a venture could florish.
The essential feature of these errors, namely the divergence of action
from intention, had little or no credibility within two of the major
psychological traditions of the time. The behaviorists would not
willingly admit of the intention, at least not as something having any
theoretical utility; and the psychoanalysts would deny the deviation,
in keeping with Freud's view that erroneous actions are indicative of
some unconscious need or purpose.

TOWARD A DEFINITION OF
HUMAN ERROR

Needs, Intentions, and Plans

Stop and think for a moment. What are you going to be doing
tomorrow? Next week? In six months' time? Next year? Two years
hence? Have you any idea? It is more than likely that you have,

---

[7]D.G. Mackay, "Complexity in output systems: Evidence from behavioral
hybrids." *American Journal of Psychology*, 86 (1973), pp. 785–806.

although as the period in question extends further into the future your answers will become increasingly more vague and uncertain. Much of what occupies our minds concerns what lies ahead, with the setting of objectives and with thinking about the means to achieve them. In short, a large part of our mental life is taken up with the making and modifying of plans. These are central to our understanding of error.

Let us take an imaginary example of short-term planning as our starting point:

> It's nearly twelve o'clock and I'm hungry. But I'm supposed to be on a diet. To hell with the diet, it's been a wretched morning and I feel like treating myself to a decent lunch. Do I want to eat French, Italian, or Chinese? Italian—I have a yearning for a large plate of spaghetti carbonara. Shall I go to Luigi's or La Dolce Vita? Luigi's—it's further away, but the parking is easier. What's the best way to get there? . . . and so on.

Although not an essential precondition, this plan of action begins, commonly enough, with the *need* to alleviate a state of tension, created in this case by a combination of hunger pangs and feelings of dissatisfaction with the frustrating morning. There are many possible ways of achieving this, but a specific *intention* is quickly formed to have a good lunch. Again, such a *goal* could be achieved by a variety of means, but one particular *plan* is favored—to eat spaghetti at Luigi's. Having made this *decision*, it only remains to choose and assemble the *action sequences* that will take our man to Luigi's by the most convenient route and for the appointed time.

The plan at this stage consists of a stated aim and a rough outline of the actions necessary to achieve it. Notice that the planner does not have to fill in the small print of each detailed operation. There is no need, for example, to instruct himself to get up from his desk, go through the door, turn right along the corridor, down two flights of stairs, out of the front door and into the parking lot . . . , etc. These largely automatic subroutines are implicit in the jottings already made on the mental scratchpad. They are manipulated in thinking by a series of verbal tags and mental images. The more we engage in relatively fixed sequences of actions, the fewer the number of "tags" required to specify them in our planning. In other words, repetition reduces the number of low level control statements necessary to guide our behavior.

Plans Have Many Levels

This plan moves through a series of levels, each involving knowledge-laden images of the world and successive choices: (1) *"I need food and the comfort it provides."* (2) *"Shall I act on this need, or not?"* (3) *"Yes, my craving for a good lunch is stronger than my will to follow my diet."* (4) *"So what do I want?"* (5) *"I have a compelling image of a large plate of spaghetti carbonara. I can taste the creamy sauce, and I can feel it sitting warm in my stomach."* (6) *"Where shall I go?"* And so on.

In their influential book, *Plans and the Structure of Behavior*, (New York: Holt, Rinehart and Winston, 1960), George Miller, Eugene Galanter, and Karl Pribram emphasized the stratified nature of human plans. They defined a *plan* as "... any hierarchical process in the organism that can control the order in which a sequence of operations is to be performed." They also argued that a plan is like a computer program, so long as that program is hierarchically organized.[8]

We Have Many Plans

In the very broadest sense, we can say that our actions are in error when they fail to achieve the objectives of our current plan. But here we run into a problem, as our imaginary example points out. Let us assume that our self-indulgent planner carries out the actions exactly as intended. He arrives at Luigi's without a hitch, avoids the noon rush, is quickly served, and consumes a vastly satisfying heap of spaghetti carbonara and sags replete in his chair. What then? In the sense that he has fulfilled his plan to the letter, his actions could hardly be said to be in error. But what about his long-term plan to lose weight? Viewed from that perspective, his impulsively conceived, yet successfully executed short-term plan to consume a calory-laden dish is clearly a mistake.

The point we are making is that our lives are governed by many plans; some of our own making, others imposed upon us, all operating at various levels and over widely differing timespans. Sometimes they nest together in close harmony, with subordinate plans fulfilling the intermediate goals set by larger plans. But at other times they

[8]G.A. Miller, E. Galanter, and K. Pribram, *Plans and the Structure of Behavior* (New York: Holt, Rinehart and Winston, 1960), p. 16.

conflict, as we have seen in our example. This host of coexisting and sometimes conflicting plans would make even a working definition of human error beyond our reach were it not for two built-in limitations to human performance. First, our physical capacity to turn personal plans into action is restricted: We can only be in one place at any time carrying out one particular set of actions. Second, we possess only a limited mental capacity for executing plans. Although there may be many stored plans competing for our attention, usually only one of them is maximally active at any moment.

Plans, Actions, and Consequences

Error, as we have seen, is not an easy notion to pin down. If we look for its meaning in the dictionary, we are sent "... on a semantic circular tour through other terms such as mistake, fault, defect and back to error again."[9] The fact that dictionaries yield synonyms rather than a definition suggests that the notion of error is something fundamental and irreducible. For our present purposes, we need, nevertheless, to probe more deeply into error's psychological meaning.

Error is intimately bound up with notions like intention, goal, and plan. The success or failure of our actions can only be judged by the extent to which they achieve, or are on the way to achieving, their planned consequences. It would seem, therefore, that any definition of error must incorporate three concepts: plans, actions, and consequences. The relationship between these three is shown in Fig. 1.1.

Plans, as mentioned earlier, govern the nature, order, and timescale of a sequence of actions, either overt or covert, leading to a particular outcome or goal. They consist of shorthand mental representations of both the actions and their likely consequences. This is shown in Figure 1.1 by the two arrows labeled *feedforward*. The two *feedback* arrows complete the cycle and indicate that future actions and the plans that organize them are likely to be modified by the outcomes of previous plans and actions.

Using this simple framework, we can construct the following

---

[9]W.T. Singleton, "Theoretical approaches to human error." *Ergonomics*, 16(1973), 727–737.

Figure 1.1   The Relationship Between Plans, Actions, and Consequences

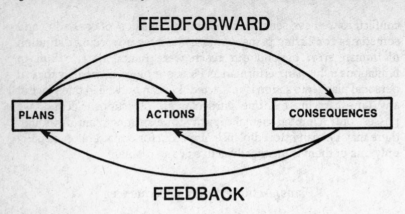

preliminary definition: An error occurs when a planned action fails to achieve its desired consequences. From this definition, and on purely logical grounds, we can distinguish four possible sequences of actions and consequences.

Sequence A: The actions proceed as planned and achieve the desired consequences.
Sequence B: The actions proceed as planned but fail to achieve the desired consequences.
Sequence C: The actions do not proceed as planned, but nevertheless achieve the desired consequences.
Sequence D: The actions do not proceed according to plan and fail to achieve the desired consequences.

Sequence A seems fairly straightforward: We make an adequate plan, carry out the intended actions, and achieve the desired goal. But are we justified in assuming that such a sequence always implies an adequate plan? Consider the following situation which, though improbable, is not impossible. You wish to be rid of someone. Although you know yourself to be the world's worst shot, you decide to dispose of your intended victim with a gun. You point your wavering weapon and pull the trigger. By chance, it so happens that the gun is on target when the firing pin hits the cartridge, and your purpose is achieved. But considering your known deficiencies as a marksman, this mode of assassination could hardly be rated as a good plan despite its successful outcome.

Similar involvements of either happy or unhappy chance are

12

also possible in the other three sequences. Although Sequence B is most likely to occur as the consequences of bad planning, we cannot always blame the plan. Recently, for example, there was the case of the Iranian businessman who took a plane to the United States in order to be reunited with his family living there. His aircraft landed on time, his immigration documents were in order, but he was not admitted into the country because President Carter had severed diplomatic relations with Iran while he was in flight. Although relations between the United States and Iran were far from cordial in the period prior to his departure from Teheran, he could hardly have foreseen that the president would take that particular drastic step at that moment in time. Here, the desired outcome of entering the United States was thwarted not by bad planning, but by a presidential decision that lay outside his powers either to control or to anticipate.

Common sense suggests that Sequence C is the most improbable of the four. Yet, by a stretch of the imagination, it is still possible to conceive of ways in which it could occur. A golfer intends to make a chip shot onto the green, placing the ball either in or as near to the hole as he can. He bungles the shot, the ball rises skyward, hits a passing bird, and drops into the hole. His intention is fulfilled even though his actions were not at all as planned.

Similarly, it is possible to find situations following Sequence D in which the actions, although deviating from the plan, could not in fairness be regarded as erroneous. The execution of our best-laid plans can be disturbed by a whole variety of "Acts of God" that are in no way foreseeable: being struck down by returning chunks of space debris, by runaway vehicles mounting the pavement, by a bottle thrown carelessly from a high building, and so on. In addition, our plans for a given time period can be superseded by more urgent ones. We intend to leave home for work, but smell gas. The fact that our subsequent actions deviate from the original plan does not make them in error. The mistake in this case would have been not to respond to this unexpected imperative.

A Working Definition of Error

Clearly, not all failures to attain a desired goal can be classed as errors. If the failure was due solely to the intervention of some chance or unforeseeable agency, it could not legitimately be called an error. By the same token, not all actions that bring about their intended consequences can be regarded as "nonerrors." In establishing the status of an error, therefore, we must distinguish it from both the unlucky and the lucky accident. Accordingly, we must modify our preliminary definition as follows. *An error occurs when a planned action fails to achieve its desired outcome, and when this failure cannot be attributed to the intervention of some chance occurrence.* Hereafter, we shall restrict our use of the term *error* to those failures that arise out of circumstances over which the individual might reasonably be expected to exercise some measure of control, and from actions for which he may be held personally responsible. The latter, of course, is primarily an issue for jurisprudence, and will not concern us further.

THE SCOPE OF THE BOOK

This book is entitled *Absent-Minded?*, yet the term *absent-minded* clearly leaves much to be desired, referring as it does to the absence of something that itself defies adequate definition. Before we can arrive at a more satisfactory label, we need to establish how these particular slips and lapses fit within the broader spectrum of human error. From our working definition, stated in the preceding section, it can be suggested that failures to achieve a desired outcome fall, very broadly, into two general categories.

1. *Errors of judgment and planning.* Where the actions go as planned, but the plan is inadequate.
2. *Actions-not-as-planned.* Where the plan is satisfactory, but the actions are not those intended.

Although we shall continue to use the term *absent-minded error* throughout the book, a more precise description of its contents would be "actions-not-as-planned." In other words, our principal focus will be upon the second category of error. Within this extensive class of mistakes, our main interest will be the interface between plans and actions. What prompts actions to depart from intentions? Can we detect any systematic patterns in the nature of these deviations? If so, what can they tell us about the underlying cognitive mechanisms?

Errors of judgment, bad planning, faulty decision-making, and other factors contributing to the first category of error, are, for the most part, outside the scope of this book.[10] Nor shall we dwell too long upon the *consequences* of errors. They are important to us only insofar as they constitute the criteria by which we recognize that a mistake has occurred.

SUMMARY

To conclude this introductory chapter, let us summarize the principal concerns of the book. Our emphasis throughout will be upon the commonplace mental lapses of everyday life as they appear in activities involving memory, thought, speech, writing, and actions in general. The reasons for studying these usually banal blunders are, firstly, that they can tell us something about the systematic determinants of human error which, in turn, may help us to limit its occurrence in the more unforgiving circumstances. Secondly, these everyday slips and lapses provide vital clues as to the mechanisms underlying the selection and guidance of skilled or habitual action. At an immediate level, however, they offer recognizable glimpses of flesh and blood people going about their real-life activities. These glimpses not only yield valuable insights into normal mental processes, they also help to bridge the formidable gap that still exists in contemporary psychology between theorizing based upon laboratory studies and the subjective experience of daily life.

[10]Peter Hall, *Great Planning Disasters* (London: Weidenfeld and Nicolson, 1980).

chapter two
THE HALLMARKS OF THE ABSENT–MINDED SLIP

Perhaps the most important distinguishing feature of absent-minded slips is that no matter how inappropriate or embarrassing they may be, these errors are nearly always instantly recognizable as belonging to our own personal repertoire of actions. We know them as our own. Obviously, they are not what we intended at that moment, but we can usually see in them a curious kind of logic, especially when we stop to reflect upon where the error was made, what it was we meant to do, and the kinds of activity we habitually carry out in those circumstances.

Our collection of absent-minded slips (taken predominantly from a British sample) indicates that act-wait-act-wait tasks like making tea are immensely productive of this kind of error. Yet certain types of mistake are never reported. We may omit to put tea in the pot, repeat the kettle boiling sequence unnecessarily, pour the tea into the sugar bowl; but is there anyone who has ever inadvertently blown down the spout of the teapot, or thrown a cup through the window, or tipped the tea over the contents of a cupboard? These are not outside the range of our behavioral possibilities; they simply do not belong in our mental library of available action programs, and hence do not occur as absent-minded slips.

Nor would we use the term *absent-minded* to describe the faltering efforts of a child struggling to make her first cup of tea. She would commit many errors: she would leave out steps in the sequence, put too much or too little tea in the pot, fill it with tepid rather than boiling water, spill things, and so on. These are the kind of blunders that any novice would make. The specific form they take is largely unpredictable, whereas for the absent-minded slip it is not. The novice's errors arise from a lack of competence, while the true hallmark of the absent-minded error is *misapplied competence*. The child has not yet mastered the necessary actions, but the mother, with her mind on other things, has total mastery of the task. Her problem, however, is that she has so many overlearned action sequences relating to the kitchen environment that the wrong one is likely to be called into play, or an action omitted because she has been "captured" by some later part of the task.

This brings us to our first point about absent-minded errors: They are a characteristic of highly skilled or habitual activities. In short, they are a problem for the expert, not the novice. Although this seems to run contrary to common sense, skills are things we acquire with much effort and practice in order to avoid making mistakes; and, of course, the expert does make fewer errors than the novice. However, it is not the *quantity* of errors we are concerned with, but their *type*. Although absent-minded errors are fairly rare occurrences when matched against the hit-and-miss mistakes of the learner, the probability of making such a slip actually increases with proficiency at a particular task. This makes them especially interesting to those wanting to understand how the mind controls our largely routine actions.

Another aspect of absent-minded errors that justifies our interest is that they are not bizarre or random events, determined exclusively by the idiosyncracies of those who commit them, or by the place and time in which they occur. Rather, they follow a clearly discernible pattern that is largely independent of the period or the perpetrator. Two quotations will serve to support our claim that absent-minded errors are a timeless and universal human failing.

The first comes from the French essayist, Jean de La Bruyere. Writing in the seventeenth century, he described the antics of one of his contemporaries, the Comte de Brancas, thus:

> He comes downstairs, opens the door to go out and shuts it again; he perceives that his night-cap is still on, and examining himself a little more carefully, discovers that only one side of his

face is shaved, that his sword is on his right side, that his stockings are hanging about his heels, and his shirt out of his breeches . . .

In his walks about town he thinks that he has lost his way, puts himself into a fret, and asks of passers-by where he is; they tell him the name of his own street, he at once enters his own house but hastily runs out again, fancying himself mistaken . . .

He plays at backgammon and asks for something to drink; it is his turn to play, and having the dice-box in one hand and the glass in the other, being very thirsty, he gulps down the dice, and almost the box as well, throwing the liquor on the board and half drowning his antagonist.[1]

Coming together in the behavior of a single person, these blunders verge on lunacy; but as we shall see when we examine the slips of less eccentric individuals, many of Brancas's aberrations have recognizable parallels in our own daily lives.

The second quotation is a charming account of an absent-minded action contributed to the *Spectator* in 1711 by an English journalist and man about town, Mr. Budgell.

My Friend Will Honeycomb is one of the Sort of Men who are very often absent in Conversation, and what the French call *a reveur* and a *a distrait*. A little before our Club-time last Night, we were walking together in Somerset Garden, where Will had picked up a small Pebble of so odd a make, that he said he would present it to a Friend of his. After we had walked some time, I made a full stop with my Face towards West, which Will knowing to be my usual method of asking what's a Clock, in an Afternoon, immediately pulled out his Watch, and told me we had seven Minutes good. We took a turn or two more, when, to my great Surprize, I saw him squirr (fling) away his Watch a considerable way into the Thames, and with a great Sedateness in his Looks put up the Pebble, he had before found, in his Fob. As I have naturally an Aversion to much Speaking, and do not love to be the Messenger of ill News, especially when it comes too late to be useful, I left him to be convinced of his Mistake in due time, and continued my Walk . . .[2]

---

[1] F.H. Pritchard, *The World's Best Essays: From Confucius to Mencken* (London: MacMillan, 1953), pp. 363–366.
[2] D.F. Bond, *The Spectator Vol. I* (Oxford: Clarendon Press, 1965), pp. 329–330. By permission of Oxford University Press.

Note the similarity between this incident and that in which Brancas attempted to swallow the dice instead of his drink. In both cases, the actions were appropriate, but the objects to which they were applied were not. Such errors bear a superficial resemblance to the spooner-isms that occur in speech, and are discussed at length in Chapter 8. Errors like these, involving complete or partial reversals, are rela-tively common in action as well. Familiar examples are unwrapping a piece of candy, putting the paper in your mouth, and throwing the candy away; or striking a match, putting the spent match in your pocket, and discarding the matchbox.

But let us return for a moment to the taciturn Mr. Budgell. As he walked away from the unfortunate Will Honeycomb, he reflected "... on these little Absences and Distractions in Mankind" and re-solved "... to make them the Subject of a future Speculation." Since the outcome of this speculation is highly pertinent to arguments pre-sented later in this book, it is worth considering them further. First, Mr. Budgell sought to distinguish between "... a Man who is Absent because he thinks of something else, from one who is Absent because he thinks of nothing at all: The latter is too Innocent a Creature to be taken notice of ..." He then considers the causes of absent-minded slips. Among them are having one's mind fixed "... on some partic-ular Science, which is often the Case of Mathematicians and other Learned Men; or is wholly taken up with some violent Passion, such as Anger, Fear, or Love, which ties the Mind to some distant Object ... or, these Distractions proceed from a certain Vivacity and Fickle-ness in a Man's Temper, which while it raises up finite Numbers of Ideas in the Mind, is continually pushing it on, without allowing it to rest on any particular Image."[3] We shall encounter these ideas again later in this chapter.

Finally, and not without a certain smugness, Mr. Budgell goes on to explain how he himself overcame any tendencies toward absent-mindedness.

> The Method I took to Conquer it was a firm Resolution to learn Something from whatever I was obliged to see or hear. There is a way of Thinking, that if a man can attain to it, by which he may strike somewhat out of any thing ... I always make myself one of

[3]D.F. Bond, *The Spectator Vol. I*, pp. 329–330.

the Company I am in; for though I say little my self, my Attention
to others, and those Nods of Approbation which I never bestow
unmerited, sufficiently shew that I am among them. Whereas
Will Honeycomb, tho' a Fellow of good Sense, is every Day
doing and saying a hundred Things which he afterwards con-
fesses, with a well-bred Frankness, were somewhat *mal a propos*,
and undesigned."[4]

Writers, if one is to believe the stories they tell of themselves, tend to
be unusually distracted individuals. The essayist Charles Lamb re-
counted a meeting he had with the poet Coleridge, who in his later
years was notoriously absent-minded and evidently as fearsome a
bore as his own Ancient Mariner. Lamb encountered Coleridge one
day on Hampstead Heath whereupon Coleridge took him into a
clump of bushes, clutched at his coat button, and began to expound
earnestly upon some difficult subject that was currently agitating his
overvexed mind. Lamb then remembered that he had an appointment
elsewhere, and seeing no other means of escape, took out a pocket-
knife and cut off the button leaving it in Coleridge's hand. Some
hours later—so the story goes—he returned to hear Coleridge's voice
still rolling and echoing among the bushes. So he took up his former
position while Coleridge continued to hold forth, still clasping the
button, and apparently not having noticed Lamb's absence.

Another given to extremes of absent-mindedness was G. K.
Chesterton who was said to have sent his wife a telegram which read:
"Am in Market Harborough where should I be?" Chesterton wrote of
himself: ". . . I have quite constantly walked into another man's house
thinking it was my own; my visits became almost monotonous."
Shades of Brancas here too.

Our emphasis so far has been upon the more unusual and
singular aspects of absent-minded behavior. If that was all there was
to it, we would be justified in consigning these lapses to the psychological wastebasket as being no more than interesting curiosities. But
even in these rather exotic incidents, we begin to discern some of the
essential characteristics of absent-minded slips of action. From what
we have seen so far, there would seem to be at least three conditions
that promote absent-minded actions.

[4]D.F. Bond, *The Spectator*, Vol. I, pps. 329–330.

1. Slips occur during the largely automatic execution of some well-established or routine sequence of actions; that is, one in which the demands upon continuous attention for moment-to-moment control are relatively small.
2. Slips appear to be associated with distraction or preoccupation. Or, more precisely, they seem likely to occur when the limited attentional resource is allocated to some external or internal matter that is unrelated to the ongoing activity.
3. Absent-mindedness appears to flourish in relatively familiar environments where there are few departures from the expected, and hence requires little in the way of outward vigilance.

These are the kind of impressions anyone could form on the basis of their own experiences and casual observations. In the remainder of the chapter, we shall present new data relating to the production of absent-minded errors lying mainly in the domain of action. Under what circumstances do they occur? What form do erroneous actions take? Are they associated with particular times of day? How frequently do they occur during the normal course of everyday life? Are some people consistently more absent-minded than others? If so, do these differences relate to such things as personality, or vulnerability to stress?

A BRIEF COMMENT ON THE
METHODS OF INQUIRY

We have used two methods to obtain our information: diaries and self-report questionnaires. Obviously, a more objective approach would be desirable; but this presents difficulties. These slips frequently occur as the result of misdirected or diminished attention, and such states would seem to be especially vulnerable to any intrusive mode of investigation. Although we can make inferences about people's intentions from watching their behavior, only the person in question has firsthand knowledge of the plans governing his or her actions, and only he or she can claim directly to recognize a deviation of action from intention. Inevitably, we must place considerable reliance upon self-reports in order to obtain data about slips of action—at least in the first instance. In view of the ephemeral nature of these lapses and the fact that they occur in familiar everday settings (which generally rules out the psychological laboratory as a suitable location), some form of diary-keeping seemed the most appropriate way to approach the question of the circumstances under which they occur.

Before considering the findings of these diary studies, it is worth making some cautionary remarks about the limitations of this technique. Aside from the more obvious problems of diary-keeping,[5] our experience suggests that there are at least three kinds of bias related to the reporting of absent-minded slips.

1. *Volunteer bias* Individuals who agree to keep a diary often do so on the assumption that they are unduly prone to absent-mindedness.

2. *Selection bias* It must be assumed that not all the slips of action committed by the diarist will get recorded. Some slips will pass unnoticed, others will be regarded as too fleeting or trivial to be of interest, while others will be forgotten before they are recorded. Only the more noteworthy, amusing, or memorable slips are likely to find their way into the diary.

3. *Recording bias* Less information will be noted in the diary than was available to the diarist at the time of making the slip. In addition, what goes into the diary report may well be influenced by the diarist's personal theory as to why the error occurred.

These difficulties clearly set limits on the kind of inferences we can draw from diary studies. Not only would it be unwise to use this material to obtain estimates of action slip frequency in the general population, the selection and recording biases suggest that we cannot even take these data as representative samples of the diarist's own behavior over the recording period. So what are diaries good for?

We believe they serve a useful function as wide-gauge trawl nets, picking up the more salient slips of action. If the trawls are extensive enough, we can reasonably expect to catch a qualitatively representative sample of action slips as a whole. Although, the quantities of any particular kind of slip cannot be interpreted as reflecting their presence in the error population at large.

Questionnaires pose a different sort of problem. Instead of asking people to comment on a specific slip that they have just made,

[5] A.N. Oppenheim, *Questionnaire Design and Attitude Measurement* (London: Heinemann, 1966).

we present them with a wide selection of possible errors and ask them to give us global judgement of how often they make any one of them. Of course, they can only respond with general impressions, and these impressions are subject to all kinds of distortion. For example, how well can a person with a bad memory remember how often he or she forgets things? How much does the last memorable slip made influence his or her impression of general susceptibility to these kinds of error? How much of what he or she tells us is true, and how much is due to his or her need to appear competent? And so on. Nevertheless, our experience is that most people respond quite readily to these questions. They do not appear to perceive them as reflecting badly on themselves, and most regard them as a normal human failings, which are often amusing and generally interesting. Assuming this to be true, questionnaires can therefore provide us with two important kinds of data. First, they give some indication of individual differences in absent-mindedness. They tell us whether people who are prone to one kind of error are also prone to others as well. Second, they provide a crude index of the relative frequency with which different sorts of error occur in everyday life. Consequently, they make valuable supplement to the diary mode of investigation.

EXTENDED DIARY STUDY

In a preliminary study, 35 volunteers (23 women and 12 men) kept a diary of the occasions in which they noticed that their actions had deviated from their intentions over a two-week period. For each of these lapses, the diarists were asked to note the time of day, their intended action, the nature of the error, and the circumstances of its occurrence. The diaries yielded a total of 433 incidents, an average of just over 12 person, with a range from 0 to 36 slips. Women recorded slightly more errors, a mean of 12.5 as opposed to 10.9 for men, although this probably reflected a greater conscientiousness in diary-keeping than a greater liability to error.

The second study involved a more elaborate—*extended*—diary form in which, as well as providing the same basic details for each slip as in the first study, diarists were also required to answer a standard set of questions in regard to every slip recorded. These questions were divided into five sections, relating to the nature of the intended actions, nature of the erroneous actions, any wrong actions that were recognizable as belonging to some other activity, their mental and physical states at the time of the slip, and the prevailing environmental conditions.

Sixty-three university students used the diaries to provide a record of their slips of action over a continuous period of seven days. They were instructed to note what happened whenever they became aware that their actions had departed from their intentions of the moment, no matter how trivial these lapses might appear. They were asked to record these details and to answer the standard questions as soon as possible after making the slip. This study produced a total of 192 slips, with an average of three per person.

The results (actual numerical values are shown in Appendix II) indicated very clearly that the activities which produced these slips were frequently and recently executed (*i.e.*, prior to the occasion when the mistake was made), and were reported as being carried out in a largely automatic way. This finding confirmed our earlier statement about the nature of the tasks which promote absent-mindedness.

In 77 of the 192 slips (40 percent), a relationship between the erroneous actions and some other activity, not intended at that time, was very clearly recognizable. This "other activity" was recently and frequently engaged in, and the responses to the questions revealed that it was seen as sharing similar locations, movements, and objects with the intended actions on the occasion the error was committed. Similarity of timing and purpose was also evident in the majority of these slips, but there was a substantial proportion (approximately 27 percent in the case of timing, and 31 percent for purpose) in which the intended activity and the task from which the intrusion had come were rated as "not at all similar." Thus, for these errors at least, the context seemed to be somewhat more influential in triggering the slips than those errors concerned with purposive overlaps.

It was also clear that slips were generally associated with either internal preoccupation or with some external distraction. Being upset, or feeling emotional and unwell, or being pressed for time were seen as being relatively unimportant in contributing to the slip.

Responses to the fatigue question, on the other hand, suggested that this was a factor that was important on some occasions, although not on others. Finally, it was evident that slips occurred in highly familiar circumstances, but that potentially bothersome factors such as heat, noise, poor illumination, and so on, were not regarded as contributing in any significant fashion to the making of the slip.

Taken as a whole, these findings confirmed our everyday assumptions about absent-minded actions. They also indicated a high degree of homogeneity in the nature of the error-producing activities and in the mental and physical conditions associated with the slips in this study. Therefore, the data provided clear support for the notion, stated earlier, that slips of action occur during the execution of highly familiar tasks requiring little in the way of conscious monitoring. In cases where the erroneous actions were identified as more properly belonging to some "other activity," it seems evident that they took the form of "strong habit" intrusions, or what others have called *strong associate substitutions*. We shall return to these in Chapter 4. The remaining 60 percent of the errors involved omissions, repetitions, and the use of wrong objects. These will be discussed in later chapters.

The results of the study provided little basis for classifying slips of action, other than the distinction between intrusion errors and others. But even here, the conditions of occurrence were remarkably similar. It would seem, therefore, that whatever form an absent-minded error takes, its conditions of occurrence have much in common. Although, we must make the proviso that we are dealing primarily here with slips of action rather than lapses of memory.

TIME OF DAY

In both the preliminary and the Extended Diary studies, the subjects were asked to record the time of day at which the mistake occurred. To discover whether there were any temporal patterns in the occurrence of slips of action, the distributions over hours of the day were plotted for each study, both separately and together. The resulting histograms are shown in Figure 2.1.

Both groups of diarists showed similar temporal distributions: a

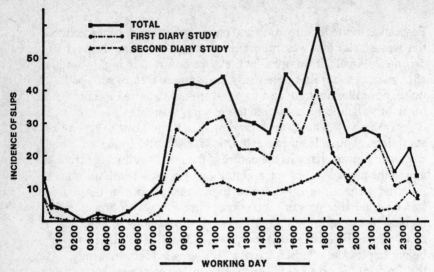

Figure 2.1 Distributions of Reported Slips of Action

rapid increase in the occurrence of slips during the early hours of the waking day, a decline between noon and 3.00 P.M., and a clear tendency to "peak" between 5 and 7 o'clock in the evening. These findings were statistically significant regardless of whether they encompassed the whole 24-hour cycle, the working day (9 A.M.–5 P.M.), or the waking day (8 A.M.–12 P.M.). The variations that existed between these two samples could reasonably be explained by their differences in life style. The preliminary diary study used a much more heterogeneous group, both in age and occupation, than did the Extended Diary study, where the subjects were all undergraduates between the ages of 18 and 25 years. Thus, the somewhat earlier "peak" for the preliminary study sample could be explained, in part at least, by the fact that many of the diarists were involved in preparing meals between 5 and 6 o'clock in the evening. Kitchens proved to be remarkably good breeding grounds for absent-minded slips.

A comparison of the hourly error occurrences for males and females is shown in Figure 2.2. It can be seen that there were no marked differences in the temporal patterns of the slips committed by the two sexes.

These hourly distributions suggest, obviously enough, that slips

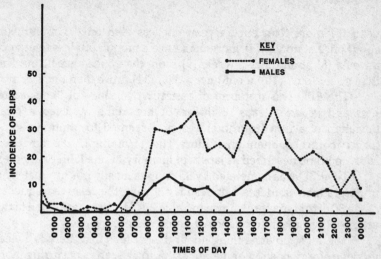

Figure 2.2 Comparing the Hourly Distribution of Slips

are most likely to occur during periods of maximum activity. There is also a hint that slips are especially probable during transitions between home and work. That is, when people are either preparing to depart for work, or immediately upon their return home. In general, these distributions appear to reflect the influence of situational factors rather than what is known about daily variations in efficiency.

THE RELATIVE FREQUENCY OF ERROR TYPES

The relative frequency with which various kinds of slips and lapses occur during daily life can be estimated. To obtain these estimates, an Error Proneness Questionnaire (EPQ) was constructed that comprised 30 items. Each item took the form of a general statement of a particular type of error, and for 26 of the items, this statement was followed by three actual examples (drawn from the diary studies). The entire questionnaire is included in Appendix I.

The respondents were asked to indicate, in relation to each kind of slip, how often they made it. To do this, they selected one of eleven possible response categories: (1) never; (2) about once in my life; (3) more than once in my life, but less than once a year; (4) about once a

27

year; (5) more than once a year, but less than once a month; (6) about once a month; (7) more than once a month, but less than once a week; (8) about once a week; (9) more than once a week, but less than once a day; (10) about once a day; (11) more than once a day.

The EPQ was made up of basically two kinds of items: *action slips* and *nonaction slips*. Eighteen of the items involved a clear deviation of action from intention, and seemed to implicate some form of control or attentional failure. The remaining 12, the nonaction slips, could be described as lapses of memory of one kind or another.

The EPQ was completed by 85 people, mostly postgraduate and undergraduate students. The results showing the relative frequency of the 30 error types are shown in Table 2.1. The items are listed in the order of their mean frequency of perceived occurrence.

The most obvious thing about this table is that there is a clear tendency for nonaction or memory slips to be seen as occurring more frequently than slips of action. These differences were statistically significant. Table 2.2 compares the numbers of action and nonaction slips falling above and below the halfway point (the median) in the frequency rankings. Specific kinds of error will be discussed in greater detail in subsequent chapters.

A BEHAVIORAL CLASSIFICATION OF SLIPS OF ACTION

An examination of 625 slips of action collected in our two diary studies suggested that a large proportion of them could be assigned to one of four behavioral categories.

1. *Repetition* Where some actions in the intended sequence are repeated unnecessarily.
2. *Wrong object(s)* Where the intended actions were made, but in relation to the wrong object(s).
3. *Intrusion* Where unintended actions other than those associated with repetitions or wrong object(s) become incorporated into the sequence at some point.
4. *Omission* Where intended actions are left out of the sequence (other than those arising from repetitions, wrong objects, or intrusions).

Table 2.1 Relative Frequencies of Error Types as Shown by EPQ Data (N = 85)

Rank	Error Type	Percent sample responding						
		Daily+	Daily	Weekly+	Weekly	Monthly+	Monthly
1.	Attending but not taking in	20.0	21.2	18.8*	10.6	14.1	9.4
2.	Forgetting plan item	4.7	11.8	14.1	27.1*	20.0	8.2
3.	Blocked on name	5.9	8.2	18.8	17.6*	23.5	10.6
4.	Forgetting intention (to do)	3.5	4.7	27.1	17.6*	22.4	12.9
5.	Forgetting intention (to say)	3.5	8.2	22.4	11.8	27.1*	12.9
6.	Should-be-doing-something feeling	3.5	8.2	17.6	18.8	9.4*	20.0
7.	Action different from intention	2.4	2.4	17.1	11.8	25.6*	17.6
8.	Recall blank on known fact	2.4	11.0	8.5	17.1	14.6*	15.9
9.	Executing unnecessary actions	2.4	8.2	14.1	15.3	15.3*	12.9
10.	Time-gap experience	2.4	4.7	15.3	20.0	14.1*	10.6
11.	Omission after interruption	0	4.7	5.9	10.6	23.5	21.2*
12.	Forget to consult reminder	0	1.2	14.1	18.8	10.6	16.5*

Table 2.1 (*continued*)

| Rank | Error Type | Percent sample responding | | | | | | |
		Daily+	Daily	Weekly+	Weekly	Monthly+	Monthly
13.	Losing place in sequence	1.2	1.2	9.4	5.9	24.7	17.6*
14.	Searching for carried object	1.2	0	8.2	3.5	18.8	24.7*
15.	Carrying object after disposal time	1.2	0	8.2	10.6	8.2	21.1*
16.	Omission of step from sequence	0	0	7.1	9.4	11.8	11.8 *
17.	Right actions but objects reversed	0	1.2	5.9	5.9	8.2	23.5 *
18.	Premature exit from sequence	1.2	0	2.4	9.4	14.1	21.4 *
19.	Familiar but unintended actions	0	0	2.4	5.9	22.4	28.2 *
20.	Wrong receptacle	0	0	3.5	9.4	14.1	14.1 *
21.	Familiar action in changed conditions	0	0	1.2	7.1	12.9	22.4 *
22.	Note need for change but continue	0	0	8.3	4.8	10.7	17.9 *
23.	Revert to abandoned plan	0	1.2	4.8	2.4	10.7	15.5 *
24.	No recollection of previous action	1.2	0	3.7	7.2	9.8	17.1 *

25.	Picked up wrong object	0	0	7.1	4.8	7.1	8.3 *
26.	Repetition of action	0	3.5	0	2.4	3.5	8.2 *
27.	Intrusion from some other activity	0	3.5	0	2.4	3.5	8.2 *
28.	Right action but wrong object	0	1.2	3.5	2.4	5.9	7.1 *
29.	Action reversal	0	0	2.4	2.4	2.4	12.9 *
30.	Wrong remembrance of place	0	0	1.2	1.2	5.9	7.1 *

+Indicates *more than*
*Indicates mean category. When situated at extreme of right hand column indicates "less than monthly".

31

Table 2.2 Comparing the Numbers of Action and Nonaction EPQ Items Falling Above and Below the Frequency Median

	Action Items	Nonaction Items
Above Median	5	10
Below Median	13	2

In order to discover the extent of agreement between different judges (*i.e.*, people other than the investigators) when they were required to allocate slips of action to these four behavioral categories, an inventory was constructed containing 100 error statements culled from the two diary studies. The judges were instructed as follows: "The only information you will have in assigning slips to categories will be brief descriptions of the errors provided by the individuals who committed them. The categories are all defined in simple behavioral terms. You will not be asked nor expected to speculate about the underlying causes of the mistakes. You merely have to decide which of the available categories best fits the described circumstances of the error. If you feel that the slip fits none of these categories, or you are not sure which one is appropriate, then you will have an opportunity to indicate this in the inventory."

The classification procedure for each slip required making a series of yes/no decisions in a standard order, as follows. The judges were first asked to decide whether or not the slip involved a repetition, then whether it was a wrong object error, then an intrusion, and then an omission. If they answered no to all four, they were asked to consider whether the slip failed to fit any of the four categories. If they responded in the negative, they were asked if they were unsure which of the four categories best fitted the slip in question. If they still answered no, they were directed to repeat the decision process again. Fifty psychologists (researchers, academics, and postgraduates) acted as the judges.

For 86 of the 100 items, more than 50 percent of the sample selected the same category, and for 56 of these items more than 80 percent were agreed on this allocation. But for 16 items, no clear majority decision was obtained (*i.e.*, 50 percent or less assignment to the most popular category). Further analysis showed that confusions occurred most often between intrusions and wrong objects, largely arising from the judges' uncertainty as to what constituted an object. However, no confusions were found between repetitions, wrong objects, and omissions.

The results of this study suggested that, for these fairly sophisticated judges at least, the four behavioral categories were adequate to classify the majority of the slips. Only 12 of the 100 items were allocated to the *none of these* category, and there were no *unsure* responses. Furthermore, with the exception of the intrusion/wrong object confusions, most items were assigned to categories with an acceptable level of agreement between judges.

Does this apparently satisfactory finding mean that we have solved the classification problem? Unfortunately, it does not. All we have shown is that there is fairly close agreement between judges concerning the surface features of a slip. These categories tell us little or nothing about the underlying causes. In short, there is no simple and direct mapping of these behavioral error types on to the underlying categories of cognitive failure. Rather, the available evidence indicates that members of the same behavioral class of error are mediated by quite different cognitive failures, and that members of different behavioral classes may share common causative mechanisms. We will elaborate upon this in later chapters.

INDIVIDUAL DIFFERENCES IN ABSENT-MINDEDNESS

Are some people consistently more liable to absent-minded slips than others? Or is absent-mindedness simply a state that all of us get into when we are preoccupied or distracted? Recently many studies have been directed at this particular issue; so it would be possible to give highly technical answers to these questions, although inevitably ones that would be hedged around with a psychologist's usual qualifications. But in view of the fact that these inquiries are still very much in their early stages, and bearing in mind that this book is addressed to the nontechnical reader as well as the psychologist, we shall restrict ourselves to the findings of the best and most thorough investigation in this area: that conducted by Dr. Donald Broadbent and his associates at the University of Oxford.[6]

Broadbent's results suggest that the answer to the first question posed above is—yes, liability to absent-minded errors bears all the characteristics of being an enduring trait rather than a passing state (although both, of course, can coexist). What is the evidence?

Broadbent's basic research instrument has been the Cognitive Failure Questionnaire (CFQ). Each of the 25 items describes an everyday cognitive failure falling within three broad areas: perception, memory, and action. The respondent is asked to indicate the frequency with which he or she makes such mistakes along a five-point scale, ranging from *Very Often* to *Never*. The CFQ has been administered to a large number of groups, covering a diversity of ages and occupations. In addition, and most importantly, Broadbent has established that the respondents' self-ratings are significantly correlated with the rating made by his or her spouse when asked to say how absent-minded that person is in the course of daily living. This demonstrates that CFQ responses have a close bearing on the reality of that person's behavior, rather than simply being a personal opinion that he or she holds about themselves. The CFQ does appear to be measuring actual absent-minded behavior.

A major finding of Broadbent's investigation was that different individuals do not seem to have specific kinds of cognitive failure. For example, those people who acknowledge that they have many lapses of memory also report making a relatively large number of errors in action and recognition as well, and conversely. Thus, susceptibility to cognitive failure appears to be determined by a general factor operating independently of the particular parts of the cognitive machinery in which it could reveal itself. Or, to put it more simply, all the items in the questionnaire were positively correlated. This result is confirmed by our own studies using a range of questionnaires, similar to the Error Proneness Questionnaire.

Further indications of the general nature of liability to minor cognitive failure or absent-minded errors come from the finding that

[6]D.E. Broadbent, P.F. Cooper, P. FitzGerald and K.R. Parkes, "The Cognitive Failures Questionnaire (CFQ) and its correlates." *British Journal of Clinical Psychology* 21 (1982), 1–16.

the total scores of a variety of questionnaires, each assessing particular forms of breakdown (in memory, attention, etc.), all correlate highly. Thus, people who score highly on a questionnaire specifically designed to measure their liability to everyday memory failures also score highly on the CFQ (which measures a variety of failure tendencies) and on our own absent-mindedness questionnaires, and vice versa.

So far, then, we have strong evidence to show that people differ widely in their proneness to minor slips and lapses. The fact that this is not simply a question of how they perceive themselves, or how they would like to present themselves, is shown by their spouses' general agreement with these self-assessments. This liability to cognitive failure is general rather than specific to any one particular domain of cognitive function.

Is this general tendency to minor cognitive failure a stable feature of the individual, or is it simply a reflection of the way people perceive themselves at the time of completing the questionnaire? To establish this, Broadbent and his co-workers gave the CFQ to the same people on two occasions separated by intervals of up to 16 months. This was done for a variety of occupational groups, and in all cases the initial and subsequent scores correlated sufficiently highly to indicate that this tendency to minor slips and lapses was an enduring characteristic rather than a passing phase.

Broadbent and his associates then considered the question of whether they were simply remeasuring some well-established personality dimension such as neuroticism, or some other consistent feature of the individual, like intelligence. Their results suggested that this was not the case. The CFQ did appear to be tapping something quite distinct from that assessed by conventional psychological tests. The only relationships of any interest were between the CFQ and the scores obtained from a modified version of the Middlesex Hospital Questionnaire (MHQ), which calls for self-assessments of mild psychiatric symptoms.[7] The correlation between the total and CFQ and MHQ scores were positive and statistically significant, as

[7]S. Crown and A.H. Crisp, "A short clinical diagnostic self-rating scale for psycho-neurotic patients." *British Journal of Psychiatry* 112(1966), 917–923. A.H. Crisp, M. Gaynor-Jones & P. Slater, "The Middlesex Hospital Questionnaire: A validity study." *British Journal of Medical Psychology* 51(1978), 269–280.

were the individual correlations between the CFQ and the Anxiety and Depression scales of the MHQ. The only negative correlation was that between the CFQ and the Obsessional Personality scale of the MHQ. That is, people with a small liability to everyday cognitive failure tended to manifest obsessional characteristics. We shall be discussing this relationship between obsessionality and absent-mindedness more fully in Chapter 7.

What does this tendency to make minor blunders signify in psychological terms? A preliminary answer is suggested by some further results obtained by Broadbent's group. The study involved a group of student nurses who were given the CFQ before spending their first period of duty in the wards. These wards were rated by the nurses for the degree of stress they induced, a factor that depended both on the amount of work demanded and the freedom the nurses were allowed in carrying out their duties. On the basis of these ratings, the nurses were divided into two groups: 48 who had worked on relatively high stress wards, and 53 on low stress wards. After completing their 6-week periods of ward duty, nurses in both groups were given the symptom inventory, the MHQ, to fill in. The results proved interesting: For those nurses who had worked on low-stress wards there was virtually no relationship between the initial CFQ score and the subsequent MHQ value; but for those who had spent their time on high-stress wards, the correlation between the two scores was both positive and statistically significant. This tells us that the level of minor psychiatric symptoms after six weeks of work is related to the earlier CFQ score *only if that work was stressful*. In other words, it would appear that liability to everyday slips and lapses (as measured by the CFQ) reflects the extent to which a person is *vulnerable* to stress. Our own evidence shows that the immediate presence of stressful factors (see the extended diary study) is not generally seen as being the cause of an absent-minded slip. Rather, the tendency to make a lot of these errors in all circumstances suggests that the person in question lacks some degree of resistance to stressful situations which is not shared by those who are less error-prone.

These interesting findings still leave open the questions of what are the determinants of this fairly stable trait of error-proneness, and why they should affect one's resistance to stress. We will speculate further on these issues in the final chapter.

SUMMARY

Absent-minded errors appear to have the following characteristics.

1. They occur in tasks in which some degree of automaticity has been achieved.
2. They are associated with distraction and preoccupation, but not with any other obvious emotional or environmental stress.
3. They occur in familiar and mostly constant environments.
4. Many erroneous actions take the form of sequences of behavior that recognizably belong to some other activity, not intended on that occasion.
5. People appear to differ characteristically in their liability to these minor slips and lapses.
6. This individual liability is not confined to one particular cognitive domain (memory, action, recognition, language etc.), but appears in all aspects of mental life.
7. There are indications that this liability to minor cognitive failure has some relationship to an individual's general vulnerability to stress.

chapter three

THE AUTOPILOTS OF EVERYDAY LIFE: INTRODUCING THE COGNITIVE DEMONS

Each day of our adult lies we perform an immense variety of tasks that once appeared to us as marvelous accomplishments, falling—or so it then seemed—quite outside our capabilities. We drive cars expertly through tangled traffic, usually without hazard to ourselves or others. We pound away at typewriters, calculators, cash registers, and computer terminals, for the most part quickly and accurately. We operate complicated industrial and domestic machinery efficiently and generally without error. We prepare appetizing and nourishing meals on demand. We read books, play musical instruments, converse in a foreign language, follow labyrinthine knitting patterns: We do a hundred and one difficult and complex things, and—what is most remarkable—we do them without any great sense of effort and, for much of the time, with our minds on other matters.

But it was not always thus. Cast your mind back to when you first sat in the driver's seat of a car. Ahead of you was an array of pedals, levers, switches, and dials whose functions you may have apprehended, and whose operations you may have coped with one at a time, but whose coordination into some effective well-timed sequence seemed quite out of the question. How could one possibly steer a straight line, operate the pedals, be in the right gear, indicate where you are turning, keep an eye on the road, and the rearview mirror all at the same time? One simply did not feel to be in possession of enough limbs and eyes, or sufficient brain power to get it all together. And, even if one did, what chances were there of surviving out on the road? Can you remember how daunting a busy highway looked before you had driven on one? But with a great deal of painful effort, a lot of practice, many silly mistakes and, if you were lucky, a patient instructor, you somehow managed it. And then, after a variable period of self-conscious pride in your new attainment (during which, incidentally, the road accident statistics suggest you were at your most dangerous), the whole business became increasingly unremarkable and routine: An activity to serve an end, rather than an end in itself.

The process we have just described at some length William James summarized, with characteristic precision, in a single sentence. "Habit," he wrote, "diminishes the conscious attention with which our acts are performed."[1] That this is a self-evident truth does not alter the fact that understanding how this transfer of control comes about still remains one of the central problems of psychology. It is also one that a careful study of the systematic slips and lapses of everyday life can do much to elucidate.

In the previous chapter, we noted that absent-minded slips distinguished themselves from other forms of error by occurring very largely during the execution of skills or habitual activities in which the demands upon our limited conscious resources are small. Although the novice makes more errors than the skilled operator, these are rarely of the absent-minded kind. As the term suggests, absent-mindedness is one of the penalties we pay for automatization. Contrary to most other types of blunder, the likelihood of making an absent-minded slip actually increases the more proficient we become at performing a particular task. It is this feature that makes slips such important clues to the organization and guidance of skilled behavior.

Furthermore, a large proportion of absent-minded errors actually take the form of intact, well-organized segments of skilled action that are suitable for the environmental context most of the time, but not when changed circumstances require some alteration of normal practice, or when new goals demand the modification of existing

[1]W. James, *The Principles of Psychology Vol. I* (New York: Henry Holt & Co., 1890), p. 114.

routines. As in political structures, the devolution of control entails certain risks, one of which is that the "provincial" governing agencies may act independently of the wishes of the central authority. In human action, likewise, the price we pay for liberating consciousness from the moment-to-moment details of the task in hand is the degree of autonomy achieved by the lower control centers.

Instead of actions being run sequentially and laboriously by a single overall controller, like a military commander who has to be concerned with the whole gamut of the army's affairs from high strategy to the siting of platoon latrines, the acquisition of a skill or habit brings with it the development of a vast staff of subordinate commanders or experts, each of whom deals exclusively in a specialist area. Consciousness is left to get on with what it is good at, namely planning, general supervision, and trouble shooting unexpected changes in the environment. But experts are notoriously blinkered individuals who will trot out their expertise at the slightest provocation, even when it is not wanted.

If we had many modes of action, we could probably afford to employ several experts in parallel operations, each working toward an intended goal. But as it is, our scope for action is severely limited by anatomical considerations. We only have one mouth, one pair of eyes, one pair of hands, two legs, two feet, and so on. Such output restrictions usually mean that only one, or at best very few, of these "experts" can have charge of these effector mechanisms at any one time. For actions to be performed correctly, the proper "expert" for the current intention has to be in the driver's seat at the right moment. But, on occasions, these conditions are not met, and our actions deviate from our intentions.

Although the primary focus of this book is upon human error, and upon absent-minded actions in particular, it is important to acknowledge at the outset that errors are the exception rather than the rule. If we are to understand more about why absent-minded slips occur, and why they take the largely predictable forms that they do, we must first have some idea of how the control mechanisms work to achieve the desired performance. In other words, we need to develop some model or blueprint of how we control our actions with only minimal conscious involvement, and with usually the intended outcome being attained.

A detailed model of this kind goes well beyond the present achievements of psychology. There are some general theoretical ideas, derived from many kinds of evidence, and especially from research on motor skills and from recent developments in the computer simulation of human performance, that will be of great use to us. For the remainder of this chapter, we shall be concerned with presenting, in very broad terms, a set of theoretical notions about the control of everyday action. Armed with these concepts, we will then, in subsequent chapters, go on to see how applicable they are to explaining the occurrence of a wide variety of actual absent-minded slips. Just as any explanation of systematic error must begin with some understanding of correct performance, so also must any theory of human action take account of these recurring patterns of error. It is a circular process. We need some theory of correct action in order to start making sense of our error data, and what we learn from a detailed analysis of these slips and lapses will enable us to flesh out and improve upon our original model of action.

BRING ON THE DEMONS

Both within the theory of action and in our subsequent attempts at explaining the slips and lapses of everyday life, we place a great deal of reliance upon a single, multipurpose notion, that of the *cognitive demon*. Before proceeding any further, therefore, it would be helpful to bring on these demons in order to make some preliminary introductions, and to say something of their intellectual forbears.

The cognitive demon emerged from a fairly recent marriage between two closely related endeavors: cognitive psychology and artificial intelligence. Cognitive psychology is the much older parent, and is concerned with explaining such mental functions as remembering, perceiving, thinking, planning, and the guidance of action. Artificial intelligence (AI) is the attempt, made possible by recent advances in computer technology and especially in its *software*, to simulate aspects of these processes using computer programs.

Although the term *cognitive demon* was first used by Selfridge, in 1959 for describing the operation of a machine that could handle

certain pattern recognition problems, its beginnings, or the beginnings of a concept very like it, go back much further. The writings of
neurologists such as Hughlings Jackson and Henry Head, and particularly to the studies of remembering carried out in the early 1930s by
the British psychologist, Sir Frederic Bartlett.[2] To explain the way in
which our recollections of meaningful material become systematically distorted over time, Bartlett employed the term *schema*
(*schemata* in the plural). Like almost everyone since, Bartlett had
misgivings about this word. The word was too definite and too
sketchy, nevertheless both the term and the notion have become
firmly rooted in contemporary psychological theorizing. Perhaps the
simplest way of substantiating this claim is to quote from two influential cognitive psychologists, the first writing in 1932 and the
second in 1979.

The first is Bartlett himself who introduced his concept of
schema in the following much quoted passage.

"Schema" refers to an active organization of past reactions, or of
past experiences, which must always be supposed to be operating in any well-adapted organic response. That is, whenever
there is any order or regularity of behavior, a particular response
is possible only because it is related to other similar responses
which have been serially organized, yet which operate, not
simply as individual members coming one after another, but as a
unitary mass. Determination by schemata is the most fundamental of all the ways in which we can be influenced by reactions and
experiences which occurred some time in the past. All incoming
impulses of a certain kind, or mode, go together to build up an
active organized setting ... There is not the slightest reason,
however, to suppose that each set of incoming impulses, each
new group of experiences persists as an isolated member of some
passive patchwork. They have to be regarded as constituents of
living, momentary settings belonging to the organism, or to
whatever parts of the organism are concerned in making a
response of a given kind, and not as a number of individual
events somehow strung together and stored within the organism.[3]

[2]O. Selfridge, "Pandemonium: A paradigm for learning" in, *Symposium on the Mechanization of Thought Processes* (London: H.M. Stationery Officer, 1959). Sir F.C. Bartlett, *Remembering*, (Cambridge: Cambridge University Press, 1932).
[3]Sir F.C. Bartlett, *Remembering*, pp. 201–202.

The second quotation is taken from Donald Norman writing on a theme very close to our own.

> Much in our everyday activities is controlled by subconscious mechanisms. We are quite unaware of how we perform our routine activities. Even that most cognitive of functions, language, resides primarily in the subconscious. As we speak, we often have little awareness of the words that will be spoken until just prior to their utterance. Even when I consciously search for a particular thought, I am aware primarily of a feeling of effort, or of will, or desire, not of a conscious selection among possible words or phrases. The times when I prepare an utterance with care prior to speaking are rare, usually reserved for some special occasion where exact words are critical. Then, the process requires considerable effort and mental rehearsal of the item: conscious preparation is the unnatural state ...
>
> I propose that skilled action sequences are controlled by sensori-motor knowledge structures: *schemas.* By schemas, I mean organized memory units, much along the lines my colleagues and I have previously proposed for perception and memory. The extension of these ideas to include motor actions seems natural, both from the demands of the situation and from historical precedent.[4]

Because Norman deliberately reiterates Bartlettian ideas, it should not be assumed that the schema notion has enjoyed continuing usage and popularity throughout the intervening years. Bartlett was writing during the dark ages of behaviorist domination in psychology when vague mentalist notions such as this tended to fall upon stony ground. If we can put a date on the revival of such ideas, it came around 1960 with the publication of an immensely influential book by three American psychologists, George Miller, Eugene Galanter, and Karl Pribram, called *Plans and the Structure of Behavior.*[5]

In this book, they proposed a now famous alternative to the Stimulus-Response (S-R) reflex, then current as the basic unit of behavioral analysis. Their unit was derived from computer program-

[4]D.A. Norman, *Slips of the Mind and an Outline for a Theory of Action* (La Jolla, California: Center for Human Information Processing CHIP 88, 1979), pp. 5–6.

[5]G.A. Miller, E. Galanter, K. Pribram, *Plans and the Structure of Behavior* (London: Holt, Rinehart and Winston, 1960).

ming and was called the TOTE unit, where TOTE is an acronym for Test-Operate-Test-Exit. The *test* phase of this information-processing cycle checks for any incongruity between the actual and desired state of affairs. If an incongruity is detected, the *operate* phase is set in motion. Then a further test is made. If the mismatch still exists, the *operate* phase is again activated—and so on until the *test* phase detects no further discrepancy between the progress of our actions and our present intention, whereupon the cycle is ended. Another important feature of the TOTE unit is that the *operate* phase can be expanded hierarchically to incorporate any number of subordinate TOTE units. See Figure 3.1 for further explanation of the TOTE unit.

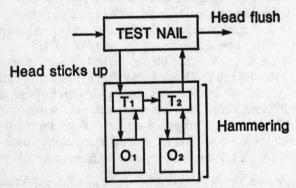

Figure 3.1 The Test-Operate-Test-Exit (TOTE) Unit

As a unit of behavioral analysis, the TOTE concept has a number of important advantages. First, the "test" notion implies that we have a clear image of the desired outcome against which to check our progress. This means that actions are oriented toward the attainment of some future goal, rather than being determined solely on the basis of immediate or past environmental events. A major weakness of the behaviorist or S-R approach was, as the Russian neuropsychologist Luria indicated, that "it . . . closed its eyes to those forms of behavior which are controlled not by the past, but by the *future*, which are constructed as the putting into effect of intentions, plans or programs, and which, as it can easily be seen, constitute the greater part of all specifically human forms of activity."[6] Second, the provision of feedback loops which shift control from the *operate* to the *test* phases, and back again, means that actions so described are highly flexible and adaptive.

Most importantly for our present purposes, however, is that the TOTE unit provides us with a means for specifying more precisely the way our schemata or cognitive demons (the two are synonymous) function. As Neisser pointed out, "A schema . . . also functions as a *plan*, of the sort that Miller, Galanter, and Pribram described in their seminal book. Perceptual schemata are plans for finding out about objects and events, for obtaining more information to fill in the format. One of their important functions in seeing is to direct exploratory movements of the head and eyes. But the schemata determines what is perceived even where no overt movements occur (listening is a good example), because information can be picked up only if there is a developing format ready to accept it. Information that does not fit such a format goes unused. Perception is inherently selective."[7]

We have just considered how ideas from computer programming enriched cognitive theorizing in the early 1960s by providing a powerful metaphor for the explanation of purposive or planned action. But the flow of ideas has gone the other way as well. In attempting to program computers to carry out pattern recognition, it has been necessary to import schemalike constructions from cognitive psychology, since it proved impossible to achieve adequate

[6]A.R. Luria, *The Working Brain* (Middlesex, England: Penguin Books Ltd., 1966), p. 246.
[7]Ulric Neisser, *Cognition and Reality* (San Francisco: W.H. Freeman and Company, 1976), p. 55.

recognition of complex scenes in the outside world on the basis of momentrary input patterns alone. Selfridge, in creating his *Pandemonium* model for learning to recognize patterns that had not been previously specified, invoked a hierarchy of demons, each of whom performed a specified task. At the bottom were subdemons who computed the similarity between the features to which each was specifically designed to respond and the image or sensory data available to all such subdemons. When a subdemon found a matching feature, he shrieked. The closer the match the louder the shriek. These shrieks were heard by demons responsible for identifying the next level of complexity, such as an individual letter. Thus, when an A-demon hears shrieks from the appropriate feature demons, he shrieks out his A-ness to a decision demon sitting above him in the hierarchy, whose job it is to identify the loudest shriek from among the shrieking letter demons. This account relates only to the idealized pandemonium with which Selfridge began his analysis, and does no justice to the adaptive power of the model. But it will serve our needs for the present.

Another schemalike notion was developed by Marvin Minsky at the Massachusetts Institute of Technology in his pioneering work on robotics and artificial intelligence.[8] He called this concept a *frame*. He proposed that, in carrying out pattern recognition, the computer must prepare itself for each new scheme from the outside world using a frame, or hierarchy of frames, that utilizes stored information to anticipate much of what will appear. Thus, if the computer is examining a playing card, it should expect to find a certain outline shape, four classes of differently colored symbols (hearts, clubs, diamonds, and spades) placed in a particular set of configurations together with the digits from two to ten, and pictures representing the court cards. Similarly, if the computer is inspecting a room, it should expect to find doors, windows, walls, floor, ceiling, and so on. Only in this way, Minsky argued, will it be able to decide between the otherwise ambiguous patterns of information available to its sensors.

Enough has been said, we believe, to show that our basic unit of theoretical currency, the cognitive demon, has a respectable intellectual pedigree. We prefer to use the term *demon* rather than *schema*,

[8]M. Minsky, in *The Psychology of Computer Vision*, ed. P.H. Winston (New York: McGraw-Hill, 1975).

although the two are quite interchangeable. Firstly, our main concern is with human error, and the natural perversity implicit in the term *demon* seems more fitting than the staid Greek word for *structure*. Secondly, the subconscious control mechanisms that we seek to describe are intensely active things, and this too is better conveyed by the image of shrieking, leaping, clamorous demons. Thirdly, the term *demon* allows us to be unashamedly anthropomorphic, which makes the exposition of these ideas a good deal easier and less technical. Finally, like many other psychologists, we find the notion of cognitive demons appealing as well as useful.

We will postpone further consideration of the general properties of cognitive demons until we have sketched out the major components of the theory of action. It should be noted that we are not restricting the word *action* solely to the observable deeds we perform within and upon the outside world. We are also concerned with the control of internalized actions such as those involved in struggling to recall a name, recognizing a face, doing mental arithmetic, or solving a crossword puzzle.

AN OUTLINE FOR A THEORY OF ACTION

As theories go, this one is of rather a low order. It generates very little in the way of precise predictions, although there are a few. As a result, it suffers the considerable failing that it cannot easily be challenged by fresh evidence. But we are prepared to live with this because of its ability to summarize in a fairly simple way a large number of the known properties of mental functioning. It is derived not only from our own and other investigators' error analyses, but also from laboratory studies of mental control processes, particularly in the field of motor skills. Contrary to much of the psychological literature, it strives to emphasize the points of agreement between various theoretical views, rather than their points of conflict. In other words, it is a theoretical composite embodying, in very general terms, much of what psychologists have learned from many different types of inquiry. As such, it deliberately cuts across traditional distinctions between areas like perception, memory, thinking, and motor learning. The cognitive demon is offered as a theoretical device that is applicable to all of these domains of mental function.

A diagram of the basic components of the theory is shown in Figure 3.2. These comprise the minimum number necessary to explain both our correct actions and our absent-minded errors. They consist of a variety of information-handling functions, linked by communication channels and feedback loops. Each of the major components is considered separately below.

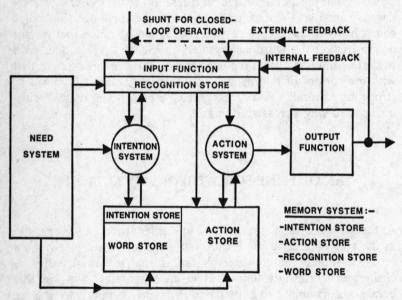

Figure 3.2 Basic Components of the Theory of Action

Intention System

The Intention System (IS) is at the head of action control. It operates in close conjunction with the Intention Store to organize plans of future action, to monitor and guide ongoing activity, to cope with changing circumstances, to review past actions, and to recover errors when they occur. At any one point in time, its operations coincide very closely with the current contents of consciousness. What goes on within the IS is largely determined by the direction and breadth (both variable) of attentional focus which switches continually between past, present, and future events. Intentional activity may be prompted by external events (via the Input Function) or by internal states (via inputs from the Need or Memory Systems).

The manipulanda of planning are usually short verbal tags describing goals ("I must buy some carrots," "I'll make a cup of coffee," "I'll call in at my mother's on my way home"). Each of these "tags" involves a large number of automatized action sequences that are not specified consciously, but remain under the control of specialized action demons (held within the Action Store). Planning, therefore, consists of making a series of jottings on the mental scratchpad. There is no need to fill in the small print of each detailed operation—these are implicit in the brief headings on the scratchpad. The more we engage in relatively fixed routines, the fewer the number of tags or jottings required to specify them. In other words, repetition reduces the number of low level control statements necessary to guide our actions. Even if we wanted to, we probably could not reconvert the smaller segments of behavior back into verbal tags because they pass beyond the reaches of consciousness into the realm of the action demon. Imagine what it would be like trying to talk someone through the act of dressing. Unless your subject knew exactly what was meant by an instruction like "Put your socks on," you would very quickly need to resort to an actual demonstration. Words soon fail when trying to describe the precise details of a highly routine activity, and this is reflected in the way we make plans.

The IS has two important properties. Firstly, it has limited capacity. This means that only one plan can be maximally active within *this* system at any one moment. Since the IS works on one thing at a time, items awaiting consideration have to be held in store until the IS is free to deal with them. Secondly, like Nature, the IS abhors a vacuum. It is always busy, at least during waking hours; what happens during sleep is more problematical. Once it has initiated a set of routine actions and handed over control to the action demons, it switches to some new concern—usually quite unrelated to the task in hand. These two characteristics, in particular, render us vulnerable to absent-minded errors.

Need System

The Need System (NS) encompasses all the basic biological springs of human action: the needs to satisfy hunger, thirst, sexual drives, and so on, as well as less clearly defined needs, such as those for nurturance or dominance. The NS is the powerhouse, the primary source of energy to drive our thoughts and actions. We will not specify its structure or contents in any detail, since this has already been done at length by many psychologists, the most notable being Freud, MacDougall, Murray, and Maslow.[9] It is sufficient for the present to point out that the NS connects directly with the Action, Word and Recognition Sto s, thus providing the mechanism for "motivated errors" or "Freudian slips". These are considered at length in Chapter 9.

Memory System

The Memory System is made up of four distinct stores: the Intention Store, the Word Store, the Action Store, and the Recognition Store. There are likely to be many more storage compartments within the total Memory System, but these four are the ones most relevant to our present discussion.

The Intention Store differs from the other three. In the first place, it acts as a kind of temporal extension to the IS. Secondly, its contents are limited, short-lived, and subject to loss or interference. To remain for any length of time in the Intention Store, an item needs to be recycled through the IS. In other words, we have to keep consciously refreshing it. You know the kind of thing—saying to yourself "Ah yes, I must remember to do such-and-such on my way home." If we fail to do this, we either forget our intention, or, if we are lucky, we are prompted by some external cue, like noticing the turn we intended to take as we are driving home. Forgetting intentions, however, is among the commonest of human failings.

Thus, the Intention Store is rather like a cluttered desktop on to

[9]Sigmund Freud, *An Outline of Psychoanalysis* (New York: Norton, 1949). W. MacDougall, *An Introduction to Social Psychology* (London: Methuen & Co. Ltd., 1908). H.A. Murray, *Explorations in Personality* (New York: Oxford University Press, 1938). A.H. Maslow, *Toward a Psychology of Being* (New York: Van Nostrand Reinhold Company, 1968).

which we throw the scraps of paper and old envelopes containing the scribbled lists of things to do.[10] Quite often, we remember to consult our lists at the right time and carry out the intended actions. Sometimes, however, we forget about the list altogether. At other times, we remember its existence but cannot find it among all the other bits and pieces. Then we are left with feeling: "I know I should be doing something, but I can't remember what it is." On yet other occasions, we retrieve the memo at the proper time and start upon the planned activity, but then part way through we lose it as when we find ourselves in a shop, or confronted by an open drawer or cupboard without the least idea of what we had come for: the "What-am-I-doing-here?" experience. And there are also times when we start working our way down our list of things to do, but at some point we fail to consult the list and wake up to find that we have become locked into some familiar sequence of actions that were not the ones we had intended.

The Intention Store, unlike the Word, Action, and Recognition Stores, does not contain cognitive demons, only fragments of conscious experience. These fragments take the form of words or images. So long as they remain intact and on the surface of the messy desktop, they are directly accessible to consciousness. But this is not true of the cognitive demons occupying the other three stores. Of these, only the word demons have some degree of conscious access; but not directly. They have to be searched for and dredged up by a special corps of retrieval demons that ply between the IS and the dark recesses of the Word Store. But even when they are successful, these retrievers can only bring up some image, not the actual word demon itself. Cognitive demons remain forever out of sight (to consciousness) in the depths of their respective pandemoniums.

The action demons, living in the Action Store, deliver preprogrammed instructions to the Output Function for carrying out routine activities. These demons, each of varying size and complexity depending on their specialized jobs, live in a kind of loosely organized chaos. If we were able to pry open the lid of this particular pandemonium, we would see a mass of writhing, struggling demons

---

[10]D.E. Broadbent, *In Defense of Empirical Psychology* (London: Methuen & Co. Ltd., 1973, p. 4.).

at the top prancing around on the bodies of dozing demons lying toward the bottom of the store. We would also notice that some intensely active demons would be glowing a bright red, others less vigorous would be a slightly duller hue, while the ones at the bottom would merely be a pale pink. The same would be true if we looked into the Word and Recognition Stores. In short, cognitive demons vary widely in their level of activation: The higher the level of activation, the more likely a demon is to be triggered into its particular mode of action.

Whereas the action demons control the effector mechanisms of the body, the recognition demons are the input specialists. Each one is tuned to respond to a particular feature of the sensory input. When it finds it, the demon shrieks up to the next set of demons in the hierarchy—just as Selfridge described it in his Pandemonium model. At the top of the heap, sits a Godfather demon who, on detecting a sufficient intensity and number of shrieks from the subdemons he oversees, delivers an appropriate percept to the IS, and carbon copies to the Action System and the Word and Action Stores.

In the case of action demons, the direction is reversed. On receiving an intention message from the IS (carried by a messenger demon who rushes around the Action Store shrieking the current wishes of the IS), the Godfather in charge of a specialist demon family kicks his subdemons into operation, and they deliver the detailed instructions to the particular part of the musculature for which they are responsible. Remember that popular action demons (*i.e.*, ones that are frequently and successfully employed) are intensely competitive creatures, and are constantly fighting with one another for an opportunity to get their hands on the output controls. Sometimes this results in dismemberments, as in Chapter 8.

In Figure 3.3, we introduce a visual notation for depicting cognitive demons. We have adopted a triangle as our standard symbol for a demon. This is to stress the hierarchical nature of their internal organization. Figure 3.3 also serves to illustrate the main differences between the way the cognitive demons operate in the three principal domains of actions, words, and recognition. Although we must take note of these differences, it needs to be stressed that for most of the time in this book we shall be emphasizing their shared characteristics, particularly in regard to the factors which influence their levels of activation.

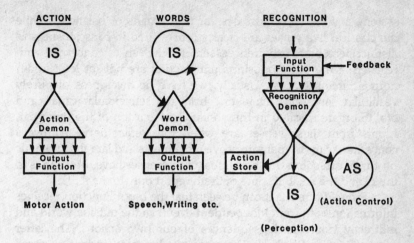

Figure 3.3 Illustrating the Variation Between Demons in the Three Principal Cognitive Domains

Action System

The Action System (AS) is simply that family of action (or word) demons currently in control of the output mechanisms. The AS, like the IS, has a definite limit upon its capacity, imposed in the case of the AS by the number and scope of the available effectors. It should also be noted that the IS does not communicate directly with the AS, but only via messenger demons. These messengers do not, in general, carry return messages from the AS to the IS. The performance of the AS can only be monitored via the feedback channels.

Output Function

This comprises the body's effector mechanisms: the muscles, joints, and associated structures that actually carry out the range of actions of which we are physically capable.

Input Function

This consists of the classical five senses—sight, sound, taste, smell, and touch—together with the proprioceptors, the muscle-skin-joint

53

system, and the vestibular system (the organs of balance). While the classical five senses are clearly represented in consciousness as distinct perceptual experiences, some of the senses concerned with registering the body's position and motion are not (at least under normal circumstances). Usually, we have no awareness of purely vestibular sensations emanating from the semicircular canals and otolith organs, located in the nonauditory portion of the inner ear. Inputs from these senses are wired into reflex nerve pathways concerned with compensatory eye movements and largely automatic postural corrections. In short, most of the senses have direct links to the IS and the AS, but some of them report only to the AS.

From Figure 3.2, it can be seen that the Input Function receives information both from independent events in the outside world and indirectly from the consequences of our own actions. The latter source is termed *feedback*. There are two kinds of feedback: *internal feedback*, the sense of our own movements and body location that is transmitted by the proprioceptors; and *external feedback*, which generally entails what we can see and hear of the effects of our actions. Because the eyes can take in a great deal of information at a single glance, while the ears can only transmit information serially, it is most often the case that conscious awareness is dominated by visual impressions.

The signals picked up from the environment and from within the body are transmitted via the Recognition Store to the IS, the AS, and the Action Store. The significance of the latter communication channel will be discussed more fully at a later point.

Closed-loop and Open-loop Modes of Control

At the top of Figure 3.2, there is a dotted arrow connecting the external feedback channel with the external inputs going directly to the IS. This is labelled "shunt for closed-loop operation," and requires some further explanation.

The IS is said to be *closed-loop* with regard to the control of ongoing action when this shunt is closed. When it is open, the control of action resides primarily with the AS. In this case, the IS is said to be operating in the *open-loop* mode of control.

In this way, the theory takes account of the fact that we have two modes of directing our actions, rather like that in a modern aircraft. That is, we can either operate directly (analogous to the pilot having his hands on the controls), or we can switch in the automatic pilot. We will use the terms *closed-loop* (CL) and *open-loop* (OL), respectively, to describe these two control modes.

It is important to stress that these two ways of controlling action are best thought of as the extremes of a dimension along which intermediate mixtures of these two states can co-exist, rather than as two distinct categories. The crucial point is that during the execution of most activities, the locus of control is continually switching between the IS and the AS. In highly skilled or habitual tasks, we will spend the greater part of the time in the OL mode, whereas in performing an unfamiliar activity this preponderance will be reversed. In the CL mode, the control of action relies heavily upon internal and external feedback for the moment-to-moment guidance of our movements. In the jargon of the control theorist, this is largely a feedback mode of operation. In the OL mode, however, the control of action is mainly of the feedforward kind. This means that motor output is largely governed by preformed instructional sequences that run off independently of feedback, at least over brief periods of time, thus leaving the IS free to concentrate upon future aspects of the task, or indeed to devote itself to matters quite unrelated to the current activity.[11]

We can illustrate these two modes of control with two scenarios: one familiar, the other, we hope, less so. Consider the case of getting from bed to the breakfast table on, say, a Monday morning. First, the familiar sequence: the alarm clock rings, the Input Function detects the sound, the appropriate family of recognition demons identify it and communicate the information to the IS. The Intention System initiates a well-established plan of action: "get out of bed, get washed and shaved, get dressed in the appropriate clothes for a Monday morning, and get me down to the breakfast table by 7.30." With varying degrees of reluctance, the appropriate groups of action and recognition demons carry out their prescribed duties in a predominantly OL mode. In other words, apart from the occasional

[11]K.S. Lashley, in *Cerebral Mechanisms in Behavior*, ed., L.A. Jeffress (New York: John Wiley, 1951). G.E. Stelmach (ed.), *Motor Control: Issues and Trends* (New York: Academic Press, 1976).

check upon the progress of action, the IS is left free to mull over the night's dreams, or to plan the day's activities. When the final test criterion is met—being washed, shaved, correctly dressed, and seated in front of a plate of cereal—the "bed-to-breakfast" tribe of cognitive demons is returned to the Action Store, and the IS gets to work summoning up other demon families.

Now consider what might happen if this familiar pattern of events is disrupted. Instead of being aroused by the alarm clock, we are awakened by thick smoke coming under the door of the bedroom. Unless we have been extraordinarily unlucky, it is highly unlikely that we have an appropriate set of demons in store specifically designed for evacuating the family to safety in the event of fire. Consequently, the IS would have to work in a mainly closed-loop mode, redeploying existing demon fragments to suit the emergency and devising entirely new sequences of action—like tying sheets together to climb out of the window. This would place a considerable burden upon verbal plan formulation (talking yourself through the actions and checking consciously upon progress), just as it is in the learning of any new skill.

So far we have outlined the basic functions of each component of the theory, and shown how they might operate together in both expected and unexpected circumstances. In the remainder of this chapter, we shall be examining the cognitive demons a little more closely. In particular, we shall describe something of their internal organization, and also the general factors which influence their level of activation.

THE ANATOMY OF A COGNITIVE DEMON

We stated earlier that cognitive demons were organized hierarchically. This is true regardless of whether they function in the action, word, or recognition domains. Now we shall attempt to specify this internal organization in more detail.

It is convenient to regard each demon, or demon family (every demon is to some extent a demon family), as being made up of TOTE units (see Figure 3.1) nesting one within another rather like a Russian doll. From Figure 3.4, it can be seen that the subordinate TOTE units are encompassed within the operate phase of the highest level unit.

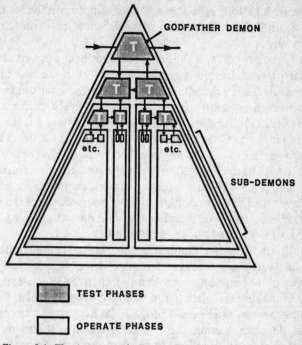

Figure 3.4 The Anatomy of a Demon Family

The Godfather demon resides within the test phase of this largest unit.

Thus each family comprises two teams of demons: those concerned with testing that a particular goal has been achieved, and those whose job it is to carry out the detailed operations necessary to achieve this desired result. Each team of demons reports to the next one higher up in the hierarchy. In this way, the locus of moment-to-moment control shifts continually between the test and operate demons. The primary task of the Godfather is to determine whether or not the overall function of the family has been fulfilled. Thus, each demon, even the Godfather, has a highly specific set of duties to perform. It is not necessary for any of them to think in the sense that the Intention System has to. Each test phase contains just enough knowledge to perform its particular decision function. There are only two outcomes: it is either satisfied with the results of the last operate

57

phase or it is not. If the latter, then it simply reactivates the operate phase until its criteria are met, or until the Intention System intervenes.

Once properly established, each family of demons can carry out its particular duties quite automatically. But in the case of the action demons, this only remains true so long as the environment in which they were intended to function stays relatively unchanging. If, for example, in the course of making a cup of coffee, it is found that the coffee jar is empty or that there are no clean cups, the whole matter must be referred back to the Intention System. One of the jobs of the IS is to spot such changes, and to plot a new course accordingly. This it usually does with only minimal demands upon its limited capacity, since most of these minor snags have been encountered before and contingency demons, suitable for dealing with familiar breaks in routine, have already been established.

If, on the other hand, it is the plan of action rather than the circumstances which contains minor changes (e.g., four cups of coffee instead of two, and one without milk), then the IS must specify, at the time of making the plan, that it will take over control at these points. In other words, the IS must program its own checks to coincide with these departures from the normal sequence. It can only do this, however, if these intentions to check are retrieved from the Intention Store at the appropriate times. If they are not, then we can safely predict that the sequence will follow its familiar pathway rather than the intended one.

FACTORS INFLUENCING
DEMON ACTIVATION

Earlier we conjured up the image of these various stores being filled with squirming demons, each glowing a different shade of red, depending upon its current activation level. One of the basic assumptions of our theory is that cognitive demons require a certain threshold level of activation in order to trigger them into action. In other words, demons need firing up before they go to work. Part of this triggering mechanism, usually the most important part, is specific to the demon's domain of functioning. Thus, as we have said, action and word demons are fired by the shrieks of messengers from the Intention System. Recognition demons, on the other hand, receive their triggers directly from the sensory input.

But in addition to these domain-specific triggering mechanisms, there are a number of general factors which influence the level of activation of *all* cognitive demons. These are shown diagrammatically in Figure 3.5, and are discussed individually below.

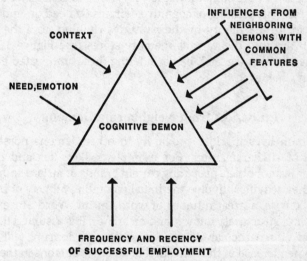

Figure 3.5   General Factors Influencing Demon Activation

Context

Familiar routines are usually carried out in specific circumstances. These situations and the expectations they induce are a powerful source of demon activation. If we find ourselves approaching a front door, we often reach for our own door key even when the door in question is not our own. In the chapters that follow, we will present a number of examples of the ways in which environmental cues can elicit actions that are generally suitable for the context, but not on that particular occasion.

Need or Emotion

It is also evident from our mistakes, particularly some of our embarrassing gaffes, that need, anxiety, or feelings of emotion can raise the activation level of particular demons. Thus, we sometimes spot the long-awaited face in the crowd at the railway barrier before its owner has actually arrived. Similarly, we can say or do something that clearly has an emotional rather than an intentional trigger. In fact, these slips of the tongue or of action are often more than just unintended, they are sometimes the very words or actions we sought to suppress. This priming of cognitive demons by need or emotion is allowed for in the theory by the pathways running from the Need System directly to the various memory stores (see Figure 3.2). As mentioned earlier, we shall be considering these "motivated errors" further in Chapter 9.

Influences from Neighboring Demons

Each demon lives in close proximity to other demons possessing identical or similar features. For example, making tea and coffee, filling hot water bottles, preparing certain brands of instant soup, and many other activities involve the initial common pathway of boiling water. Likewise, a great number of words in the Word Store share similar letter structures, sounds, and meanings. It is assumed that the activation of a particular demon, regardless of domain, will bring about some increase in the activation of all other demons in the store that possess common features. The closer the identity between these shared features and the greater their number, the larger will be the degree of activation induced.

Frequency and Recency of Prior Employment

Irrespective of the other influences upon it, the activation level of a cognitive demon at any moment will reflect the number of times it has been successfully used in the past. The recent past will have greater influence than will more remote occasions. In other words, busy demons will tend to maintain a higher level of activation than idle ones.

It should be noted, incidentally, that old and little-used demons do not die, they merely get rusty. We are constantly being surprised by the way we retain skills that we have not practiced for many years. Unlike the fragments of plans held in the Intention Store, cognitive demons seem to be fairly permanent structures within memory. And again unlike the Intention Store, there appears to be no obvious limit on the number of demons that can be stored.

Of all the general factors influencing activation, the frequency and recency one is the least specific. Other factors such as context and need will vary from situation to situation and from person to person, but the effects of prior use are always present. As a consequence, we are able to make one very broad prediction from this model: Erroneous actions will tend to be more commonplace (*i.e.*, have occurred more frequently in the past) than those intended on the occasion the mistake was made. This prediction applies not only to actions, but also to false recognitions and to those times when we struggle to recall a name or a word. In the former case, the false perception is likely to be more familiar than the correct one; and in the latter, the intermediate words that we dredge up in our search are likely to be more widely used than the target word or name.

This phenomenon of *banalization* or *strong associate substitution*[12] is evident in all forms of human error, as we shall be demonstrating in the chapters that follow, and clearly reflects the influence of a powerful and pervasive bias in human cognitive function. The idea that human action is intrinsically conservative represents one of the constantly recurring themes of this book.

Having established the theoretical framework by which we hope to organize and explain the slips and lapses of everyday life, as well as the mental processes that give rise to them, let us now turn to the errors themselves. In each of the six chapters that follow, we shall be examining a distinct class of absent-minded mistake. We begin in the next chapter with one of the most commonly occurring, the slip of habit—in thought, word, and deed.

---

[12]S. Timpanaro, *The Freudian Slip* (London: N-B, 1976). L.B. Chapman and J.P. Chapman, *Disordered Thought in Schizophrenia* (Englewood Cliffs, New Jersey: Prentice-Hall, 1973).

chapter four
SLIPS OF HABIT

The German novelist, Freytag, tells the story of an academic who was so bad at acknowledging acquaintances in the street that he had been drilled by his sister to raise his hat and bow when she pulled at his coat. One day when his sister was away, he was returning home, deep in thought, from a visit to a friend's house. Fearing that he would not bother to feed himself, his solicitous hostess had wrapped up a piece of chicken and put it in his overcoat pocket. As he walked along, he was pursued by a dog who tugged at his coat in an attempt to get at the chicken. Whenever the dog tugged, the professor raised his hat and bowed, and as the dog continued to tug, he was heard to say, "Thank you, dear, I did bow."

A slip of habit is one in which our actions, words or, less obviously, our thoughts are diverted by the lure of some well-trodden pathway. These departures invariably take the form of highly organized, intact sequences that are clearly recognizable as belonging to some other context or activity, but which do not form part of our current intentions.

The impression one gains from a close examination of these errors is that the more frequently a particular routine is set in motion and achieves its desired outcome, the more likely it is to recur uninvited as a slip of habit. William James likened habits to "great flywheels."[1] Once set in motion, they require very little additional energy to keep them going. But the price we pay for this momentum is a reluctance to change direction when altered circumstances or new destinations demand it.

The first part of this chapter will be concerned with slips of action, and with identifying the psychological and environmental factors that promote their occurrence. Then we shall look at the degree to which these various forms of strong habit intrusion are apparent in slips of the tongue and pen, and in lapses of thought as well. Any coherent segment of thought, word, or action that emerges unintended can provide important clues to the otherwise secretive mechanisms that govern our subconscious mental processes. In particular, they can tell us more about the structure and operation of the hypothetical cognitive demons, introduced in the previous chapter.

SLIPS OF ACTION

Strong habit intrusions are perhaps the commonest of our unintended actions. In the Extended Diary Study, discussed in Chapter 2, 40 percent of the errors recorded by the diarists were identified by them as belonging to some other activity; that is, they took the form of intrusions. The fact that these "other activities" were rated as being very frequently and recently engaged in clearly suggests that these errant segments of action were strong habits, and the nature of the erroneous actions themselves confirms this. (See Appendix II.)

The diarists were also asked to rate the degree of similarity between their intended actions (on the occasion that the strong habit intrusion occurred) and those involved in this *other activity*. These two tasks were judged as sharing very similar locations, movements, and objects. Similarity of timing and purpose was also evident in the majority of these slips, but there was a substantial proportion of them (approximately 27 percent in the case of timing, and 31 percent for purpose) in which the intended activity and the task from which the

[1]W. James, *The Principles of Psychology*, Vol. I. (New York: Henry Holt & Co., 1890), p. 121.

intrusion had come were rated as *not at all similar*. Thus, for these errors at least, contextual factors seemed to be somewhat more influential in triggering the slips than those concerned with purposive overlaps.

As shown by the other results of the Extended Diary Study (presented in Chapter 2), action slips of all kinds occur most often in extremely familiar surroundings (or other environments that share common features) during the execution of some well-practiced task that makes few demands upon conscious attention, thus leaving the Intention System free to devote most of its limited capacity to other matters. Under these conditions, the Intention System is prey to one of two kinds of attentional capture; by some pressing internal consideration (preoccupation), or by some engaging but unrelated external happening (distraction). In either circumstance, we may be left temporarily at the mercy of the most energetic cognitive demon in the neighborhood.

Since *attentional capture* appears to be an essential prerequisite for the occurrence of a slip of action, it would pay us to consider the nature of this condition a little more closely.

Attentional Capture

The philosopher, Sir William Hamilton, has provided a graphic account of extreme states of preoccupation or abstractedness.

> Archimedes, it is well known, was so absorbed in geometrical meditation that he was first made aware of the storming of Syracuse by his own deathwound, and his exclamation on the entrance of the Roman soldiers was: *Noli turbare circulos meos!* In like manner Joseph Scaliger, the most learned of men, when a Protestant student in Paris, was so engrossed in the study of Homer that he became aware of the massacre of St. Bartholomew, and of his own escape, only on the day subsequent to the catastrophe. The philosopher Carneades was habitually liable to fits of meditation so profound that, to prevent him sinking from inanition, his maid found it necessary to feed him like a child. And it is reported of Newton that, while engaged in his mathematical researches, he sometimes forgot to dine. Cardan, one of the most illustrious of philosophers and mathematicians, was once upon a journey, so lost in thought that he forgot his way and the object of his journey. To the questions of his driver whether he should proceed, he made no answer; and when he

came to himself at nightfall, he was surprised to find the carriage at a standstill, and directly under a gallows.[2]

For most people, not being great mathematicians or scholars nor having the servants willing to indulge them, such profound states of preoccupation are rare. But we have all known what it is like, albeit briefly, to be in a "brown study," to be so immersed in our thoughts that we become temporarily oblivious to our surroundings and our actions. Two of the commonest indications of this in our collection of absent-minded slips are continuing to carry objects that should have been disposed of earlier and searching for something that one is actually carrying or wearing. Here are some actual examples.

> "I left the bedroom carrying yesterday's underwear which I had intended to dispose of in a container in the bathroom before going downstairs for breakfast. However, on this occasion, I reached the kitchen before I realized I was still carrying the cast-off clothes."

> "After having a quick cup of coffee in the Staff Room, I went to the sink and washed the cup but, instead of putting it in the cupboard where it belongs, I kept it in my hand and walked back to the classroom with it."

> "I went looking for my glasses. Then I realized I had them on."

> "I took out my pen and continued to search for it in my case."

Another common occurrence, though not actually an error as such, is the time-gap experience. This is where we "come to" in the course of driving a car, or taking a walk, or when carrying out some routine task to discover that, for the moment at least, we have no recollection of the places that we have just passed through or of the things we have just done.

> "I noticed that we were approaching the Watford Gap service area. I had no idea we had come so far. The previous stretch of highway was a complete blank to me."

> "I found myself at the end of Union Street without any recollection of the previous few minutes of the walk. I knew the way I must have come, but had no clear mental picture of having done so."

[2]Quoted by W. James, *The Principles of Psychology, Vol. I*, p. 419.

66   Slips of Habit

"I came out of the bathroom and then had to feel my chin to check whether or not I had shaved."

A closely related experience which again does not reveal itself in action is that of apparently attending to something, but not taking it in. Usually this occurs when reading. Our eyes seem to have been following the words on the page, but on asking ourselves what the passage contained, we draw a complete blank. The same thing happens when we are watching TV, though here it is often hard to notice that anything has been missed, or when people are talking to us.

In a study using the Error Proneness Questionnaire (see Appendix I), 85 subjects were asked to indicate how often they made thirty different kinds of action slip and memory lapse. The most common item was the attending-but-not-taking-in experience we have just been discussing. Twenty percent of the sample judged it as occurring more than once a day. No other mental lapse or slip of action approached this degree of frequency (see Table 2.1). The time-gap experience was ranked tenth in terms of estimated frequency.

Implicit in the theory of action, presented in the previous chapter, was the notion that the Intention System needs to carry out a number of checks (via the closed-loop shunt shown in Figure 3.2) upon the progress of routine actions in order to keep them on track. It is reasonable to assume that rigor and timing of these checks will depend, to some extent, upon the nature and urgency of the other plans and parallel mental activities currently being handled by the Intention System. During the execution of routine activities, our minds are generally occupied with fairly transient and mundane affairs: we may be wondering if we fancy a boiled egg for breakfast, or whether we should take an umbrella to work, or we may be idly reviewing the events of the previous day, or what we would like to do that weekend. In such thoughts as these, there are usually plenty of lulls and natural breaks into which to slot the necessary checks upon the task in hand. Occasionally, however, these musings are far from idle. We may be totally absorbed in worrying about a child's health, or in plotting the demise of the boss, or in playing back to ourselves fragments of emotionally charged conversations. When this happens, it is highly likely that the Intention System will fail to carry out its monitoring duties as scrupulously as our plans require. It may specify an intention incompletely; or it may omit to refresh a stored intention so that it gets forgotten; or it may neglect to retrieve and activate a stored intention at the proper moment. Any of these oversights can result in the guidance of action being snatched by some highly charged cognitive demon who has been lying in wait for just such an opportunity.

External distractions can likewise appear in many guises, and exert varying claims upon the limited capacity of our conscious attention. Some, like the doorbell or the ringing of a telephone, can be handled by restructuring our current activities—turning down the gas under the milk pan, or taking the kettle off the stove—so that we can deal with the interruption. Other distractions can either be ignored or dealt with rapidly. But some, like the screaming of a child, capture our attention to the exclusion of almost everything else. Once in a while, these attentional imperatives crop up in situations that require us to continue our routine activities, such as driving a car, or more seriously, when piloting an aircraft.

A recent examination of British civil aircraft accidents (see Table 1.1 in Chapter 1) revealed a number of instances of pilot error which closely resembled absent-minded behavior in that they involved slips of action rather than errors of judgment.[3] A significant number of these slips were committed while the crew were dealing with genuine emergencies, such as the failure of an engine in a multiengine aircraft, or when the same asymmetric condition was deliberately induced by an instructor during a training exercise. By themselves, these events were not sufficient to have caused the ensuing crashes. The critical factor appeared to be the degree to which they captured the attention of the crew members, thus setting the scene for an erroneous response substitution to take place.

Although we can only speculate about their precise causes, accidents such as these give credence to the notion that attentional capture, by some important distracting event, can lead to erroneous and probably strongly associated responses being made. It will be noticed that these training accidents date back several years. Today, most pilot training organizations do not conduct inflight training

[3]J.T. Reason, in *Adult Learning*, ed. M. Howe (London: John Wiley, 1977), p. 40.

exercises involving asymmetric approaches. This owes much to the advent of sophisticated aircraft simulators in which such maneuvers can be practiced more safely and at less cost; but it also has something to do with the high accident rates associated with this type of training exercise.

Conditions Provoking Strong Habit Intrusions

If the present line of investigation has any practical value, it is to highlight the ease with which such dangerous slips of action can occur, and to identify the conditions in which they are most likely. Our collection of absent-minded slips suggests that strong habit intrusions can be divided into two broad categories according to the nature of the conditions which triggered them. In one group, the primary impetus for the errors arises largely from established linkages between the demons within the Action Store. In the other, the precipitating factors stem mainly from the external circumstances prevailing at the time. In the one case, therefore, errors appear to be driven predominantly by internal factors; and in the other by external factors. The distinction between these two groups is an extremely fuzzy one, since internal and external factors are both likely to have played some part in provoking any one particular slip. It is in the nature of routine actions that they should, for the most part, be tied to specific environmental situations. Nevertheless, for the purposes of classifying the conditions promoting strong habit intrusions, this distinction remains a useful one, and will form the basis of the subsequent analysis.

Internal Factors

Errors in this category tend to be characterized by inertia, rigidity, or perseveration. We are indeed creatures of habit, and this is perhaps nowhere more obvious than in the way we continue to employ tried and trusty action sequences in situations that demand newer ones. In short, we often fail to notice (or forget) the need for a change of routine. In terms of our theory, this means that the Intention System does not give the appropriate tug on the reins of action, so that like a driverless horse pulling a milk cart, we continue along our usual route. This failure to divert the course of action from the familiar path generally occurs in two kinds of situations: when a *change of goal* necessitates a departure from normal routine, and when *changed circumstances* demand some modification of a preestablished action pattern.

Intended departures from routine. These slips tend to take two main forms: overshoots and wrong turns. Overshoots are when we begin on some well-established sequence with the intention of exiting before its usual termination, but carry on as usual. William James described a typical instance:

> Very absent-minded persons on going to their bedroom to dress for dinner have been known to take off one garment after another and finally get into bed, merely because that was the habitual issue of the first few movements when performed at a later hour.

Following are some related examples from our collection:

> "I intended to change from jeans into a dress. I undressed completely as if I were going to bed."

> "I meant to take off my shoes, but I took off my socks as well."

> "I intended to go home a different route in order to stop at a shop. My 'different' route meant taking another turn off my usual circle. I was on my bike. I entered the circle, went past the turn I wanted and took the normal one home. It took about 15 seconds of pedaling down the wrong road (normally the right one) before it clicked."

> "I was making coffee for two good friends knowing very well they take it black. Nevertheless I put milk in both their coffees. I normally take it with milk."

> "I had decided to cut down my sugar consumption and wanted to have my cornflakes without it. However, I sprinkled sugar on my cereal just as I had always done."

> "I brought the milk in to make myself a cup of tea. I had put the cup out previously. But instead of putting the milk into the cup, I put the bottle in the fridge."

> "Suffering from some sort of flu bug, I returned home from work at around midday, hoping to get to bed for a few hours. I was

tired and feeling ill. All I needed to do was set the alarm and get into bed (I had something important to do that evening). However, as soon as I picked up the alarm clock, I was triggered into my going-to-bed-at-night routine. I checked all the doors to see that they were locked, set the central heating system, did my usual bathroom bit; and it wasn't until I found myself winding up my watch that I caught up with myself again."

Some of these errors are more like wrong turns than overshoots; they are more akin to selecting the wrong road at a Y-junction than not turning off before one's usual destination. But again, it is the most familiar route that is generally taken in error.

"I intended to pick up a knife to cut the potatoes, but actually picked up the teatowel. I wanted to cut the potatoes I had just peeled for boiling. Normally when I prepare french fries, I dry the potatoes with a teatowel before cutting them. On this occasion I was doing boiled mashed potatoes."

"I meant to get my car out, but as I passed the back porch on my way to the garage I stopped to put on my boots and gardening jacket as if to work in the yard."

"I intended to phone a friend in Leeds, but I started to dial my home phone number in London."

"I set out to drive from Leicester to Birmingham, a journey that entails going south a few miles on the M1 motorway before cutting across to the M6. But instead of turning south, I turned north. I drove 10 miles or so before I realized my mistake. Just before this, I had been making weekly journeys to Manchester, and my customary route was northwards along the M1."

There is another type of error falling into this general category which, although it occurs fairly infrequently, does so with sufficient regularity to deserve mention. These slips involve not so much an overshoot or a wrong turn, but a complete about-turn of the direction of action. Here are three examples from our collection.

"I intended to take off my shoes and put on my slippers. I took my shoes off and then noticed that a coat had fallen off the hanger. I hung the coat back up, but instead of putting on my slippers I put my shoes on again."

"I ladled soup into the soup bowl, and then started to ladle it back into the pan again."

"I got the correct fare out of my purse to give the bus driver. A few moments later I put the money back into the purse before the driver could collect it."

Changed circumstances. The locations in which we carry out well-established routines can change in a way that requires a modification of our normal pattern of action. Sometimes we fail to notice these changes, or forget about them, and continue exactly as before, or as we had previously intended.

"We now have two refrigerators in our kitchen, and yesterday we moved our food from one to the other. This morning I repeatedly opened the refrigerator that used to contain our food."

"On starting a letter to a friend, I headed the paper with my previous home address instead of my new one."

"I borrowed my friend's key in order to get his football from his room. I began to run upstairs to my own room instead."

"I looked at my wrist in order to check the time, but I wasn't wearing a watch."

"Throughout January, I kept writing checks with last year's date on them."

"I walked into the bathroom intending to have a bath. One of my roommates was in the tub so I returned to my room and decided to go shopping. I put my coat on, picked up my towel, and went back to the bathroom."

"I decided to make pancakes for breakfast. Then I remembered we didn't have any syrup so I decided not to bother. Five minutes later, I started getting together the ingredients for pancakes, completely forgetting about my earlier change of mind."

External Factors

Another powerful trigger to unintended actions is the environmental cues associated with long-established routines. A typical case is when we wander into some familiar location, like the bathroom or bedroom, with the intention of getting something. Then we "wake up" to find ourselves carrying out some habitual activity closely linked to that particular place, but having nothing to do with our original intention.

When the Intention System is engrossed in something other than the concerns of the present, we operate in a state of weakened intentionality. Then the control of action can be *captured* by certain aspects of a familiar environment, or by other external factors that are wrongly identified as belonging to such a place. We are driven by environmental signals acting directly upon the relevant demons within the Action Store, and this unwitting behavior runs along the grooves dug within these locations by the routines we habitually carry out in them.

The strong influence exerted by these external triggers can be seen in three classes of unintentional behavior. The first is straight-forward *environmental capture* in which our actions, though not in keeping with our current plans, are appropriate for the situations in which they occur. The second class we have labelled *mistaken capture*. Here the strong habit intrusion is best explained by assuming that a highly activated demon, or set of demons, has responded to certain features of the immediate surroundings that are similar to those in its normal place of operation, but which are not actually present. The third category are *freewheeling intrusions*. These are not, strictly speak-ing, errors since they generally occur when we have no immediate intention to fulfill, except perhaps to wait for something to happen.

Environmental capture.

"I have two mirrors on my dressing table. One I use for making up and brushing my hair, the other for inserting and removing my contact lenses. I intended to brush my hair, but sat down in front of the wrong mirror and took out my contact lenses."

"I went into my room intending to get a book. I took off my rings, looked in the mirror, and came out again—forgetting to pick up the book."

"I went upstairs to sort out and bring down the dirty washing. I came down without the washing, having tidied the bedroom instead. I went upstairs again to collect the washing, but some-how got sidetracked into cleaning the bathroom. I forgot about the washing until I returned to the basement and saw the washing machine."

"Late one evening, I ran the bath and prepared the towels, etc. I went into the bedroom to undress, but then I got into bed, forgetting the bath."

"On leaving the room to go to the kitchen I turned the light off, although there were several people there."

"I stopped at a gas station to fill up. I got out of the car, unlocked the gas cap, put in the gas, and paid for it. I then relocked the gas cap, but locked the car door—instead of opening it to get in."

"I was recovering from an unpleasant operation and in order to get fit my husband persuaded me to take up cycling, and I tend now to cycle everywhere. On Saturday mornings, I ride to the city through two large parks. On this particular Saturday, I was amazed to see people staring at me as I crossed the playing fields on a footpath. Then I realised—the bike had a puncture and on that occasion I was in my car. Having forgotten that I was not on my bike, I had followed my customary cycling route."

The last error could, of course, be equally appropriate for the "changed circumstances" category. This only serves to emphasize the point we made earlier about the fuzziness of the distinction between internal and external triggering factors. It also illustrates how difficult it is to identify any one cause for a particular slip. Usually there are a number of likely candidates. We can only hope to indicate the commonly recurring patterns among these causative factors, rather than attempt to make a precise determination of the origins of any one error. In most cases, there simply is not enough evidence to decide one way or the other.

Mistaken capture.

"As I approached the turnstile on my way out of the library, I pulled out my wallet as if to pay—although I knew no money was required."

"Walking up the front path to my friend's house, I pulled out my own front door key and was just about to place it in the lock when I realized my mistake."

"I put some money into a machine to get a stamp. When the stamp appeared I took it and said 'Thank you'."

Freewheeling intrusions. There are times when we do not have any particular plan for the immediate future. We find, for instance, that there are a few minutes to spare before we need to go out, or before we receive an unexpected visitor or phone call. Or it could be that there is some unpleasant task that we ought to be doing, but which we have postponed because we cannot face the prospect of starting on it right away. In these circumstances, we tend to wander around rather aimlessly, usually immersed in our thoughts. Often these meanderings take us into familiar locations. Then we "come to" and are mildly surprised to find we are eating an apple we did not want, or cleaning our teeth, or brushing our hair—or any number of things we did not specifically intend to do, but which were strongly associated with the familiar location into which our drifting had taken us.

An interesting parallel to these quite normal freewheeling intrusions is found in patients suffering from massive lesions of the frontal lobes: that part of the brain concerned with planning and the maintenance of intentional activity. The Russian neuropsychologist, Luria, described what happened in the case of one such patient: ". . . when asked to light a candle, (he) struck a match correctly but instead of putting it to the candle which he held in his hand, he put the candle in his mouth and started to 'smoke' it like a cigarette. The new and relatively unstabilized action was thus replaced by the more firmly established stereotype. I have observed such disturbances of a complex action program and its replacement by elementary, basic behavior in many patients with a clearly defined 'frontal syndrome'."[4] With such extensive injury as these patients had suffered, it is difficult to pinpoint any one cognitive factor as being responsible for the unwanted intrusion of the inert stereotypes or strong habits; but the problem seems to lie mainly in the inability of the damaged frontal lobes to formulate or to sustain an organized plan of action. The goal directed linkages between one action demon and the next seem to be weakened, or perhaps never established, so that the correct course of action is readily diverted along well-trodden, associated paths. The condition of these patients also suggests an

[4]A.R. Luria, *The Working Brain* (Middlesex, England: Penguin Books Ltd., 1966), pp. 199–200.

answer to the question: What do we need an Intention System for? Without it, we would be like pieces of flotsam swept along on the currents generated by the dominant action demons and their environmental triggers. We will come back to this issue in the final chapter. In the meantime, we will turn to the very similar patterns of strong habit intrusion that we find in speech and writing.

SLIPS WITH WORDS

A few examples from our collection should be sufficient to demonstrate that strong habit intrusions in speech and writing show a close resemblance to the action slips considered above.

> "I said 'Henry Miller' (the novelist) when I meant to say 'Henry Murray' (the psychologist)."

> "I have repeatedly addressed my younger daughter by her elder sister's name. It also happens the other way round, but not so often."

> "I wrote 'calls round' instead of writing 'calls a particular object'."

> "I meant to ask my son about the whereabouts of his brother. Instead I asked him where *he* was."

The list of such instances is potentially endless, but these few are probably adequate to show the influence of internal and external triggering factors that are closely analogous to those we have just been discussing for slips of action. In addition to these general characteristics, however, there are some features of word slips not shared by unintended actions. Two examples will illustrate this.

> "I intended to write 'genes', but wrote 'jeans' instead. I was thinking about washing my jeans."

> "I wrote 'hear' instead of 'here'. The following sentence was about hearing something."

Both of these slips appear to have been triggered by acoustic rather than semantic cues. In the first case, there is evidence of cross-talk between the Intention System and the largely automatic writing program. In the second, the cross-talk comes from that part of the Intention System preparing what was to come next. The cross-talk component of these slips is by no means peculiar to errors with words, but the phonological triggering certainly is. These errors, together with the retrieval failures we shall be discussing in Chapter 6, provide important insights into the way word demons are structured, organized, and activated.

Another interesting feature of word slips is the ease with which they can be induced in others by leading them into carefully prepared traps. Children's word games, in particular, often involve tricking the unwary (or even the not so unwary) into saying something nonsensical. The following question-and-answer game is fairly typical.[5]

> Q. What do we call the tree that grows from acorns?
> A. Oak.
> Q. What do we call a funny story?
> A. Joke.
> Q. What do we call the sound made by a frog?
> A. Croak.
> Q. What is another word for a cape?
> A. Cloak.
> Q. What do we call the white of an egg?
> A. Yolk (sic!).

The regularity with which even moderately vigilant adults fall into this verbal trap shows how difficult it is to avoid. Four powerful error-inducing tendencies appear to be operating together to trigger the incorrect response "yolk". First, the preceding questions serve to prime all those word demons possessing the acoustic feature of rhyming with "oak". Second, the "egg" demon is likely to have been more closely associated in its past use with "yolk" than with the correct answer "albumin". Third, the word "albumin", even aside from its associations with "egg", is likely to be a relatively underused one; hence its demon will have a low level of activation compared to

---

[5]Quoted by G.A. Kimble and L.C. Perlmuter, "The problem of volition." *Psychological Review* 77(1970), 361.

the one for "yolk". Finally, the inclusion of the word "white" in the question precludes its use as an answer. Our general experience with questions is that they do not usually contain the answer.

Such games provide a useful means of assessing the relative contributions of these different error-producing factors. This can be done experimentally by systematically manipulating each of these various priming factors independently, and relating this to the observed occurrence of the predicted error. Moreover, if we can program others to commit these verbal slips, it can hardly be claimed that they were unconsciously motivated.

As noted earlier, clinical studies can provide a valuable sidelight on the factors contributing to strong habit intrusions. It has long been known that the apparently bizarre utterances of schizophrenic patients contain a large number of *clang* words. That is, they show a tendency to substitute words that are strongly associated (either semantically or acoustically) to the preceding ones rather than those appropriate for conveying the desired meaning. Bleuler cited the case of a woman patient who, when asked to list the members of her family, began with "father, son," but then ended with, "and the Holy Ghost." Two American investigators, Loren and Jean Chapman, have argued that schizophrenic thought and language demonstrate an excessive yielding to the normal bias of strong associate substitutions. The same tendencies are also present in normal controls, showing up most clearly when the subject is given insufficient information to make the correct response, or when the task is too difficult.

The Chapmans carried out a study in which both schizophrenic and normals were required to select the correct response on a multiple-choice vocabulary test. The test comprised 120 items, 60 of them contained incorrect "strong associates", and the other 60 items did not. The following is an example of an item with associate.[6]

Shoot means the same as
A. Rifle (associate)
B. Rug (irrelevant)
C. Sprout (correct)
D. None of these.

[6]Quoted by L.B. Chapman and J.P. Chapman, *Disordered Thought in Schizophrenia*, p. 119.

And below is an example of an item without an associate.

Scale means the same as
A. Pin (irrelevant)
B. Yell (irrelevant)
C. Climb (correct)
D. None of these.

Normal subjects achieved equal scores on both subtests. But the schizophrenic subjects did markedly better on the "no associates" test. This finding and other related studies support the general conclusion that schizophrenics are unusually prone to strong habit intrusions.

What is there about schizophrenia that renders its sufferers more liable to strong associate substitutions? The tentative answer, based upon a number of studies, is that they show a reduction in both the breadth and the flexibility of their attentional focus. Whereas attention in normals is occasionally misdirected by transitory pre-occupations or distractions, that of schizophrenics appears to be predominantly tuned to internal events, hence the control of speech output is more susceptible to falling by default under the control of contextually triggered strong associates.

LAPSES OF THOUGHT

Errors in thought are less easy to detect than those in words or action, since a great deal of our thinking is not directed toward the solution of any particular problem. And even when it is, there are not always right and wrong answers. In everyday life, it is more usual not to think in any purposive or deductive way so long as all is running smoothly. Under these conditions, we drift along on a current of habit, associative connections, routine and impulse: "... the uncontrolled coursing of ideas through our heads," as John Dewey described it.[7] The inferences and judgments that we make in this

---

[7] John Dewey, Quoted by N. Bolton. *The Psychology of Thinking* (London: Methuen & Co. Ltd., 1972, p. 5).

undirected mode of thinking are rapid, involuntary, and largely outside conscious awareness. It is only when this smooth flow is interrupted that we become conscious of the need to think explicitly and productively; or, as the expression has it, it is only then that we need to "stop and think."

Ninety years ago, William James created the enduring metaphor of a "stream of consciousness" in which the progress of our thoughts was likened to the flights and perchings of a bird. The resting places are composed of images, usually of a fairly concrete nature, and the places of flight "... are filled with thoughts of relations, static or dynamic, that for the most part obtain between the matters contemplated in the period of comparative rest."[8]

Although in thought, as distinct from speech or action, the connections that can be made between the objects of our thinking are not, in theory, constrained by time and space, or by the rules of syntax, they are by no means random, even when we are thinking to no particular purpose. As Thomas Hobbes wrote in 1651: "When a man thinketh on anything whatsoever, the next thought is not altogether so casual as it seems to be. Not every thought to every thought succeeds indifferently."[9] The succession, in fact, is very far from being accidental.

When our minds are apparently running along of their own accord, we can occasionally step out of this stream and ask ourselves why our thoughts have followed that particular course rather than some other. In tracking back to find an answer, we usually discover that the direction of our thinking has been governed by long-established associative principles. The first of these is *similarity*: Our thoughts run easily from one idea to another that resembles it. Another is the principle of *contiguity*: " ... objects once experienced together tend to become associated in the imagination so that when any one of them is thought of, the others are likely to be thought of also, in the same order of sequence or co-existence as before."[10]

A third factor that propels our thoughts is *interest*. To quote William James once more: " ... our musings pursue an erratic course,

---

[8]W. James, *The Principles of Psychology Vol. I* (New York: Henry Holt & Co., 1890), p. 243.

[9]Thomas Hobbes, Quoted by W. James, *The Principles of Psychology, Vol. I* p. 595.

[10]W. James, *The Principles of Psychology Vol. I*, p. 561.

swerving continually into some new direction traced by the shifting play of interest as it ever falls upon some partial item in each complex representation that is evoked."[11] He illustrated this with a personal example. Upon looking at his clock, he found himself thinking about a recent resolution in the Senate (1879) concerning bank notes. In attempting to establish how this had come about, he recalled that the sight of the clock conjured up an image of the man who had repaired its gong. This, in turn, suggested the jeweler's shop where the man had worked. The image of the shop prompted him to think of the gold shirt studs he had bought there. This led him to thinking of gold and its declining value, which had brought him to the bank notes recently discussed in the Senate.

This explains the unlikely link between the clock and the Senate resolution; but why did his thoughts take this route rather than any of the myriad other directions indicated by the principles of similarity and contiguity? James provided the following answer.

> "Each of these images offered various points of interest. Those which formed the turning points of my thoughts are easily assigned. The gong was momentarily the most interesting part of the clock, because, from having begun with a beautiful tone, it had become discordant and aroused disappointment. But for this, the clock might have suggested the frien' who gave it to me, or any one of a thousand circumstances connected with clocks. The jeweller's shop suggested the studs, because they alone of all its contents were tinged with the egoistic interest of possession. This interest in the studs, their value, made me single out the material as its chief source, etc., to the end."[12]

The point has been made, and in any case is obvious enough: Despite their apparent freedom to make "flights" and "perchings" between any points within the imaginable universe, our thoughts, in reality, tend to be shackled by habit and the principles of association which fashion it. From the ground, an aircraft seems to possess an unlimited scope for three-dimensional movement; but, as the trainee pilot soon discovers, this freedom is mostly illusory. Even when restrictions are not imposed by the traffic regulations of invisible airways, there still

---

[11]W. James, *The Principles of Psychology Vol. I*, p. 573.
[12]W. James, *The Principles of Psychology Vol. I*, p. 573.

remain those dictated by the structure of the aircraft itself: it can only climb at a given rate, cruise within a certain speed range, and its maneuvers must not exceed the mechanical limits of its engine and airframe. And so it is with our thoughts.

So far we have discussed the undercurrents which carry our thoughts in fairly predictable directions when we are not forcing them toward some end. Now let us examine a real-life instance of purposive thinking which, if not actually in error, can hardly be taken as a model of deductive reasoning.

A Case of Convoluted Thinking

The following personal example (JR) is fairly typical of the lapses of thought to which people not usually regarded as stupid can sometimes fall prey. It is worth recounting at some length since it nicely exemplifies those occasions giving rise to the "How-silly-of-me! Why-didn't-I-think-of-that-before?" feeling that comes with the often sudden realization that our reasoning has pursued some unnecessarily convoluted path.

The right front tire of my car was badly worn, so I decided to exchange the wheel for the spare. I jacked up the car and attempted to loosen the nuts securing the wheel. But these had been tightened by some muscle-bound mechanic and refused to budge. I tried various ways to shift them: brute force, penetrating oil, and more brute force. Finally, I resorted to hammering at the spanner. Nothing worked. Not only were the nuts seized tight, but the wheel turned whenever I exerted pressure on the spanner. This, I concluded, was the root of the problem. If I could prevent the wheel turning, the nuts would surely be unable to resist my efforts. My subsequent thinking went something like this: Putting on the handbrake won't help because that only works on the rear wheels; and the same applies to putting the car in gear. So I'll have to use the brake pedal. But I can't do that and work on the nuts at the same time. What about using something heavy to keep the brake pedal depressed? No, I don't have anything handy that is heavy enough. I know. I'll get my wife to sit in the car with her foot down on the pedal. Ah! She won't be able to get in through the driver's door because the jack is blocking the way. And if she tries to get in from the other side she might rock the car off the jack. I'll have to bring the car down and take the jack away so she can get in . . . So I lowered the jack,

and it was only when all four wheels were firmly back on the
ground that it dawned on me: I had accidently solved the
problem of the turning wheel.

Some of our everyday thinking, like that involved in reckoning
change or deciding whether the refrigerator in the showroom will fit
into the gap between our kitchen cupboards, can lead to obviously
wrong answers. But outside of formal exercises in logic or mathe-
matics, such clearcut distinctions are not easy to find. In life, as
opposed to the classroom, lapses of thought tend to be more subtle.
As this example shows, our thought processes are less likely to be
guilty of formulating incorrect solutions than of arriving at inefficient
and inelegant ones.

Of course, a more proficient tire changer would have started to
loosen the wheel nuts before jacking up the car. But that is not the
point at issue: ridiculous or not, we have just described a piece of
natural thinking. In our example, the lapse consisted of continuing
along a circuitous route that by-passed the immediate and obvious
remedy—until it was hit upon by chance. This is an instance of what
Edward de Bono, the exponent of lateral thinking, has termed the
monorail mistake.[13] The logic followed in trying to solve the turning
wheel problem was not obviously faulty; the error lay in moving
along a single track from one idea to the next, and in failing to
consider those relevant factors which were part of the total situation.
In other words, this piece of directed thinking revealed the same kind
of associative biases that channel our thoughts when we are not
trying to steer them in any particular direction.

Our thoughts can be likened to a small boat with a rather
inadequate outboard motor. A lot of the time we switch the motor off
and allow ourselves to drift with the prevailing currents and tides.
Every now and again, we want to get somewhere in particular; so we
switch on the motor and attempt to navigate an appropriate course.
But the motor is rather underpowered, and in any case it keeps
cutting out from time to time. Then we are subject to the same forces
that carry us along when we have no special destination in mind.

[13]E. De Bono, *Practical Thinking* (Middlesex, England: Penguin Books Ltd., 1976).

Rigidity in Problem-Solving

The ease with which our thinking can become mechanized is especially evident in the way we attempt to solve an apparently similar series of problems. This tendency to continue to apply previously successful methods to problems that can also be solved in simpler and more elegant ways was demonstrated in a classical series of studies by A.S. Luchins, working in New York during the 1940s. These studies are unique in psychology in that the same basic technique was used on more than 9,000 subjects, both children and adults. In this case, at least, we can be confident that the principal findings are extremely robust.

Luchins, a refugee from Nazi Germany, was concerned with the blinding effects of habit and with what happens when a habit "... ceases to be a tool discriminantly applied but becomes a procrustean bed to which the situation must conform; when, in a word, instead of the individual mastering the habit, the habit masters the individual."[14] Specifically, he sought to measure the effects of mental *set* (he preferred the German word *Einstellung*) upon the way subjects tackled a set of water jar problems. His standard 11 problems are shown in Table 4.3.

People were told that there were two or three jars (usually three) of varying size, and their task was to figure out how to obtain a stipulated amount of liquid using only the jars provided for each problem. These problems were presented in a fixed order, and the subjects worked out their answers using paper and pencil. The first problem in the series was for instructional purposes only. The appropriate solution is to take the larger jar (29 quarts—Jar A) and pour away three quantities, each one equal to the capacity of the smaller jar (3 quarts—Jar B). That is, they should fill the smaller jar from the larger one three times. What is then left in the larger jar is the required amount. Subjects were required to solve the remaining problems without further assistance.

Problems 2–6 were the Einstellung, or habit-inducing trials, since they could only be solved by one standard method. In each

[14]A.S. Luchins and E.H. Luchins, "New experimental attempts at preventing mechanization in problem solving." *Journal of General Psychology* 42(1950), pp. 279–97.

Table 4.1. Luchins Water Jar Problems

Problem	Given the Following Jars as Measures (in Quarts)			Obtain This Amount of Water:
	Jar A	Jar B	Jar C	
1	29	3		20 QUARTS
2	21	127	3	100 "
3	14	163	25	99 "
4	18	43	10	5 "
5	9	42	6	21 "
6	20	59	4	31 "
7	23	49	3	20 "
8	15	39	3	18 "
9	28	76	3	25 "
10	18	48	4	22 "
11	14	36	8	6 "

case, the solution was to take the largest jar (Jar B), subtract the first jar once (Jar A), and then the last jar (Jar C) twice. Thus the solution can be represented as follows: $B - A - 2C$.

Of particular interest was the manner in which the subjects attempted to solve Problems 7 and 8. These could be answered by the familiar $B - A - 2C$ method, but a simpler and more direct means was also available for both of them. This was $A - C$ for Problem 7, and $A + C$ for Problem 8. The primary measure was the percentage of subjects who continued to use the Einstellung solution ($B - A - 2C$) on these two test problems.

In his first study, Luchins used three groups. The experimental or set group solved all 11 problems in order. The control group, however, simply started with Problems 7 and 8. This was to establish how they would be solved by people in whom no prior set had been induced. A third group was treated in the same manner as the "set" group, except that before Problem 7 each subject was instructed to write "Don't be blind" on the answer sheet. This, they were told, was " ... to make you aware of the fact that you must be cautious; you must watch out and see that you do not act foolishly while solving the subsequent problems." The results for Problems 7 and 8 are shown in Table 4.4.

Table 4.2. Percentage of Subjects Responding to Problems 7 and 8 with Einstellung Solution

Group	Percent
Control	0
"Set"	81
"Don't be blind"	63

The first point to notice is that none of the control subjects used the inefficient $B - A - 2C$ solution. They all used the more direct A $- C$ or $A + C$ methods. But 81 percent of the subjects in the "set" group used the Einstellung solution. The "Don't be blind" instruction to the third group reduced the proportion of mechanized solutions to 63 percent.

Problem 9 differed from any of the other "test" items in that it could not be solved by the established $B - A - 2C$ procedure. Only the $A - C$ method would work. The reason for putting this problem here was to force people to consider alternative modes of solution. If this was successful, it should reduce the number of Einstellung solutions for Problems 10 and 11. These, like Problems 7 and 8, could be solved by two methods. The results for Problems 10 and 11 are shown in Table 4.5.

In the set group, there was a drop from 81 percent Einstellung solutions on Problems 7 and 8 to 55 percent on 11 and 12. The drop

Table 4.3. Percentage of Subjects Responding to Problems 10 and 11 with
Einstellung Solution

Group	Percent
"Set"	55
"Don't be blind"	30

in the "Don't be blind" condition was from 63 percent to 30 percent.
These habit-breaking procedures obviously had some effect, but
even both together failed to eliminate the Einstellung in 30 percent of
the subjects within the "Don't be blind" condition.

Not only did Luchins try variants of this test on an enormous
number of subjects, but he obtained essentially similar results on a
variety of other tasks as well. These involved geometric problems,
words hidden in letters and paper-and-pencil maze tests; but they all
shared the same basic problem—first a series of problems with
a unique solution, then a set of "test" problems which could be solved
by either the old procedure or a new, simpler one. Just as in the
water jars experiment, subjects showed a strong bias toward applying
the familiar, clumsy solution. Clearly, therefore, this mechanization
of thinking is both quick to develop and hard to dislodge.

THE SUCCESSFUL MODIFICATION OF
STRONG HABITS AND THEIR
CONSEQUENCES

There are a few errors in our collection which suggest that although
strong habits strenuously resist attempts to change them, they can,
with a great deal of effort and concentration, eventually be modified
to suit new conditions or goals. But when the original circumstances
are restored, these now inappropriate modifications sometimes
show, in their turn, a stubborn resistance to change. Two personal
examples (JR) will help to make the point clearer.

I had recently acquired a dictating machine and was busy getting
the hang of writing letters on it. To gain some confidence with

the machine, I would scribble the letters in rough, and then record them. In reading them on to the tape, however, I was very scrupulous about including such things as 'comma', 'semicolon' and the like. After I had been using the machine for a few days, I gave a lecture in which I read out a passage from a book. It was only after I had read a sentence or two that I realized—to my acute embarrassment—that I was also reading out all the punctuation marks as if dictating into the recorder.

I pulled up outside a friend's house on a quiet residential street and parked the car facing the wrong way for the traffic flow. On leaving the house with the friend, I drove off still staying on the wrong side of the road without noticing the fact. Indeed, I wondered why the vehicle coming toward me was on my side of the road. Then I realized what I was doing and pulled into the curb—pretending to park in front of another house to save face. Two things seem to have contributed to this slip. The first was that I had been attending very closely to what was being said to me, and the second was that I had just returned from driving for eight days in France, where I had become accustomed to having the driver's side nearest the curb.

In our previous discussion, we stressed the pervasive influence of the frequency of past successful employment as a factor leading to the unintended appearance of an established output pattern. But the interesting feature of these two slips is that recent modifications of well-established skills—reading aloud and driving on the left side of the road—seem to have overriden frequency considerations. It appears as if, in certain circumstances, the effort required to modify an existing routine leaves powerful residues for sometime after the change of procedure is no longer necessary.

HABIT: A MIXED BLESSING

Habit, like many other things in the human condition, carries with it both enormous benefits and great penalties. Unlike most other creatures, man comes into this world with relative few automatic performances wired into his nervous system. Our range of potential activity is so vast that we can only acquire these instinctual equivalents as the result of painful and laborious practice once we are here. But, as William James remarked: "If practice did not make perfect, nor habit economize the expense of nervous and muscular energy, (we) would be in a very sorry plight."[15] Henry Maudsley gave us an inkling of what this plight would be: "If an act became no easier after being done several times, if the careful direction of consciousness were necessary to its accomplishment on each occasion, it is evident that the whole activity of a lifetime might be confined to one or two deeds ... A man might be occupied all day in dressing and undressing himself; the attitude of his body would absorb all his attention and energy; the washing of his hands or the fastening of a button would be as difficult to him on each occasion as to the child on its first trial; and he would, furthermore, be completely exhausted by his exertions."[16]

But it is equally true, as this chapter has sought to demonstrate, that habit constitutes an immensely productive source of human error. The circumstances in which these errors are made can, as we shall see in Chapter 10, exact terrible punishments. Yet, to some extent at least, we can guard against the slips of habit by appreciating the conditions under which they are liable to occur. We will never eliminate them altogether, but we can hope to reduce their number by increasing people's awareness of what triggers them, and to minimize their consequences by making critical environments more forgiving of error.

Perhaps the most sinister feature of this dark side of habit, however, is not so much the way it diverts our actions as the restrictions it can impose upon our thinking. Slips of action are obvious, mostly inconsequential and usually easy to put right. Habits of thought, on the other hand, are insidious in their onset and subtle in their influence. Because they are not readily detectable, they have a tendency to become self-perpetuating. This is all right so long as we remain in the same place tackling the same problems. But the world is not generally so obliging, and if there is a single message to be had from this chapter it is that the more entrenched a habit has become, the greater is its likelihood of emerging at a time when it is neither wanted nor appropriate.

---

[15] W. James, *The Principles of Psychology* Vol. I, p. 113.
[16] Quoted by W. James, *The Principles of Psychology* Vol. I, p. 155.

chapter five
RECOGNITION FAILURES

In April, 1958, a Viscount airliner approaching Prestwick Airport crashed into a hillside at Tarbolton, Ayrshire, killing all on board. In December of the same year, a Britannia aircraft on a test flight struck the ground at Christchurch in Hampshire. There were only two survivors. In both cases, the pilots reported their altitude to air traffic control as being 10,000 feet higher than it actually was.[1,2]

The occupants of these two aircraft, like others before and since, were victims of the notorious "killer" altimeter, shown in Figure 5.1. From its tragic history, it is clear that this instrument was unwittingly designed to makes its occasional misreading inevitable. The main problem is that it has three pointers of differing length sharing the same range of numbers (0–9) on the dial. The shortest pointer indicates the height of the aircraft in units of ten thousand feet, the next longest in thousands of feet, and the longest in hundreds. With this knowledge and some effort, you can probably establish that the height indicated on the altimeter shown in Figure 5.1 is a little over 24,000 feet.[3]

---

[1]D.E. Broadbent, *In Defense of Empirical Psychology* (London: Methuen & Co. Ltd., 1973), pp. 3–4.

[2]J.T. Reason, in *Adult Learning*, ed. M. Howe (London: Wiley, 1977), pp. 21–44.

[3]J.M. Rolfe, "Psychology and aviation medicine", unpublished paper (Farnborough, England: R.A.F. Institute of Aviation Medicine, 1962).

Figure 5.1 Altimeter

A number of factors conspire to make this instrument easy to be misread by ten thousand feet. Since each pointer moves steadily around the scale, the smallest pointer will be approaching one when the next largest reaches nine. It is therefore very easy to read an indicated height of 9,000 feet as 19,000. In everyday life, we are accustomed to reading a pointer to the nearest digit, and this habit is hard to break. Also the difficulty is further compounded by the relative lengths of the pointers, which are inversely related to the size of the units they signify. To read the instrument, we are required to look at the pointers in the reverse order of their size. This in itself hardly feels natural, but it also means that the largest errors are likely to be associated with the smallest and least visible pointer. Third, the construction of this instrument is such that the smallest, yet most significant pointer, can be occluded by either of the other two at various points on the dial. Small wonder, therefore, that it produces recognition failures. Less understandable is why aircraft are still being fitted with this lethal altimeter.

Verbal communications can be readily misperceived at the best of times, and more so when there is additional noise and distraction; hence the specialized and restricted vocabularies used in aviation and in other circumstances where the cost of getting the message wrong can be great. The possible ambiguity present in even the simplest spoken instruction is demonstrated by the case of the captain of a four-engined aircraft who, on discovering that No. 4 engine was on fire, asked the flight engineer to "feather four," and was appalled to find that the engineer had feathered all four engines.

In periods of high activity, when the risks of ambiguity and misinterpretation are at their greatest, it obviously pays to restrict communications to those matters relevant to the task. This lesson was painfully learned by the kind-hearted aircraft captain who, on the takeoff run, looked across at his depressed first officer in the right hand seat and told him to "cheer up." The unhappy first officer though he had said "gear up" and promptly raised the undercarriage before they had left the ground.[4]

A close examination of a number of well-documented catastrophic lapses (see Chapter 10) suggests that mistakes of this kind are usually embedded within a complex network of causal factors which interact in such a way as to bring a relatively minor lapse to unnatural prominence. This was the case with the Nairobi jumbo jet incident, discussed in some detail below.[5]

Shortly after dawn on September 3, 1974, a British Airways Boeing 747 was approaching Nairobi Airport after a nine-hour flight from Zurich. The time was just before 5 o'clock in the morning and the flight deck, already hot and dry, was filled with the glare of the rising sun. The captain, a man with over 30 years commercial flying experience, was piloting the aircraft. The co-pilot was handling most of the air-to-ground communications.

The aircraft was equipped with an autopilot/flight director system which among other functions has the capability for automatic capture of a preselected altitude. With this equipment, it is possible to carry out either a partial or a fully automatic landing, provided the

[4]J.M. Rolfe, "Ergonomics and air safety." *Applied Ergonomics* 3(1972), 75–81.
[5]Boeing 747–136 G-AWNJ. Report on the incident near Nairobi Airport, Kenya, on 3 September 1974. (*Aircraft Accident Report 14/75* London: H.M. Stationery Office, 1975).

destination has an Instrument Landing System (ILS) and the appropriate navigational aids. Nairobi Airport, which was unusually high at 5,327 feet above sea level, was equipped with ILS on Runway 06. When an aircraft's position over the nondirectional "Golf Golf" beacon was confirmed by visual reference or by radar, the permitted procedure for an ILS approach was to descend to 7,500 feet after leaving the beacon, and then to hold that altitude until the glide path has been intercepted. After this, the descent of the aircraft would be controlled automatically until the point of landing. This information was available on the airport approach charts located beside the Captain on the flight deck.

When the aircraft was about 150 nautical miles from Nairobi, the Captain carried out the "top of the descent briefing" in which he reviewed the approach charts, noted Nairobi's height above sea level and checked the appropriate safety heights for the area. He also discussed with his flight deck colleagues the availability of diversion airfields. Of these, Entebbe was the most likely. The commander announced his intention of carrying out an automatic approach using the ILS with a manual landing once the runway had been sighted.

About 90 miles from Nairobi, the Captain commenced the descent from 37,000 feet. They were cleared to descend to 10,000 feet. At this point, they were in visual contact with the ground and remained so until passing the volcanic crater east of the "Golf Golf" beacon when they flew into a low cloud. It was at this stage that further descent clearance was given to intercept the localizer beam and complete the ILS approach. The actual transmission from the Nairobi radar controller was: "Speedbird zero two nine you are passing the golf golf beacon this time. Descend seven five zero feet . . ." Neither pilot heard the clearance correctly and believed they were cleared to descend to "five, zero, zero, zero feet." The co-pilot accordingly made the following transmission without hestitation: "Roger speedbird zero two nine cleared to five thousand feet . . ." Critically, this message was neither corrected nor acknowledged by the radar controller.

On receiving this clearance, the commander disconnected the auto-throttle and put the aircraft into a descent. At the same time, the co-pilot dialed 5000 into the Altitude Selector of the autopilot. The effect of this setting was to cause the aircraft to descend on automatic pilot until it reached this preselected altitude—an altitude that was actually 327 feet below the height of the airfield.

While the aircraft continued to lose height, the flight deck crew was engaged in a burst of intense activity. All of them were convinced that the flight path had been programmed correctly. At 2,500 feet above the ground, they heard a terrain audio warning. They noted the warning, but were not alarmed by it since it occurs at least once on each approach. The next two warnings came within two seconds of one another. In the first case, the ILS deviation warning lights on each pilot's instrument panel lit up. Because it was unexpected, the captain's first reaction was to believe it to be a false alarm. Then the Decision Height warning tone began to sound. Almost immediately afterwards, the aircraft broke out of the cloud and they saw the ground, but no runway, some 200 feet below them. It was at this moment that the realization of their error struck the commander " . . . like the kick of a horse in the stomach." With great presence of mind, he checked the rate of descent on the elevators, disconnected the autopilots and eased the throttles into the three-quarters position—which he judged to be adequate for the overshoot but not enough to disturb the passengers with too violent a maneuver. It was later estimated that, at its lowest point, the aircraft came within 70 feet of the ground some six miles ahead of the runway.

The immediate causes of this near disaster are fairly easy to identify: the pilots misheard the clearance altitude and set an incorrect value on the autopilot, the radar controller did not correct or even acknowledge the co-pilot's readback, and the pilots failed to respond to the automatic warnings showing that they had departed from the ILS glide-path and were too close to the ground. The most puzzling fact is not that they misheard the transmission from the Nairobi Air Traffic Control—the initial "seven" of the clearance height was extremely indistinct and could only be heard later by the pilots on the third replay of the tape—but that they accepted a clearance height which they knew, or at least had known some minutes earlier during the briefing, to be below the actual height of the airfield. How could such a lapse come about?

The subsequent investigation revealed several factors likely to reduce crew efficiency: fatigue, glare, time of day, preoccupation with worsening weather conditions and the unwelcome possibility of diverting to Entebbe.[5] It was also discovered that the co-pilot was suffering from a residual gastric disorder picked up a month earlier in New Delhi, for which he had been taking unauthorized medication that included drowsiness and nausea among its known side effects. But why did this particular error occur rather than some other?

The captain himself offered two very plausible reasons.[6] First, as far as he could tell, the co-pilot was carrying out his duties promptly and efficiently, and under those circumstances, it was quite usual for a busy captain to have, in his words, " ... a coiled spring reaction to an anticipated flight requirement, the altitude content of which is set by the co-pilot after he has received his clearance." Second, he believed that the misheard clearance was accepted by both pilots, despite their prior briefing, because it was the kind of intermediate clearance they were used to receiving in many other airports in the world. To their tired and preoccupied minds, five thousand feet sounded right because it was the altitude their past experience had led them to expect in the approach phase of a flight. In this, as in many other errors, we see the influence of the pervasive bias that causes us to overlook small but crucial changes in otherwise familiar circumstances, and to make the usual rather than a suitably modified response.

Throughout this chapter, we shall be emphasizing the close similarities between the slips of habit, discussed earlier, and recognition failures. Both occur, we argue, due to the activation of strong rather than appropriate cognitive demons, a take-over that is made possible by automaticity (*i.e.* a high level of organization and autonomy within these wrongly emergent demons) and by attentional *capture*. As in slips of habit, recognition failures can take the form of either intrusions or exclusions. In the former, the error consists of mistaking one object for another. In the latter, the mistake involves missing some feature of the sensory input because it is embedded in a familiar context that is more usually responded to as a whole. For example, when the subjects in an experiment were asked to cross out all the "t's" in a short passage of printed prose, they missed a disproportionately large number in the word *the*, since the definite

---

[6]Personal communication with the captain of the Boeing 747 involved in the Nairobi incident.

article tends to be read as a single unit rather than as three individual letters.[7]

But whether the misperception involves a wrong identification or an omission, the nature of the mistake demonstrates a marked bias toward accepting a percept that is more familiar, or more expected than the correct one on that occasion. As in action or word selection, the factors which mostly determine the form of the erroneous impression are frequency and context, though sometimes we can also detect the influence of need or emotion.

Recognition failures reveal themselves both in action and in perception. In the latter, the wrong impression is realized before it is acted upon. Because these misperceptions are usually short-lived, being corrected almost immediately by additional sensory evidence, they are hardly noticed during the normal course of everyday life. But slips of action are more memorable, and it was these rather than simple misperceptions that were recorded by our diarists.

EVERYDAY SLIPS OF ACTION ARISING FROM RECOGNITION FAILURES

On the basis of the short error descriptions available to us, it is difficult to be sure whether a wrong action was due to the incorrect response selection or to a recognition failure. However, there are a fairly large number of slips in our collection (approximately 11 percent) whose characteristics clearly favor the latter alternative. In these, the mistake consists of reaching for, approaching or placing something into an object that is physically similar to the one intended. Here are some actual examples.

> "I intended to pick up the deodorant, but picked up the air freshener instead."

> "I found myself pushing someone else's shopping cart at the supermarket."

> "Instead of opening a tin of Kit-E-Kat, I opened and offered my cat a tin of rice pudding."

[7]Alice F. Healy, "Detection errors on the word 'the': Evidence for reading units larger than letters." *Journal of Experimental Psychology: Human Perception and Performance* 2(1976) 235–242.

"I raised the egg in the egg cup to my lips instead of the orange juice."

"Instead of switching on the bathroom heater, I switched on the exhaust fan."

"I flicked my cigarette ash into my coffee cup instead of into the ashtray."

"When seasoning the meat, I sprinkled it with sugar instead of salt."

"Instead of pouring the tea into the tea cups, I poured it into the milk jug."

"On several occasions while preparing breakfast, I have sprinkled instant coffee over my cereal instead of putting it into the mug."

"On coming through the barrier at the station, I handed the ticket collector an old bus ticket instead of the train ticket."

"I filled the washing machine with oatmeal."

Though usually trivial, these slips can sometimes have damaging and expensive consequences, as in the next example.

"I checked the water and oil levels in the car engine. Both needed topping off. I removed the oil filler cap—the radiator cap was already off—and went to get the oil can and the water container. I then poured two pints of oil into the radiator. The car eventually needed a new radiator and water pump."

On other occasions, the results can be acutely embarrassing.

"I stopped at a roadside cafe to use the toilet. I saw what I thought was MEN on the sign over the door. When I got inside, the place looked horribly unfamiliar and I rushed out again—to the astonishment of passers-by. I looked at the sign again. It said WOMEN. In my haste, I had only taken in the last three letters."

"A few weeks ago, during a particularly busy day, I was about to drive from one meeting to another and to my great discomfort found that as I was saying goodbye to a fairly distinguished group of people at my car, I got into the back seat to drive away. I am often chauffeur driven—but not on this occasion."

Occasionally, it is not an object that is misrecognized, but its aspect.

"I put my dungarees on back to front."

"Instead of pulling the plug out of the back of the electric coffee pot, I pulled on the spout and burned my hand."

"I opened the box of matches upside down, dropping all the matches on the floor."

In these examples, the errors could reasonably be attributed to a combination of inattention during the performance of a routine task and perceptual similarity between objects or their aspects. But there are other slips which seem to arise from the active part of a stored intention, the verb as it were, becoming detached from its proper setting and incorrectly applying itself to another object for which the particular act is roughly appropriate. Thus, these detached intention errors appear to possess two components: the existence of a stored intent to carry out some activity plus contextual triggering from another object for which the same kind of action is suitable. Below are some recognition failures which seem to fall into this category.

"My 11-year-old daughter had wandered downstairs unable to sleep, and after a chat I set off to see her back to bed. Going through the hall, vaguely conscious of something live walking behind me, I opened the front door and kindly said 'Out you go.' I'd briefly confused her with the cat."

"I went to my room to get a watch I hadn't worn for some time to bring it downstairs and fit it with a new strap. While looking for the watch, I found a bracelet I liked but had forgotten about. I went down with the bracelet instead of the watch, and opened the package with the strap as if to fit it to the bracelet."

"I intended to place my hairbrush in its usual place by the bookcase. I put my boyfriend's lighter there instead."

"I intended to close the window as it was cold. I closed the cupboard instead."

Another type of recognition failure is "jumping the gun." When we are keyed up to expect a particular signal or event, like athletes waiting for the starter's signal, some other change occurs in our immediate environment and we respond to it as if it were the thing anticipated. For example:

"I was waiting at home for an important phone call which I expected at any minute. The front door bell rang, and I rushed to pick up the phone."

"I was sitting in my car waiting for a red light to change when the cigarette lighter on the dashboard popped out. On hearing the noise, I began to move forward even though the light was still red."

Occasionally, descriptions of recognition failures contain a hint that unconscious motivation was involved, as in the next example.

"I intended to bring the file with my computing notes to the university so that I could go on the computer at 11:30. When I got there, I discovered that I had brought the wrong file and had to give computing a miss. I don't understand and don't like computing."

In certain slips of action, it is not an object that is confused, but time, or the day of the week.

"I got up at 7 o'clock instead of 8 o'clock, one hour too early."

"I woke up, got dressed, but when I got to the bedroom door I realized it was my morning off and I could have stayed in bed."

"I got up and took the bus to work only to realize later that it was Saturday. I don't work on Saturdays."

The one thing that all of these recognition failures appear to have in common is inattention. Just as some degree of conscious attention needs to be invested in checking that the desired actions have been correctly selected, so it would also seem necessary for establishing the accuracy of our perceptions. Inappropriate recognition demons can be activated by rough approximations to the expected class of stimuli. And sometimes, in the presence of detached intentions or when tuned to expect a particular signal, these approximations may be quite remote from the correct perception. In the one case, the link is established by the nature of the detached intention; in the other, any sudden change in the environment can suffice to trigger the prepared action.

MISPERCEPTIONS

When we are engaged in some routine activity with our mind on other things, it is quite possible, as we have seen, to act on the basis of a recognition failure. The problem here is not usually the inadequacy of the sensory information, but the fact that conscious attention is directed elsewhere, thus allowing already activated recognition demons to gain control over the perceptual mechanism. With its limited capacity occupied by pressing but unrelated matters and lulled by the familiar rhythm of an habitual task, the Intention System is only alerted to the error when action departs sufficiently from the plan to create some attention-grabbing incongruity, such as the sight of tea filling a sugar bowl.

Perceptual failures can also occur, though more rarely and with generally fleeting consequences, when we are paying close attention to the sensory information. These recognition failures usually arise because the data reaching our senses is of insufficient quantity or quality to allow us to form an immediate and accurate perception. The information may be presented too briefly, or be too noisy or sparse to permit an unambiguous impression. But active recognition demons will be searching this degraded input hungrily for features that match their particular specifications. If one of these demons is already close to its triggering point due to influences from past use, the environmental context, stored intentions, or the Need System, it will only need very little in the way of partial sensory information for it to achieve at least momentary control of the perceptual apparatus. We all know the experience of "seeing" a sought for face in the crowd at an airport or railway station. But as the wrongly identified person draws nearer, they bring with them disconfirming visual clues that eventually oust the wrong impression—though if we have a strong need to see that particular face, the false perception often puts up a stubborn resistance against the contrary evidence.

The tenacity of false impressions in the face of incompatible sensory facts is evident from a study of train drivers who had passed danger signals.[8] An engine driver who has made the same journey many times develops a strong set of expectations about events and signals further down the line. At the beginning of the journey, he may well be alert to departures from the expected. But as the run progresses, and he becomes tired or anxious about making up lost time, he may neglect a signal which he does not expect, or misinterpret one that conflicts with his preconceptions.

In the Ludlow train collision of September, 1956, the driver ran past a caution signal and two signals at danger without reducing speed. In the official report, it was suggested that the driver " ... may have been lulled, to some extent, through his long experience of working over the line, by the expectation of a clear run through Ludlow as is usual with this train." At Lewisham, in the following year, a driver ... passed a number of cautionary and stop signals without slowing down. The train collided into the rear of a ten coach electric train. Ninety lives were lost and 109 people seriously injured. The driver survived and at his trial stated that he had expected a green 'go' signal " ... because I have never been stopped there in the whole time I have been travelling."

It has been suggested that erroneous impressions, or "false

[8]D. Russell Davis, "Railway signals passed at danger: The drivers, circumstances and psychological processes." *Ergonomics* 9(1966), 211–222. D. Russell Davis, "Human errors and transport accidents." *Ergonomics* 2(1958), 24–33.

hypotheses," are especially likely to be accepted immediately follow-ing some period of stress or high anxiety. When an emergency has been successfully negotiated, there is a natural tendency to relax one's vigilance. Similarly, toward the end of a long trip, one often feels as good as home. This end effect could well have contributed to the disastrous multiple train collision at Harrow and Wealdstone in October, 1952, which cost 122 lives.[9] The driver of a train from Perth was approaching the end of his long journey when he passed a color signal at caution and two semaphore signals at danger without apparently noticing them. At the official inquiry, it was estimated that this lapse of attention must have lasted for at least a minute. It may be supposed that after a difficult trip, during which he had been delayed by fog and a late start, the driver was induced into a false state of security by the clearance of the fog and the prospect of an easy, uninterrupted run into the London terminus. The same kind of premature relaxation seems to have occurred in the case of the motorist who, on returning home from a long journey, swung into the identical driveway of his neighbor's house and hit a tree which, as far as he was concerned, ". . . just couldn't have been there."

We mentioned earlier that false impressions can be retained even though there is a mass of sensory evidence to the contrary. Once it has formed a hypothesis that fits in with our needs and expectations, the Intention System sometimes shows a marked reluc-tance to abandon it. As Einstein once said, "If the facts don't fit the theory, then the facts are wrong." How else can one explain the following incident reported by a police sergeant patroling a stretch of highway?

> We coned off an accident for 200 yards. There were two police cars with blue flashing lights, two breakdown trucks with amber flashing lights, two hazard lights working in advance of the accident and one set of blue spinning lights 400 yards ahead— and a Hillman came through everything at 60 mph, right over the top of a red light on one of the cones. When I stopped him, he said he thought the lights were advertisements.[10]

[9]L.T.C. Rolt, *Red for Danger* (London: Pan Books, 1978), pp. 280–281.
[10]Motorway police sergeant, in *Drive* 15 (Autumn, 1970), p. 71.

FACTORS THAT DETERMINE
FALSE IMPRESSIONS

While everyday experiences and accident reports offer up varied examples of recognition failure and yield clues as to how these false impressions are shaped, it is only in the laboratory that these factors can be studied systematically. In these artificial but controlled conditions, the perceptual act can be broken down into its component parts and, at the same time, we can manipulate the strength of those variables which may determine its outcome. Following, we shall be briefly considering what has been learned from experimental studies about the influences that cause our false impressions to take one form rather than another. Four factors, in particular, seem to be of importance: frequency, incongruity, context, and need.

Frequency

According to the theory of action described in Chapter 3, the likelihood of a cognitive demon springing unbidden into action or perception is directly related to the number of times it has been successfully employed in the past. Let us see how this assumption stands up to the experimental evidence.

With most of the objects that confront our senses, it is virtually impossible to estimate their frequency of occurrence with any degree of certainty. But this is not true of words. Thanks to the painstaking efforts of previous researchers, we possess reasonably accurate figures for the number of times a given word or name appears in written English.[11] As a result, many of the studies concerned with effects of familiarity upon perception have compared people's ability to recognize words of high and low frequency in the language. Usually these words are presented, either to the eyes or to the ears, in some attenuated form so that the chances of correct detection are well below 100 percent.

In an experiment by Broadbent,[12] subjects were required to

---

[11]E.L. Thorndike and I. Lorge, *The Teacher's Word Book of 3,000 Words* (New York: Teachers College Press, 1944).

[12]D.E. Broadbent, "Word frequency and response bias" *Psychological Review* 74(1967), 1–15.

write down the words they thought they heard on a taped list. The noise level of the recording was carefully adjusted so as to permit only about 30 percent likelihood of correct recognition. Half the words in the list were of high frequency in English, and the other half of low frequency. The findings are summarized in Table 5.1.

Table 5.1. The Results of Broadbent's (1967) World Frequency Experiment

Stimulus word	Percent correct	Percent HF* errors	Percent LF* errors
High frequency	32.5	32.3	15.8
Low frequency	12.8	41.7	19.2

*HF = High frequency; LF = Low frequency. These numbers indicate the percentage of high and low frequency words, not necessarily in the original list, that occur as wrong guesses.

There are two points to be noticed about these results. First, high frequency stimulus words were nearly three times as likely to be detected correctly. Second, when the wrong word was identified it was twice as likely to be a high frequency word than a low frequency word; and this ratio of 2:1 remained roughly the same regardless of whether the stimulus word itself was of high or low frequency. This and many similar studies clearly demonstrate the primacy of past experience in shaping both our correct and incorrect perceptions.

Incongruity

Another way of showing the powerful effects of expectation upon recognition is to present people with a stimulus in which a highly familiar configuration has been deliberately rearranged to make it incongruous. Two American psychologists, Bruner and Postman, did this with playing cards.[13] They measured how long it took subjects to recognize cards in which the normal colors had been reversed as compared to normal cards. In certain cards, like the three of hearts, the hearts had been printed in black instead of red; while in other

[13]J.S. Bruner and L. Postman, "On the perception of incongruity." *Journal of Personality* 18(1949), 206–223.

cards, like the two or six of spades, the spades were printed in red.

Each card was shown to the subjects at gradually increasing exposure times, starting with a very brief ten milliseconds and going up in small steps to one second (1000 milliseconds), and they were asked to indicate when they thought they had recognized the card. The results showed dramatic differences in the recognition times (thresholds) for normal and reversed-color cards. While 100 percent of the normal cards had been recognized by 350 milliseconds, only 89.7 percent of the doctored cards had been correctly identified at the longest exposure of 1000 milliseconds. On average, recognition thresholds for the color-reversed cards were four times greater than those for normal playing cards.

Some explanation of why it took the subjects so long to recognize the incongruous cards can be found in the different ways people dealt with the color reversals. Four kinds of reaction were found. The first of these the investigators called the *dominance* response. Essentially, this consisted of a denial of the incongruous elements. Thus, when faced with a red six of spades, a subject may report with much confidence, the "six of spades" or the "six of hearts", depending upon whether he was tuned to the shape of the pips or their color. A second technique they termed *compromise*. Here, subjects resolved the conflict between the expectation and the reality by reporting a red six of spades as either a purple six of hearts or a purple six of spades. A third reaction was called *disruption*. In this case, the subject fails to resolve the conflict satisfactorily and responds with increasingly bizarre comments, like "I don't know what the hell it is now, nor even for sure whether it's a playing card," at a point well above his normal recognition threshold. Finally, there is *recognition* of the incongruity. This is generally preceded by a vague sense of wrongness that is difficult to articulate, then gradually the nature of the rearrangement comes to be appreciated.

These findings provide convincing evidence of the principal theme of this chapter, namely that perceptual organization is strongly influenced by expectations built up as the result of previous transactions with the environment. When these deeply ingrained expectations are violated, as in this experiment, the perceiver manifests a good deal of resistance to accepting the incongruity.

Context

The influence of immediate context is easily demonstrated by Figure 5.2.[14] Here the same stimulus is perceived as an *H* or an *A*, depending

TAE CAT

Figure 5.2   Demonstrating the Effect of Context Upon Word Recognition

upon its setting. This is an example of what has been termed *top-down* information processing, because higher level knowledge determines the way inputs from specific feature demons are perceived. Its converse is *bottom-up* processing.[15] That is, minor demons identify specific features at the lowest level of processing. These are combined by higher-level demons into patterns such as letters, and are put together to form words and sentences.

An experiment by Tulving, Mandler, and Baumal set out to investigate how these two modes of processing interact.[16] Their material was nine-word sentences. The first eight words were there to provide a context for the ninth, critical word. Here is an example: "The huge slum was filled with dirt and *disorder.*" Subjects were given either none, four, or eight of the context words and then shown the target word for a very short period. Thus, for the sentence given above, subjects in the various conditions would see the following:

8-word context:	The huge slum was filled with dirt and disorder.
4-word context	Filled with dirt and disorder.
0-word context	disorder.

[14]J.R. Anderson, *Cognitive Psychology and its Implications* (San Francisco: W.H. Freeman and Company, 1980), p. 43.

[15]See also G. Reicher, "Perceptual recognition as a function of meaningfulness of stimulus material." *Journal of Experimental Psychology* 81(1969), 275–280. D.D. Wheeler, "Processes in word recognition." *Cognitive Psychology* 1(1970), 59–85.

[16]E. Tulving, G. Mandler, and R. Baumal, "Interaction of two sources of information in tachistoscopic word recognition." *Canadian Journal of Psychology* 18(1964), 62–71.

The target word (*disorder*) was presented at exposures of 140 milliseconds down to zero. Figure 5.3 shows the percentage of

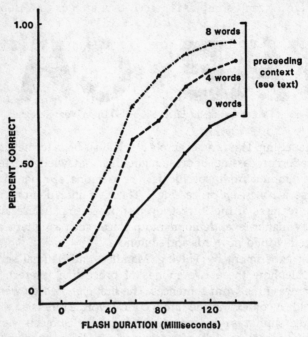

Figure 5.3

correct identifications of critical words as a function of their exposure period and the number of preceding context words. It can be seen that the probability of correct detection increased both with the amount of context and the duration of the presentation. Even in the zero-millisecond exposure, where subjects could only guess, they were performing 16 percent better with an 8-word context than with a zero-word context. But note also that the benefits of context are greater with longer exposures—more than 40 percent at the 60-millisecond exposure and about 30 percent at the 140-millisecond exposure. It is evident that subjects were using context to reduce the amount of bottom-up processing needed to identify the word.

This experiment shows that we can use prior sentence context to assist us in word recognition. With the aid of context, we need to extract less information the word itself to identify it. In fact, we can use the rest of the sentence to fill in missing words—as in the previous sentence. Did you spot the missing *from*?[17] Even if you did, it is unlikely that you had any trouble making sense of the sentence. Context works the other way as well. Take a look at the sentence printed below.

> I LOVE PARIS IN THE
> THE SPRINGTIME.

Did you notice anything wrong with it? Perhaps you spotted the extra *the*, but it probably did not leap out of the page at you.

Need

We have seen that recognition failures, like correct perceptions, are shaped partially by context and what is familiar, and therefore by what we expect to perceive. As William James put it, "Perception is of definite and probable things." But there is also a wealth of experimental evidence to suggest that we not only perceive what we expect to perceive, but also what we *want* to perceive.

A typical study of this kind was carried out by Levine, Chein, and Murphy.[18] Having deprived subjects of food for varying lengths of time, they showed them a number of ambiguous drawings behind a ground glass screen. Some of the pictures represented food articles, others neutral objects or meaningless designs. The subjects were asked to give a verbal association for every picture. With black-and-white pictures, the number of times some article of food was mentioned in connection with the picture increased after three hours without food, and increased still further after six hours. A control group, who were shown the pictures on a series of occasions shortly after eating, exhibited no such trend toward an increase of food-related associations.

In a subsequent set of experiments carried out by McClelland and Atkinson, observers were situated in front of a screen on which,

[17]P.H. Lindsay and D.A. Norman, *Human Information Processing: An Introduction to Psychology* (New York: Academic Press, 1972, p. 133).

[18]R. Levine, I. Chein and G. Murphy, "The relation of the intensity of a need to the amount of perceptual distortion." *Journal of Psychology* 13(1942), 283–293.

they were told, faint pictures would be projected.[19] Their task was to report what they saw. In most cases, nothing was actually projected onto the screen; but occasionally vague blots were shown. Once again, more food responses were given after longer periods of food deprivation.

It has been observed many times that the recognition of objects is more rapid when they are related to some interest, value, or need of the observer. For example, hungry or thirsty subjects recognize words related to their needs more readily than other words. Subjects with a high need for achievement (as assessed by personality measures) spot success-related words faster than neutral ones; while the same is not true of less ambitious individuals.[20]

These studies and our everyday experiences would seem to justify the assumption built into our theory of action: that recognition demons no less than action or word demons can be primed by the Need System, thus increasing their chances of usurping the perceptual mechanism. We will examine this issue again in Chapter 9 when we revisit the Freudian slip.

SUMMARY

To summarize the story so far: The nature of recognition failures testifies to the existence of well-organized and independently active recognition demons that are capable, on occasions, of gaining control over perception even when this is unmerited either by the information available to our senses or by our current intentions. Two conditions, in particular, seem liable to provoke these failures: inattention and inadequate sensory information. The former results from internal activity, the latter is largely a function of the external world.

It is evident from the frequency with which recognition failures lead to slips of action during routine activities that there is some characteristic of habitual behavior that disposes us to form the

[19]D. McClelland and J. Atkinson, "The projective expression of needs: I. The effect of different intensities of the hunger drive on perception." *Journal of Psychology* 25(1948), 205–222.
[20]F.H. Allport, *Theories of Perception and the Concept of Structure* (New York: John Wiley & Sons Inc., 1955), pp. 375–406.

occasional wrong impression. In most cases, the mistaken objects are clearly illuminated and quite distinct; so that we cannot blame our senses. The most likely candidate is the fact that these activities encourage our minds to occupy themselves elsewhere, so that we fail to allocate the small degree of attention necessary to check that our actions and perceptions are running according to plan. Perhaps the most interesting feature of these perceptual confusions, and the wrong actions that arise from them, is the indication they give of the need to keep available some small part of the limited attentional resource (see Chapter 11) for monitoring perception, even in the case of highly automated tasks. Recognition demons, like action demons, need to be kept in check, if only on a very loose rein.

The other factor leading to perceptual failure is the presence of ambiguous sensory messages that contain features relevant to more than one recognition demon. Presenting the eyes or the ears with a vague stimulus is like tossing a bone to a bunch of hungry dogs. Each one claims a part of it, but it is usually the strongest and most active that snatches the whole bone for himself—even when it was meant for another.

These particular wrong impressions are hardly errors as such, since the information provided is usually insufficient to form a correct appreciation. Nevertheless, they bring into sharp relief the intrinsic factors that bias our perceptions in predictable directions. All recognitions, whether true or false, emerge from a transaction between the available sensory data and the pre-established knowledge structures, the demons, set up to accommodate them. When we are attentive and the sensory information is adequate, we usually perceive things as they really are. But when one or other of these conditions is not met, our impressions are fashioned by that recognition demon which is currently the most active.

No surprisingly, therefore, recognition failures are generally neither random nor unlawful. Their nature is governed by the same forces that determine correct perception. Our perceptual apparatus is geared to handle the expected, so it is hardly remarkable that its failures should tend toward the expected rather than the unexpected, toward the familiar and banal rather than the novel or bizarre. Sometimes, as we have noted, these biases toward perceiving the probable are overridden by *wishful thinking*, and we see what we want to see rather than what is actually there. But whether it is expectancy or need, or a combination of both, the point we seek to emphasize is that given only a moderate knowledge of a person's state of mind, we stand a good chance of predicting the directions along which his or her perceptions could err.

POSTSCRIPT: DISMANTLING THE DEMONS

Fully-fledged recognition demons are the product of a long process of construction that begins at birth and continues every day of our lives. But this does not mean that they are rigid structures, resistant to change. Perhaps more so than other kinds of cognitive demon, those concerned with recognition are peculiarly vulnerable to various forms of interference, and in particular they find it difficult to withstand sustained use.

In the normal course of events, recognition demons are not called upon to function for more than a brief moment in the center of the perceptual stage. Even when we believe ourselves to be concentrating hard upon something, our attention is continually wandering, though it may not stray very far. In a short space of time, many recognition demons will be employed—and that is the way they prefer it. If they are forced to remain in the limelight for too long, they dwindle in stature and influence. Paradoxically, too much sustained activity tends to dismantle them.

You are probably aware of the strange effect that is caused by repeating the same word over and over to yourself. Try it: choose any word, preferably with at least three syllables, and keep repeating it out loud. After a short while, the word begins to sound rather odd. One part of your brain even begins to doubt that it has heard it before. In some curious way, this continued repetition quickly strips the word of its familiarity and even meaning. It is as if we have fatigued that particular recognition demon to the point where it has become partially de-automatized. The effect is short-lived, but is quite marked while it lasts.

This same procedure of focusing attention unnaturally (to the Western mind at least) upon a single entity is common to many forms of meditation (see also Chapter 11). Some meditators repeat a word (*mantra*) to themselves. Others focus their attention upon the feel of their breathing. Others stared fixedly at some object, like a stone or a vase. Still others scrutinize their navels. But whatever the precise manner of this concentration, the essentials are the same. Attention is deliberately narrowed down to one specific point—or, in our terms, to one particular group of recognition demons.

One of the common outcomes of this exercise is that the object thus attended to starts to revert back to its basic sensory qualities. It begins to move toward, though probably never reaches, "the buzzing, blooming confusion" that objects must convey to the eyes of the newborn child. The effects may carry over to other perceptions as well. We can look out of a window and instead of seeing fields, houses, trees, we may see patches of green, brown, blue, and ochre, more like an Impressionist painting than our usual perception. Colors often seem fresher and more intense. Objects may lose their "object-ness." The experience is generally regarded as pleasing, though to some it can be alarming. Not all can achieve these effects, but they are sufficiently often reported by meditators of all persuasions to indicate that they are the consequence of sustained but focused attention combined with physical relaxation, and would seem to be brought about in part by the disintegration of recognition demons.

Those who would like to read more about these experiences and the methods by which they are achieved, should consult the footnotes given for this chapter.[21] For our present purposes, however, these phenomena are interesting for the additional light they throw upon the nature of recognition demons.

---

[21]C. Naranjo and R. Ornstein, *On the Psychology of Meditation* (New York: Viking, 1972). John White, ed., *Frontiers of Consciousness* (New York: Avon, 1974). A. Deikman, "Experimental meditation", *Journal of Nervous and Mental Disease* 136(1963), 329–343. Mahesh Yogi, Maharishi, *Transcendental Meditation* (New York: Plume, 1975). A. Neher, *The Psychology of Transcendence* (Englewood Cliffs, New Jersey: Prentice-Hall Inc., 1980).

chapter six
MEMORY BLOCKS

Of all the minor breakdowns in cognitive function, the one that probably occurs the most frequently and causes us the greatest concern, both as a source of embarrassment and as an apparent symptom of mental decline, is the failure to retrieve from memory something we *know* to be there. It seems to happen most often with names—the "You know . . . what's his name?" experience. We recognize the face and may know a great deal about the person; but somehow the right name fails to pop into consciousness. Others may do so, but we recognize them as being wrong. William James, as ever, has provided us with the best description of this unpleasant "It's-on-the-tip-of-my-tongue" state.

> Suppose we try to recall a forgotten name. The state of our consciousness is peculiar. There is a gap therein; but no mere gap. It is a gap that is intensely active. A sort of wraith of the name is in it, beckoning us in a given direction, making us at moments tingle with the sense of our closeness, and then letting us sink back without the longed-for term. If the wrong names are proposed to us this singularly definite gap acts immediately so as to negate them. They do not fit into its mold. And the gap of one word does not feel like the gap of another . . . They rhythm of the lost word may be there without the sound to clothe it; or the evanescent sense of something which is the initial vowel or consonant may mock us fitfully, without growing more distinct.[1]

[1] W. James, *The Principles of Psychology Vol. I* (Henry Holt & Co., 1890), p. 251.

In the bulk of this chapter, we will be reporting the findings of two studies bearing on this *tip-of-the-tongue* (TOT) phenomenon that have been carried out recently at the University of Manchester by Deborah Lucas, a member of our research group. In the final part, we will attempt to relate these memory blocks to the characteristic forms of the absent-minded error, and consider how the theory proposed in Chapter 3 can help us to understand some of these aggravating lapses. But first we need to summarize the rather sparse information that already exists on this topic in psychological literature.

A BRIEF SUMMARY OF THE RESEARCH FINDINGS

For over a hundred years now, ever since the methodical Ebbinghaus sat down to force-feed his memory with lists of meaningless letter clusters (nonsense syllables) and to make systematic tests of how well he subsequently recalled them, psychologists have been conducting laboratory studies of memory.[2] The literature on the topic is vast. We have learned an enormous amount about how people memorize lists of words, nonsense syllables, and the like under controlled conditions, and this has provided much useful information about the structural aspects of memory. Unfortunately, this research has not told us a great deal about the way we use memory in the course of everyday life. Although we are required to learn and retain new material on occasions—phone numbers, addresses, bus schedules, and so on—most of our daily interactions with memory involve trying to gain access to something that is already there. The state of the art with regard to our understanding of the real-life uses to which memory is put was summed up recently by an eminent cognitive psychologist, Ulric Neisser.

> It is therefore discouraging to find that nothing in the extensive literature of the psychology of memory sheds much light on [the everyday uses of memory], so that anyone who wishes to study the problem must start from scratch. . . . It is an example of the principle that is nearly as valid in 1978 as it was in 1878: If X is an interesting and socially significant aspect of memory, then psychologists have hardly every studied X.[3]

[2] A. Baddeley, *The Psychology of Memory* (New York: Harper and Row, 1976).
[3] U. Neisser, in *Practical Aspects of Memory*, eds., M.M. Gruneberg, P. Morris and R.N. Sykes (London: Academic Press, 1978), p. 4.

This is perhaps an overly pessimistic statement, but it is certainly relevant to our present concern with blocking on names. Freud called this state *paramnesia* and attributed it to unconscious repression, as we shall discuss in Chapter 9.[4] But aside from a rather cursory investigation carried out by Woodworth in the late 1920s and early 1930s, and an obscure and still untranslated study by a German psychologist, Wenzl, in about the same period, no one bothered too much with this TOT phenomenon until the mid 1960s.[5] Then, in 1965, Hart published a paper on the *feeling of knowing* (FOK) phenomenon, or the extent to which we are sure that what we search for is actually in our memory store. He carried out a series of experiments which indicated that the strength of this FOK was a reasonably good guide to how subjects subsequently recalled the particular item. Since human memory is clearly fallible, it makes sense to presume that these feelings of knowing serve a useful purpose in telling us how worthwhile it would be to seek some forgotten name or word.[6]

In the following year, two American investigators, Brown and McNeill, made a systematic study of the TOT state itself.[7] They induced these states in their subjects by giving them definitions of infrequently used words, and asking them to supply the word in question. When this procedure elicited a TOT state, the subject was then asked to make guesses about the nature of this target word, the number of syllables, initial letters, and so on. Their results showed that people in TOT states had correct knowledge of some of the letters in the word, the syllabic structure, its phonological characteristics, and the location of the primary stress. The nearer the subject came to successful recall, the more accurate was this intermediate information. And when he was on the verge of recall, the subject could distinguish between those words popping into the mind that resembled the sought-for one, and those that did not. In the re-

[4]Sigmund Freud, *The Psychopathology of Everyday Life*, trans. Alan Tyson (Middlesex, England: Penguin Books Ltd., 1975).

[5]R.S. Woodworth, *Psychology* (3rd ed.), (New York: Holt, 1934). A. Wenzl, "Empirische und theoretische Beitrage zur Erinnenungsarbeit bei eschwerter wortfindung." *Arch. Ges. Psychol.* 97(1936), 294–318.

[6]J.T. Hart, "Memory and the feeling-of-knowing experience." *Journal of Educational Psychology* 56(1965), 202–216.

[7]R. Brown and D. McNeill, "The 'tip-of-the-tongue' phenomenon." *Journal of Verbal Learning and Verbal Behavior* 4(1966), 325–337.

mainder of the chapter, we will refer to these as *intermediate solutions*, and the sought-for word as the *target*.

In 1973, this work was extended by Yarmey into the putting of names to famous faces.[8] He found that subjects in the TOT state generally had an accurate knowledge of the first letters of the target name, initial letters of similar sounding names, and a fairly clear idea of the number of syllables. He also found that, in searching for such a name, the subjects made use of contextual cues such as the famous person's profession, where they had seen him or her and how recently. Since the mid-1960s, a steady trickle of studies on this topic has emerged, but still relatively few in comparison to conventional learn-and-recall experiments.[9] Below we have listed the principal findings of these studies.

1. TOT states indicate that retrieval from memory is a matter of degree. It is not an all or nothing affair. In these states, we tend to remember at least some part of the word or name we are seeking without necessarily finding all of it.
2. The intermediate solutions that people produce in TOT states are likely to share similar sounds or structures to the target word. But on many occasions they can also be ones with similar meanings.
3. FOK judgments are reasonably good indicators of subsequent success at retrieving the target, whether this is achieved through outside prompts (cued recall) or by recognition.
4. FOK is probably an impressionistic judgment based on the number of attributes that the person feels he or she knows about the target. However, this judgment depends not only on the attributes of the specific target, but also on the sense of familiarity the person has regarding the *class* of items to which the target belongs.

Now let us turn to the studies carried out by Deborah Lucas. The first of these was exploratory in nature. Unlike the Brown and McNeill and the Yarmey investigations, the subjects' responses to the search-triggering material were largely open-ended. The subjects were

[8]A.D. Yarmey, "I recognize your face but I can't remember your name: Further evidence on the tip-of-the-tongue phenomenon." *Memory and Cognition* 1(1973), 287–290.

[9]M. Gruneberg, in *Aspects of Memory*, eds., M. Gruneberg and P. Morris (London: Methuen, 1978), pp. 186–209. M. Eysenck, *Human Memory* (Oxford: Pergamon Press, 1977).

invited to say what they knew about the people depicted in the photographs used as stimulus material, and their comments were recorded. We were concerned not only with what the subjects knew about the person in question, but also with the order in which these items of information emerged.

FEELINGS-OF-KNOWING, NAMING AND THE BODY-OF-KNOWLEDGE: FILM STARS' FACES

The focus of interest in this study was face-name associations. In addition, it had two broad aims. First, to examine the relationship between subjective FOK ratings and the subject's subsequent success in retrieving the correct name, with or without help. The second aim was to explore the *body-of-knowledge* (BOK) that, in some way, must underlie a face-name association. Every face or name we recognize has some stored information connected with it; where the person lives, what the person is like, what the person's job is, and so on. We know from personal experience that when we block on a name, we will try various strategies to retrieve it. And one of these strategies is to review what we know about that person. A question of some interest is which strategies are the most effective in unblocking a name.

Two methods were used in this investigation. One was the method of cued recall, where the investigator provided subjects with various facts about the name, and then saw which proved most effective in prompting the correct retrieval. A second, more indirect method was to invite the subject to tell all that he knew about the film star whose name was sought, and then examine what it was he could remember and in what order it emerged. In other words, we hoped to gain some idea of how the knowledge was stored in his mind, and the way, if at all, in which the name of the person was related to it.

Because of the exhaustive nature of the study, only five male subjects were used. Their average age was 33 (with a range from 21 to 58 years), and all professed to have a strong interest in the cinema and its stars. The stimulus material consisted of full-face, black-and-white photographs of 30 male and 30 female film stars of the 1940–

1960 era. They were chosen so as to provide a wide range of familiarity. For each star, there were two cue cards. One consisted of the initial letters of the star's first and second names, with dashes to indicate the number of missing letters. The second set of cue cards were essentially the same, except that the first two letters of both names were given.

The study was divided into four stages. In the first, each subject was asked to sort a pile of 30 pictures of male stars into two piles: "recognize" and "don't recognize." They were asked to do this as quickly as possible, and it was stressed that the sorting should be done purely on the basis of facial recognition to avoid, as far as possible, any attempt at name-searching in this phase. Second, they were asked to rate each face on a scale from 0 to 10 in response to the question: "How certain are you that you know this person's name? Even if you can't remember it now, indicate how strongly you feel you *could* name this person." In the third stage, the subject took the pile of photographs they said they recognized and tried to produce, for each face, a name and a number of facts about the person in question. In the final stage, any photographs that the subject could not name from the "recognizable" pile, and all those from the "don't recognize" pile were treated as follows.

(a) The subject was told to choose one or more questions from a prepared list. The experimenter then provided the information to answer each question that was asked. The type and order of the questions asked was recorded. These questions covered such topics as the films the actor had starred in, the TV series he had appeared in, examples of the roles played, personal details of the star, initial letters of the first and second names, last letters of these names, the number of syllables in each name, and any other question the subject wished to ask not covered by these categories.

(b) When the subject could not name a face after two or three questions, the subject was shown the first cue card for 10 seconds. And, if that failed, they were shown the second cue card. If recall occurred it was noted. If the subject still could not recall the name after receiving all of this information, the subject was put out of his (only males in this study) agony by being told.

The whole procedure was then repeated some days later for the 30 female stars. Depending upon the verbosity and/or expertise of the subject, the sessions took between 20 minutes and an hour to complete. The main results are summarized below.

The FOK Ratings
and the Retrieval of Names

The manner in which the subjects retrieved (or failed to retrieve) the star's name was divided into 8 categories.

1. Recognize face; give name immediately
2. Recognize face; retrieval delayed; self-cued recall
3. Recognize face; retrieval delayed; externally-cued recall
4. Recognize face; unable to retrieve name, even with external cues
5. Don't recognize face; give name immediately
6. Don't recognize face; retrieval delayed; self-cued recall
7. Don't recognize face; retrieval delayed; externally-cued recall
8. Don't recognize face; unable to give name, even with external cues

Figure 6.1

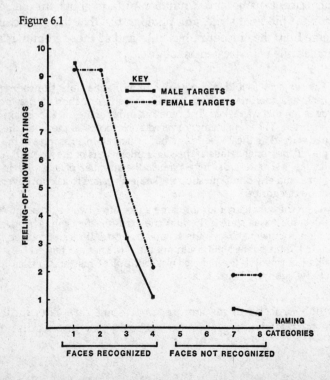

These categories constitute all the logical possibilities. In practice, one would not expect categories 5 or 6 to occur unless the photograph had been wrongly assigned to the "don't recognize" pile in the first stage. This did not, in fact, occur.

Figure 6.1 shows the relationship between the FOK ratings and these eight retrieval catgories, plotted for male and female stars separately. The results are very clear: the greater the feeling of knowing, the more readily the subject retrieved the name. This confirmed earlier findings.

Figure 6.2 shows the percentage of the total number of re-

Figure 6.2

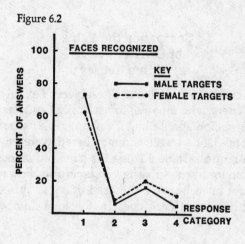

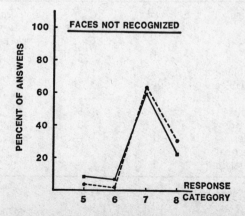

sponses that fell into each retrieval category. The small proportion of responses falling into category 2 reflects the comparative rarity of TOT states in this particular study. The most interesting finding is the large percentage of responses falling into categories 3 and 7, those in which correct recall is affected through the aid of external cues. The percentage of responses in category 7 is 60 percent, which suggests that the correct answers were often given on the basis of successful guessing. Being film buffs, and knowing a lot about the population of names from which these were drawn, they were probably able to obtain the right names on the basis of the lexical prompts given on the cue cards.

Comparing the Value of Different Cues in Aiding Retrieval

Two kinds of cue were available to the subjects. Lexical ones, giving initials, last letters, and number of syllables; and semantic ones involving information about films, TV shows, roles, personal details, and the like. Both kinds, it will be remembered, were provided at the subject's own request. Table 6.1 lists the cues and shows how often they were asked for by the subjects. The table also shows the number of effective cues in each type (*i.e.* those leading to correct retrieval), and the effectiveness of each cue (*i.e.* the total number asked for

TABLE 6.1. Total Numbers and Effectiveness of the Cues Requested

CUES		Total Cues Asked for	No. Effective Cues	Effectiveness of Cues (Total ÷ No. Effective Cues)
Lexical	Initials	80	23	29%
	Last letters	5	1	20%
	Syllables	14	1	7%
Semantic	Films	26	6	23%
	TV Shows	1	0	0%
	Roles	0	—	—
	Personal Details	0	—	—

divided by the number of effective cues). It is clear from these results that lexical cues were asked for more frequently and yielded more effective results than did the semantic cues. Most useful of all were the initial letters of the target's name. This gives further support to the guessing hypothesis mentioned previously.

The Body of Knowledge

The possible body of knowledge concerning each star was sub-divided under eight headings: type of film or TV show (*i.e.* Westerns, comedies, etc.); particular film and TV shows (*e.g.* titles, plot details, etc.); type of role (*e.g.* bad guy, lover, etc.); co-stars; personal details (*e.g.* past and present spouses, physical description, scandals, etc.); era/ contemporaries; subject's personal opinions and comments. The transcribed recordings were independently assessed by two judges, and a final coding agreed between them.

No consistency was found between subjects in the order in which these items emerged. But there was a significant concordance in the frequency with which each category occurred in the subjects' discussion of the star. These use-of-category frequencies differed only slightly for male and female stars, and are shown below in their respective rank orders (1 being the most frequent, and 8 being the least).

Male Stars	*Female Stars*
1. Subject's comments	1. Personal details
2. Particular films	2. Particular films
3. Personal details	3. Subject's comments
4. Type of role	4. Co-stars
5. Type of film	5. Type of film
6. Particular role	6. Type of role
7. Co-stars	7. Particular role
8. Era	8. Era

The use of these categories was consistent both within and across subjects. The largest discrepancy in the two sets of rankings is the importance of co-stars. These are given more often for female than for male stars. The correspondence of these rankings gives some hint that, in the realm of film stars at least, knowledge is organized in a fairly systematic fashion. The other possibility is that some aspects of this body of knowledge are intrinsically more memorable than others, or that some kinds of information are more stable (*e.g.* subjective impressions, particular films, etc.) and hence remain more salient in memory.

The TOT State

From the tape recordings of the subjects' spontaneous remarks while they were in a TOT state, it was possible to distinguish three different retrieval strategies, as well as some curious failures of recognition. However, it must be remembered that only relatively few subjects achieved this state, and that not all of them spoke aloud while they were struggling for a name. Nevertheless, these different techniques are of interest since they bear closely on our later discussion.

Lexical strategy
"There's a 'D' and an 'F' in his name—Dirk?" (TARGET: Kirk Douglas)
"Italian sounding name. Speaks with a foreign accent. Spanish. Second name starts with 'L'—Lomas?" (TARGET: Fernando Lamas)

Contextual and semantic strategy
"He starred in a film called 'Hobson's Choice', also in the 'Hunchback of Notre Dame' . . ." (TARGET: Charles Laughton)
"Had a TV series. Appeared with Jack Lemmon in 'The Apartment' " (TARGET: Shirley MacLaine)

Multiple name strategy
"She evokes so many names. It's not Patricia Roc, I don't think. It could be Patricia Roc, but it's somebody more familiar . . . I wonder if it's Yvonne de Carlo? No, not quite." (TARGET: Maureen O'Hara)

Failure to recognize the correct name
"I associate his face with James Cagney movies, as a gangster's side-kick." (TARGET: James Cagney)
"This is one of the Susans. Now it's *not* Susan Hayward. It's Susan . . . Red-haired. I've temporarily forgotten her name." (TARGET: Susan Hayward)

The lexical strategy fits well with the findings of Brown and McNeill when subjects were retrieving unfamiliar words after being given their definition. The contextual strategy conforms closely to what Yarmey found when getting subjects to put names to famous faces. But both investigators confined their subjects' possible responses into prescribed categories. Such a method would not, for example, reveal the multiple-name strategy, where many different possibilities are tried out on the mental ear. Nor would it reveal the interesting failures of recognition given in the last category.

Taken as a whole, these findings reaffirm the value of lexical strategies, particularly procedures like alphabetic first-letter searches in resolving certain tip-of-the-tongue crises. However, this method has its limitations as the following personal example will show. Two of us were struggling to recall the name of André Previn. Naturally, we tried the alphabetic technique, but with no success. The TOT state continued for hours until the target popped up of its own accord. The reason for the failure is apparently simple. There is no acoustic equivalent of the French "A" in André within the English alphabet.

This study proved to be a useful starting point, but as with most other psychological enquiries it raised more questions than it answered. One thing it did indicate, however, was the need for more naturalistic investigations of the TOT state than had hitherto been employed by those following the experimental tradition of Brown and McNeill. The next investigation carried out by Deborah Lucas involved a diary study of TOT states, along the lines of the Extended Diary for slips of action discussed in Chapter 2.

TIP-OF-THE-TONGUE DIARY STUDY

Thirty-five people were persuaded to keep a diary of their *resolved* TOT states (*i.e.* where the target had been found successfully) over a period of one month. Fourteen men and eighteen women acted as diarists, their average ages being 33 and 36 years respectively. A mean of 2.3 resolved TOT states were recorded for each subject over the diary-keeping period (there were no significant differences between men and women), producing a total of 75 TOT's in all.

The subjects were required to answer a number of standard

questions in regard to each resolved TOT state. These included the nature of the target, the intermediate solutions, the number of times they actively searched for the target, the strategies they used in resolving the TOT, the last time (prior to the current TOT state) they had recalled the target, and whether any word or name which they knew to be wrong kept occurring to them during their searches for the target.

This last question turned out to be crucial for the subsequent analysis. In the case of 40 TOT states, there was persistent interference by a wrong word or name, and in 35 there was not. For convenience, we will identify the former as *interference TOT's*, and the latter as *non-interference TOT's*. It soon became clear from the answers to the other questions that these two TOT states were quite distinct species. In our presentation of these findings, therefore, we will treat these two TOT states separately. Before examining the quantitative findings, however, let us look at the intermediate solutions that led to the eventual resolution of these TOT states. It was possible to identify four types of pathway to this final solution: mostly phonological, mostly semantic, multiple-name strategies, and mixed strategies. Below are some examples of each. The intermediate solutions are given in the order in which they occurred, and the target is italicized.

Mostly phonological pathways
Margaret, Muriel, *Mary*
Roydell, Royston, *Roysell*
McGill, McGill, Maretta, Maggie McGill, *Maggie*
Andrea, Angela, Anthea, *Alison*
Bumble-bee, Bumble, *Bunbury*
Eva, Esther, *Evelyn*
Pot-pourri, *Pomander*

Mostly semantic pathways
Retaliate, Immunity, *Resistance*
Alone, Unaided, *Initiative*
Picasso, Correrra, *Guernica*
Water-line, *Damp-proof course*
Handling, Boatswain, Nail polish, Buffer, Beautician, Beauty Parlor, Hairdresser, *Manicurist*

Multiple-name strategies
Ice-pick, Ice-axe, Ice-bolt, *Ice-screw*
West Highland Terrier, *Jack Russell Terrier*
Patrick Cargill, Patrick McGoohan, Inspector West, *Patrick Allen*
Holt's Brewery, Ansell's Brewery, *Marston's Brewery*
Seven Stars, Hayrick, Eagle and Child, *The Gables*
"Stranger at the Door", "Family at War", *"Testament of Youth"* (British
TV series)

Mixed strategies
Mulligatawny, Soup, *Mrs. Mulligan*
Jimmy Reid, Reid, *Neil*
Rombart, Mille, *Melita*
Embellish, Ripieno, *Continuo*

These examples reveal the various ways in which our minds
focus in on the target using either phonological and semantic associations, or mixtures of both. In addition, they confirm the earlier
finding that one strategy that people frequently use to find a forgotten name is to try out on the mental ear a string of names linked
either by a common part name, or by their inclusion in a particular
class of items (*e.g.* TV series, breweries, etc.).

Now let us return to the differences found between interference
and non-interference TOT states. These show up most clearly in the
type of successful strategy used to resolve them. Before presenting
these results, however, it is necessary to explain that these resolution techniques could be grouped under three general headings:
Internal strategies (alphabetic search, generation of similar words,
recall of contextual information, trying to form a mental image of the
target, etc.); *Pop-ups* (where the target comes to mind apparently
spontaneously); and *External strategies* (asking others, looking up the
target in a dictionary or encyclopedia, accidentally hearing or seeing
the target, etc.).

Figure 6.3 summarizes the differences between interference
and non-interference TOT's in their manner of resolution. The first
point to be noticed is that irrespective of these differences, the three
resolution strategies were employed about equally often in finding
the target: 38.7 percent for internal methods, 32 percent for pop-ups,

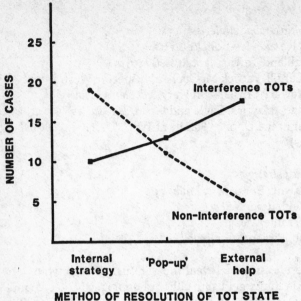

Figure 6.3

METHOD OF RESOLUTION OF TOT STATE

and 29 percent for external methods. But while the proportion of pop-up solutions remained roughly the same for both interference and non-interference TOT's, there was a large and statistically significant variation in the relative success of internal and external strategies for these two states. Non-interference TOT's were resolved more often by internal means, while the majority of the interference TOT's needed some external help to find the target.

If we now focus on the internal strategies, it will be seen from Figure 6.4 that significant differences existed between the two kinds of TOT state in the particular method that eventually yielded the target. Whereas non-interference TOT's were solved by a variety of means; those 10 (25 percent of the total) interference TOT's in which an internal strategy proved successful were, in 8 out of the 10 cases, achieved through the generation of similar words. Both alphabetic searches and the recall of contextual information were of little or no use, as was attempting to form a visual or acoustic image of the target. We have no ready explanation for this finding, but it further endorses the belief that we are dealing with two distinct forms of TOT state.

126

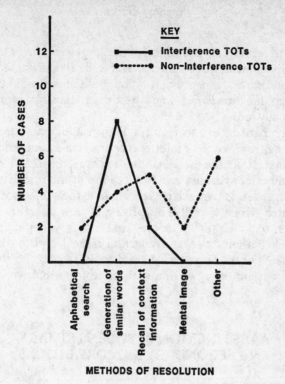

Figure 6.4

Another interesting source of variation between the interference and the non-interference TOT states was in the number of searches that were made for the target during the period prior to its successful retrieval. That is, the approximate number of occasions that the subjects consciously sought for the target. For both categories of TOT, the majority of targets were found in no more than two searches. But whereas the greatest proportion of non-interference TOT's were resolved in a single search, a substantial number of the interference TOT's required more than this. In other words, irrespective of the mode of retrieval, targets in the interference state took a longer time and presumably greater effort to find.

In all other measures taken, these two kinds of TOT state did not differ significantly. There was a slight tendency for interference targets to have been recalled (prior to the TOT state in question), a

127

longer time earlier than non-interference targets. But in both groups the majority of the targets had been last recalled somewhere between 1 month and three years previously. In both states, it was contextual information that the subjects knew best about the target word before it was actually found.

A comparison of the features known about the target word (before it was retrieved) for interference and non-interference targets showed that structural information—such as the first letter, end letter, number of syllables, and the location of the primary stress—was not regarded as particularly accessible to the subjects at the start of the search. This was a little surprising in view of earlier findings, and the use to which such phonological features were put during the search itself. Perhaps this was a reflection of the degree to which such characteristics of the target word are directly available to consciousness. We may not *know* we know these features, but we use them nonetheless.

A DISTINCTION BETWEEN PRIMARY AND SECONDARY MEMORY BLOCKS

Let us begin this distinction by stating some general assumptions about the way we normally call words and names to mind. Unless what we search for is unfamiliar (a foreign word, a strange name, or an infrequently used word), the way in which we summon it to consciousness is a largely automatic procedure. If we are asked for the names of our children, or the town in which we live, or our telephone number, or the name of our street, the answer springs to mind immediately. We do not usually have to make any deliberate attentional effort to find such information. With these frequently practiced retrievals, it is as if the messenger demons who listen at the keyhole to the Intention System can rush into the Word Store, select the appropriate cognitive demon, remove from it the conscious fragment for the Intention System or deliver it directly to the Action System, before any direct request has been made. Most of the time, the process occurs with remarkable ease, rapidity, and accuracy. But every now and again, the mechanism breaks down. This hiccup in the automatic retrieval process is what we would call a *primary* memory block. *Secondary* blocks involve something over and above this, as we shall discuss later.

Primary Memory Blocks

These, we would argue, arise as the result of some failure in the automatic retrieval mechanism. The result is that we come up with the wrong word (as in slip of the tongue substitutions), or only some part of it, or with nothing at all. Such breakdowns could have a variety of causes. It may be that the retrieval machinery has become a little rusty from underuse. Or that some small but necessary part of the attentional component is lacking because of distraction or preoccupation with something else. In either case, one of two things will ensue. Either the correct word or name will be recovered almost immediately, so that we barely notice the lapse. Or that we are forced to bring the bulk of our attentional resources to bear on the search for some period of time. As soon as focal consciousness is implicated in the retrieval, we move into the realm of the secondary memory block.

Secondary Memory Blocks

In this state, we formulate a specific intention to find a given word or name, knowing that the automatic search procedure has broken down. The Intention System reviews what is known about this target, and communicates these often fragmented pieces of information to the Word Store via the messenger demons. Once down in the store, we can imagine the messengers rushing around shouting out these partial attributes to the assembled word demons. Some of these will be slumbering, but many will be intensely active and showing a great deal of interest. By the nature of these demons, a considerable number may well regard themselves as matching, at least in part, the incomplete (and possibly inaccurate) descriptions being paged by the messenger demons. Some will claim to fit the phonological bill, others will believe themselves to be in the right semantic ballpark, and still others will feel they fit both sets of criteria.

Now, the evidence presented earlier indicates that a large proportion of these retrieval failures are remedied at this stage. The messenger returns to the Intention System with the appropriate piece of conscious currency. This is matched, possibly against some appropriate recognition demon, and the search is ended (although wrongly on some occasions). But, quite often, this word or name is rejected, and the messenger returns once more to the Word Store to find a better alternative.

As this searching procedure continues, the Intention System begins to form new hypotheses that may result in misleading specifications. For example, a person looking for the name "Joel" may emphasize the latter rather than the former part of the name, and look for a first name beginning with "L". Or, in deciding upon a contextual search, the Intention System may find itself confronted with additional blocks: "You know . . . she co-starred in that Western . . . I've forgotten what it's called . . . with that mean looking fellow . . . what's his name?" The ways in which this search can break down are many and various; but one in particular is relevant to our present concern, namely the distinction found between interference and non-interference TOT states.

Two personal examples will help to set the scene. One of us (JR) has had repeated difficulties in retrieving the word meaning to dither or defer action (*procrastinate*). On many occasions, a conscious search for this word has produced *prevaricate*. This has structural and, in some small degree, semantic features in common with the target word. When this is rejected, the next word that invariably crops up is *prognosticate*. Here we get a better structural match, but the semantics are clearly wrong. What is interesting about this process, however, is that it repeats itself so often. It is almost as if a learned connection has been made between these wrong words and the Intention System's specifications. It seems as though past activation has fired up the *prevaricate* word demon to respond to the call for *procrastinate*. An interesting feature of this particular problem is that the first five letters of the target *procr* occur (according to the Concise Oxford Dictionary) in only two other words in English, *procreate* and *Procrustean*. This together with the fact that *pre* is a very common prefix might explain how this particular learned block occurred in the first place. If the messenger had, on some earlier occasion, entered the store with a set of semantic attributes and the knowledge that the word began with "P", it is not difficult to understand how the relatively active *prevaricate* demon (active by virtue of its common prefix, and perhaps also by some recent use) came to offer itself as a likely candidate. Once accepted, if only briefly, its level of activation increased still further until, eventually, it became a chronic blocking agent in the search for *procrastinate*. It may well be that all or most interference TOT's have similar origins. In other words, some forms of memory blocking may be due to strong associate substitutions of the same kind that we see in slips of action and recognition. It is quite reasonable to regard these persistent but incorrect intermediate solutions as errors; that is, as unwanted deviations from an intended path.

The second example involved a search for a film title: "Deliverance." In this case, the conscious specifications were quite extensive. It was known that the film starred Jon Voight and Burt Reynolds; that it concerned the unhappy exploits of four suburbanites in hillbilly country; and that the film poster portrayed the vivid image of a hand emerging from a river holding a shotgun. It was also felt, although not very strongly, that it was a single-word title.

The first intermediate solution to occur was *intemperance*. This sounded right, but was clearly not the target. Nevertheless, there was a strong sense of being on track. The next intermediate was *intolerance*. Since this was the title of a classic film, the messenger had clearly been searching in the right semantic quarter. Again, it "sounded" right, but could not be the correct answer. Further searches only succeeded in yielding the same two intermediate solutions, probably because they fitted so closely to the phonological characteristics of the target. Eventually, the correct title was found by a roundabout contextual route some days later.

The interesting feature of this particular memory block, aside from adding further support to the idea of strong associate substitutions as blocking agents, was that, at the outset of the search, there was no conscious awareness of the fact that the target ended with *-erance*. Yet the two intermediate solutions that kept recurring closely showed that this knowledge was available at some level in the system. This bears out our earlier remarks that we may often use correct phonological cues of which we appear to have no conscious awareness.

We are suggesting, therefore, that whereas non-interference TOT's may arise for a variety of cognitive reasons—and hence, as the diary data have shown, be amenable to a variety of strategies—the interference TOT states are slips of habit in the memory search domain. Active demons, sharing phonological and/or semantic attributes with the partially defined target, may, by virtue of being in a

more active state than the sought-for word, usurp its position. Even if it is then rejected, its activation level will have increased still further through its recent usage. It will therefore have a tendency to recur, which in turn will energize it even more. Faced with such a learned blockage, the only sensible strategies are either to stop searching (which is the layman's general remedy for all TOT states), or to seek the solution from some external source.

SUMMARY

In addition to discussing the general problem of memory blocking, and presenting some new data on the topic, the main purpose of this chapter has been to demonstrate that certain TOT states yield intermediate solutions that bear a close resemblance to the slips of habit discussed in the two previous chapters. As in other such errors, we would expect these intermediate solutions to be more commonplace in the particular circumstances of the search than the target. This idea is currently being investigated by Deborah Lucas.

chapter seven
LOSING TRACK OF PAST ACTIONS: REPETITIONS AND OMISSIONS

In the previous three chapters, we have focused mainly upon one very common class of absent-minded error, the strong habit intrusion, and we have discussed its appearance in many different guises—as slips of word and deed, as lapses of thought, as recognition failures, and as blocks to the retrieval of known items from memory. Now we turn to another type of mistake, the principal characteristic of which is a failure to keep track of one's position in a planned sequence of actions. Once again, these actions are usually part of a highly routine task in which the demands upon conscious attention are minimal; and, as before, the occurrence of an error is likely to be associated with preoccupation or distraction on the part of the Intention System. However, as we shall see below, the precise mechanisms of these place-losing errors are somewhat different from those that underlie the strong habit intrusion.

The most dramatic form of this kind of error is when we suddenly realize that we have no idea of what we have just done, and hence do not know exactly what to do next. In most tasks, a quick look at what we are doing will supply us with sufficient information to judge our progress. But on some occasions, this visual evidence is lacking and we draw a complete blank, as in the following examples taken from our collection.

"I was spooning tea into the teapot, and I realized I had no idea of how many teaspoonfuls I had just put in."

"I didn't know if I had put water into the kettle. I had to lift the lid to check."

"In the shower this morning, I 'came to' to find that I didn't know whether or not I had washed my hair. It was wet and there was no way of telling. I could have washed it and all the suds could have disappeared down the drain. I certainly had no recollection of anything except what I had just been thinking about."

Another class of absent-minded errors that clearly fall into this general category are *repetitions*, in which some actions in an intended sequence are repeated unnecessarily. Our findings (see Table 2.1 in Chapter 2) suggest that repetitions do not occur particularly often: they were ranked 27th out of 30 possible error types in terms of their relative frequency. But they are reported with sufficient regularity in our collection to constitute a distinctive and, as we shall indicate later, a theoretically interesting class of slips. Approximately 3 percent of our collection of absent-minded slips were repetitions, some of which are listed below.

> "I was cleaning the car windows. I started with the windshield and then went around the car cleaning the other windows. When I got to the front I started cleaning the windshield again quite unnecessarily."

> "I took out a cigarette, put it in my mouth and lit it. I then took out a second cigarette and was about to put it in my mouth when I realized what I was doing."

> "I combed my hair in front of the hall mirror, got my coat and then went to the mirror again to comb my hair although I had just done it."

> "I put salt and pepper on my food, helped my child to cut her steak and proceeded to sprinkle salt and pepper on my plate for the second time."

> "I intended to call my cousin and then a friend. I called my cousin and when I had finished I picked up the phone and called him again."

> "I turned off the heating before going to bed. I then put the milk bottles out and went to switch off the heating again when I realized it was unnecessary since I had just done it."

> "I called my son to give him his medicine when he reminded me I had already given it to him earlier on."

> "I always shampoo my hair twice. On this occasion I found myself shampooing it for the third time unintentionally."

> "I went upstairs to get a book. I put it on the table, made myself a cup of tea and set off upstairs to get the book again."

> "I started taking off my nightdress in order to get into the bath when I realized I had already bathed and was ready for bed."

Although all of these slips share the same behavioral feature, the unnecessary repetition of an action, it seems on the face of it unlikely that they share the same underlying cause. Some of them we can attribute to plain forgetfulness, others could result from judging oneself to be not as far along in a sequence as one really is, still others may arise from the fact that the intention which prompted the action is not set at rest by having executed the planned behavior, and there are others, particularly the final example, which appear to result from this kind of environmental capture we discussed in Chapter 4. This multiplicity of possible error-producing mechanisms raises a problem that will confront us throughout this chapter; namely, that descriptions of this kind do not provide sufficient information for us to determine the unique causes of any particular slip. All we can do is suggest a number of possibilities, based upon the model of action described in Chapter 3, which could have brought about any specific place-losing error.

This difficulty of the same *behavioral* class of error having a number of possible underlying causes is especially true of the third category of slips relevant to place-losing: *omissions* (where intended actions are left out of a planned sequence). It could be argued that *all* deviations of action from intention involve an omission in the sense that they constitute a failure to carry out a particular action *at the time specified by the plan*. But even if we restrict ourselves to those omissions in which a necessary action is not done (as distinct from those in which the planned actions are replaced by others, as in strong habit intrusions or repetitions), there are still many possible reasons why they could have occurred. Consider the six examples below, all of which are clearly omissions in the more specific meaning of that term.

"When I got back from shopping, I found the letter on the hall table that I had intended to mail."

"I intended to take my pills, get my coat and go out. I put my coat on and left, forgetting to take my medicine."

"I bought something and started to leave the shop without waiting for my change."

"I got into bed with my slippers on."

"I wrote out a check and put the check book back into my bag without tearing the check out."

> "I intended to put the key in the lock and open the door. I put the
> key in but did not turn it and tried unsuccessfully to open the
> door."

The first example is one of a very common class of omission in which
an item in a plan is forgotten and hence not executed. The failure
here would appear to lie in the retentiveness of the Intention Store.
In the case of the second slip, there are at least two possibilities:
either that the planned item "take my pills" was lost from the
Intention Store; or that this intention remained intact, but was pre-
empted by the more familiar routine of putting on a coat prior to
leaving the house. In other words, this slip may have been a strong
habit exclusion, probably associated with preoccupation or momentary distraction. The next two slips are *premature exits* in which one
proceeds to the next stage of a planned sequence without having
completed some earlier phase, possibly because the Intention System
is more concerned with what is coming next than what is currently
happening. The last two slips, on the other hand, seem more typical
of *nosy supervisor* errors in which the Intention System makes a
cursory spot check on the progress of a largely automatic task and
comes up with the wrong answer: In both cases that the activity was
further along than it actually was. Another possibility, particularly in
the case of the key-turning error, was that some unrecorded external
event occurred which, though not directly attended to, was subconsciously counted in as part of the door-opening sequence in lieu of
the key-turning.

In considering the possible causes of these repetitions and
omissions, we have touched upon a number of factors. The next
section looks at these more closely in relation to our theory of action.

POSSIBLE CAUSES OF
PLACE-LOSING ERRORS

The Nosy Supervisor Syndrome

In Chapter 4, we considered how slips can arise from the failure of
focal attention to switch to the task in hand at the appropriate
moment. When this happens, the reins of action are likely to be

snatched up by some local active demon. What is less intuitively obvious, however, is that slips can also be produced by exactly the opposite process; that is, when the Intention System attempts to find out what is going on at a time when control is best left to the Action System. The situation is not unlike a supervisor going to a worker on the factory floor and asking how he or she is getting along. In the course of answering the question, the operator makes a mistake because his or her rhythm of work has been disturbed. Or, as sometimes happens, the supervisor is inattentive to the answer given, and comes away with a false impression. And sometimes the supervisor does not even stop for an answer, or fails to hear the one that is given.

Restating this in terms of our action model, we can say that many absent-minded errors occur because the Intention System is in the *wrong control mode*. Most often, mistakes happen because the Intention System is running open-loop at a point when it should have been making a closed-loop check. These are errors of inattention. But overattention, or attention paid at the wrong moment, can also produce slips. In this case, the Intention System goes closed-loop at a time when it would have been better to have stayed in the open-loop mode. Or, to put it bluntly, there are occasions when the Intention System should have minded its own business.

Anyone who has concentrated too closely on what his feet are doing when running downstairs two at a time will know how disruptive too much attention paid to a largely automatic activity can be. Giving too much attention to some component of a highly skilled performance is a sure way of making it falter, as every top-class musician or athlete will know. For a novice, it may help to focus upon one aspect of the whole, such as trying to improve one's service in tennis; but for the expert this can be disastrous. In such cases of overattention, the outcome can be a complete rendering of the delicate fabric of the skill; but more subtle errors can arise in everyday activities when the Intention System merely makes a cursory check upon the progress of the task at some inopportune moment.

Making tea is a good example of the kind of activity that is especially susceptible to place-losing errors. This is a task in which a series of largely automatic actions need to be carried out in the right order, and where there are periods of waiting for something to happen—the kettle to boil or the tea to brew. Furthermore, it is also a procedure in which a quick visual check on one's progress does not always yield the right answer. Judging from the pattern of errors in our collection, two kinds of wrong answer are likely. Either we conclude that we are further along than we really are, and, as a consequence, omit some necessary step like putting tea into the pot or switching on the kettle. Or, we conclude that we are not as far along as we really are, and then repeat an action, like setting the kettle to boil for a second time when we have a pot filled with freshly made tea. The interesting thing about these omissions and repetitions is that if we had not made these checks upon progress, our tea-making action demons would probably have carried us through without a hitch.

Program Counter Failures

In order for largely automatic actions to be carried out successfully, the Action System needs an automatic device, analogous to a program counter in a computer, that keeps track of the point reached in the sequence. Logically, this process could fail in one of two ways. It could count in some extraneous event as part of the intended sequence, giving rise to an omission error. Or it could fail to count in a correct action, thus causing it to be repeated.

Our error collection contains a number of examples that could fit the former possibility. They are mostly characterized by an omission error that is contingent upon some unexpected event or interruption. Here are two fairly typical examples.

> "I picked up my coat to go out when the phone rang. I answered it and then went out the front door without my coat."

> "I walked to my bookcase to find the dictionary. In the process of taking it off the shelf other books fell onto the floor. I put them back and went back to my desk without the dictionary."

Another reason for omissions is that the "program counter" may take a thought, an intention to do something, as the deed. There are three slips in our collection which suggest that something along these lines can occur, although plain forgetfulness is always an alternative explanation.

"I intended to check the water output from the washing machine. But I must have only partially checked because when I left the machine I heard the wrong sound. The hose had twisted and water was flooding the floor."

"When I settled down to write, I found I had everything except my pen—which I was convinced I had picked up."

"I had come back in the middle of the day to write at home. It was a wet, damp miserable day and the house felt cold, so in addition to raising the central heating, I turned on the gas fire in my work room. After I had been working for a while, the room began to feel hot and stuffy, and I distinctly formed the intention to turn it off. Later, I went out to make some coffee and on returning to the study, I was surprised to see that the fire was still on. I was convinced I had turned it off soon after framing the intention; but I clearly hadn't."

Examples of the second kind, the repetition errors, are harder to find, partly because these lapses are comparatively rare anyway, and partly because when they occur it is hard to distinguish the possibility of program failure from the nosy supervisor problem, discussed previously. However, our collection contains one rather curious example that might have arisen from the failure to "count off" a particular action, or in this case repeated actions.

"I intended to put two spoonfuls of sugar into my coffee, but put in seven or eight instead."

This error bears some resemblance to the motor perseverations described by Luria in patients suffering from deep lesions in the premotor areas of the brain.[1] Particularly conspicuous in them were the frequent repetitions of circular movements in drawing or writing. As in the error above, the Action System fails to apply the stop rule after the intended sequence is complete.

Unresolved Intentions

Sometimes, when we have failed to act upon a stored intention at the proper time, we experience a vague sense of unease, a feeling that we

[1]A.R. Luria, *The Working Brain* (Middlesex, England: Penguin Books Ltd., 1966), pp. 176–186.

should be doing something, but we are not sure what. This feeling suggests that in framing an intention to do something, a state of tension is created which is directly related to this, as yet, unfulfilled intention. For the most part, this tension is kept at a moderate level, just sufficient to help in preserving the stored intention until it needs to be executed. Once the intended actions have been carried out satisfactorily, the associated tension disappears. Thus, we can envisage a continuous series of cycles in which the formation of an intention generates a variable amount of specific tension that is normally discharged once the desired outcome has been achieved. Of course, since we are largely future-directed creatures, there will always be some intentional tension present in the cognitive system; but we can assume that it is highly specific to particular intentions.

It seems quite possible, however, that occasionally the execution of the intended act, even when performed satisfactorily, does not entirely remove the related tension. Some residue remains which subsequently causes the associated action to be repeated unnecessarily. Similarly, the converse is also a theoretical possibility. On some occasions, the formulation of an intention may generate insufficient tension leading to the omission of these actions from a plan.

When the consequences of not performing a certain planned action are seen as likely to cause damage or injury, then it is reasonable to suppose that a larger than usual amount of tension attaches to this intention. Under these circumstances, we may deliberately repeat the action a number of times in order to reassure ourselves that the feared outcome will not occur. To put it another way, with these high-risk intentions it may take a number of repetitions to dissipate the tension experienced on these occasions as anxiety. Most of us, before leaving on vacation, go around the house a number of times checking that doors are locked, windows shut and that the electricity, gas, or water is turned off. It is also quite likely that some of us have even returned home after setting out on our journey for one more check, just to be on the safe side. These deliberate, anxiety-reducing repetitions are not the same as absent-minded repetitions, but they do provide additional evidence for the existence of unresolved intentional tension as a possible mechanism for some of these place-losing slips.

All of us are prone to making repeated checking actions once in a while; occasional repetitions such as these lie well within the so-called normal range of behavior. But in some people suffering from obsessive compulsive reactions, this meticulousness is taken to pathological lengths. To a certain extent, these individuals could be regarded as suffering from an excess of present-mindedness, the complete opposite of normal absent-minded carelessness. Such patients have particular difficulty in completing any activity. For example, they may not be able to turn off a tap without coming back to it several times, turning it on again and then off, to make sure that it is properly turned off. Letters cannot be mailed without the envelope being opened and resealed a number of times. The routine business of everyday life may become quite impossible because of the time taken to check and recheck each stage of the procedure. The following case history illustrates this.

> One patient of this kind took two and a half hours to shave; much of this time being taken up in checking the exact setting of the razor, in making sure that all the adjustable parts were screwed to a particular degree of perfect balance and tension. Similarly, when punching a card either to clock in or to clock out at work, the card had to be taken back six to a dozen times to make quite sure that it had been properly punched, and that the time and the date upon it corresponded accurately with the actual hour and day on which the operation had been undertaken.[2]

This crippling form of obsessionality probably constitutes the extreme of a dimension along which all of us may be placed; though most people will occupy the middle ground, being neither excessively meticulous nor inordinately careless, but given to occasional bouts of compulsive checking when the dire consequences of an oversight appear to justify it. Both Broadbent's group and our own have independently obtained evidence to show that particularly absent-minded people tend to show low scores on questionnaire measures of obsessionality in general, while the reverse is true of those who claim a relatively low susceptibility to absent-mindedness. This merely underlines the point made earlier that obsessionality,

[2]D. Stafford Clark, *Psychiatry for Students* (London: George Allen & Unwin Ltd., 1964), p. 79.

being a form of present-mindedness, is not a condition that is conducive to slips of inattention. Although, as we have sought to indicate in this section, there are features of obsessional behavior, particularly the notion of unresolved intentions, that suggest means by which certain kinds of absent-minded place-losing errors may arise.

Anticipatory Leaps

In verbal activities such as speaking or writing, it sometimes happens that our thoughts run faster than our lips or hand and we find ourselves jumping ahead to a word that we had in mind, but for which the present moment is not right. As a result, we omit a word or phrase that should have been there. The same kind of error appears to occur quite frequently in action as well. When we are carrying out a planned sequence of subtasks, we occasionally exit prematurely from one routine and move on to the next, leaving out some necessary intermediate step. Slips of this kind were ranked 18th in regard to their relative frequency of occurrence among our list of thirty absent-minded error types. (See Table 2.1 in Chapter 2.)

A large number of the premature exits in our collection involved failing to switch off appliances, or getting into the bath or into bed with unwanted clothes on. Below are some other examples of a similar nature.

> "I filled up at a gas station and then drove off, leaving the gas cap on the roof of the car."

> "I intended to turn on the kettle and to go into the sitting room to wait for the kettle to boil. Instead, I switched on the kettle and poured cold water on to the tea."

> "The dog was sleeping peacefully when I decided he needed a walk. I went to the hall to get the leash, then walked out of the front door carrying the leash, but without the dog."

> "I drove myself and my wife to the station. I got out and she drove away with my keys in the ignition."

One possible cause of the anticipatory leaps is that an already primed action demon, lining up to take a turn for the Action System, jumps the queue because he has received the small amount of additional activation necessary to exceed his triggering threshold. In speaking or writing, .this can come from similar structure or phonological characteristics, such as a word with the same initial letter, in the prior context. For actions, this additional activation could also arise from many quarters: from having one's thoughts on what is going to happen next, from something in the previous actions, from the tension attached to the stored intention, or from a current state of need. We cannot often be sure precisely what this triggering factor is, but the theory of action allows for a number of such possibilities.

Not Remembering Previous Actions

Most people attribute their place-losing errors to forgetfulness. They say, for example, that they *forgot* they had made the bed earlier, and so went to make it again; or that they *forgot* where they put down an item that they had in their hands a moment ago; or that they *forgot* to take their socks off before getting into bed. We would wish to argue, however, that this term is not altogether appropriate in this context. To have forgotten something implies that it was once remembered, but is now lost or irretrievable. But there are good reasons for assuming that a large part of successfully completed routine activities are not stored in memory in the first place, or only for a brief period. A more suitable way of describing this experience, therefore, would be as a failure to remember, rather than forgetting.

The defining feature of largely automatic activities is that they are only attended to in an intermittent fashion, if at all. William James stated that " ... an object once attended to will remain in memory, whereas one inattentively allowed to pass will leave no traces."[3] Subsequent research has caused us to modify this statement only slightly to allow for the fact that some classes of unattended stimuli can be later recalled, but, for the most part, such inputs are held very briefly in the *working memory* and are soon lost to the system.[4] Thus, if we remember anything at all of previous routine actions, these

[3] W. James, *The Principles of Psychology Vol. I* (New York: Henry Holt & Co., 1890), p. 427.
[4] A. Baddeley, *The Psychology of Memory* (New York: Harper and Row, 1976).

recollections will at best be fragmentary, probably corresponding to those periods in which the Intention System made a closed-loop check on current progress. There is, in any case, little functional value to be had in storing all aspects of *correctly* executed routines, even if we possessed sufficient capacity to do so, which, of course, we do not. What we are most likely to remember, if quizzed at the completion of such a task, is what we were feeling or thinking about during it, rather than what we were actually doing. We could no doubt reconstruct what was done from our general knowledge of the activity; but that is not the same thing as recalling it directly.

This inability to recall the details of a highly skilled or habitual act was clearly expressed by Samuel Butler. In the following passage, he describes what is likely to remain in the mind of a concert pianist or violinist regarding the piece he or she has just played.

> At the end of his performance, his memory would appear to be no less annihilated than was his consciousness of attention and volition [while playing]. For of the thousands of acts requiring the exercise of both the one and the other, which he has done during the five minutes, he will remember hardly one when it is over. If he calls to mind anything beyond the main fact that he has played such and such a piece, it will probably be some passage which he has found more difficult than the others, and with the like of which he has not been so long familiar. All the rest he will forget as completely as the breath which he has drawn while playing.[5]

In another place, Butler considers the more commonplace activity of writing, and what is remembered by a practiced writer immediately after he has finished.

> He will probably not remember the formation of a single character in any page that he has written; nor will he be able to give more than the substance of his writing if asked to do so. He knows how to form each letter so well, and he knows so well each word that he is about to write, that he has ceased to be conscious of his knowledge or to notice his acts of volition, each one of which is, nevertheless, followed by a corresponding muscular action. Yet the uniformity of our handwriting, and the manner in which we almost invariably adhere to one method of

[5] S. Butler, *Life and Habit* (London: Jonathan Cape Ltd., 1878), pp. 4–5.

forming the same character, would seem to suggest that during the momentary formation of each letter our memories must revert (with an intensity too rapid for our perception) to many if not to all the occasions on which we have ever written the same letter previously—the memory of these occasions dwelling in our minds as what has been called a residuum—an unconsciously struck balance or average of them all—a fused mass of individual reminiscences of which no trace can be found in our consciousness, and of which the only effect would seem to lie in the gradual changes of handwriting which are perceptible in most people till they have reached middle age, and sometimes even later. So far are we from consciously remembering any one of the occasions on which we have written such and such a letter, that we are not even conscious of exercising our memory at all, any more than we are in health conscious of the action of our heart.[6]

Although written over a hundred years ago, these passages have been quoted at some length become they embody many of the principal features of our theory of action. What Butler calls the *residuum*, we have termed cognitive demons; but aside from this and other small differences in the mode of expression, the relationship he describes between consciousness (the Intention System) and the residuum (or cognitive demons) is perfectly compatible with the theoretical arguments set out in Chapter 3. The basic point in both accounts is that, once established, action demons no longer have direct access to consciousness. Communication between the Intention System and the Action Store is along a one-way channel: from the Intention System to the Action Store, but there is no return traffic. The only way we can acquire conscious knowledge (and hence the possibility of long-term storage) of the performance of action demons is via the closed-loop shunt. (See Figure 3.2 in Chapter 3.) But this only tells us of the consequences of of demonic activity, not of the demons themselves.

Up to the present, we have concentrated largely upon the possible causes of place-losing errors. In the remainder of this chapter we shall turn our attention to more practical issues. We will begin by considering what actors have to say about "drying up" on the stage, then we will examine one of the commonest errors made by

[6]S. Butler, *Life and Habit,* pp. 6–7.

railway signalmen, and conclude with a brief look at some recent studies of place-losing in old people.

ACTORS' "DRIES"

Deborah Lucas, whose research on everyday memory failures we discussed in the previous chapter, recently interviewed a small group of professional actors in Manchester on the subject of that stage nightmare, the "dry", or forgetting one's lines. Below are some excerpts from the transcript of that discussion. These have been tidied up a little to make them more understandable (and the expletives deleted), but the sense has not been tampered with.

> "I find that when I'm on stage, saying lines and receiving them, that it's almost like being on automatic. Not that, hopefully, your acting is automatic; but you just don't think about the lines that are coming. I've only ever dried once, and that was in 'King Lear.' I was playing the Fool. Lear was on and Goneril made an entrance. I said something to Lear and then she said something to him, after which I was supposed to say something to her. But I had been listening so intently to what she was saying to Lear that when she finished her speech, I just looked at her and thought 'What's she looking at me like that for?' And then I realized it was my line, and it sort of came out."

> "I was on stage with just one other person, and he jumped three pages ... the lines were very similar. I knew there was something, but I couldn't quite put my finger on it, and it took me about three lines of dialogue before I realized what had happened. I took him back, and he managed to adjust when we'd got to the place we'd already been to. [Question: Was he surprised, or did you know that he knew he'd gone wrong?] He began to be aware of it when I was trying to lead him back."

> "If you let your mind wander to the hat in the front row, or think 'I did that rather well tonight', it's absolutely fatal. Or if you suddenly realize that there's something in the text you haven't noticed before. There's a sort of blinding 'Oh! Of course, that's what it's all about.' When that happens you may hear someone speaking, and then realize it's you."

> "I had a conversation with A, and then B had to join in. Then A and B carried on a conversation together, and I was supposed to

come in a few lines later. I found myself listening to what they were saying, like a member of the audience. When it came to my turn to speak, I didn't know what to say because I had been listening as myself rather than as the character in the play."

"Yes, I suppose if you could trace the process of learning it would be like setting up a long complicated mechanism whereby one thought triggers another, which triggers another, and so on. That's why you don't—you can't—think about what's coming up. You just let the triggers happen. And I suppose where that goes wrong is when you start thinking outside that sequence. That throws you. Or the triggers can be very similar to later triggers. I've known someone go from the first into the second act of the play, simply because the dialogue at those points was rather similar, or the thoughts are the same and you suddenly find yourself in Act 2."

"One old actor told me ages ago, 'Now listen, old chap, if you ever dry do a tap dance.' And I said, 'What for?' He said, 'Well they're so busy looking at your bloody feet that you can remember what the lines are.' And that was okay until I fluffed at Stoke. I was doing Llewellyn in 'Henry IV', and I was on stage with Gower. We'd been working very hard on three heavy shows, and we were all tired. I started off on a great, long rambling speech of Llewellyn's and, right in the middle of it, I started to concentrate on Gower so much that we both got mesmerized. I stopped, and a voice in my brain said, 'Do a tap dance, Philip.' But my feet were rooted to the spot, and I kept looking straight into his eyes. I was hypnotized almost. I went through the whole process of saying to myself, 'Right, in another second they're going to start shuffling and getting uncomfortable, so I'd better do something.' I opened my mouth, expecting 'aaaargh' to emerge, but out came my lines and I was alright. But it was frightening because I was looking into this person's [Gover's] eyes and nothing seemed to move inside me."

"That's exactly like my first dry on the professional stage. I was the boatman in 'Ten Little Niggers'. At the end of the play, the judge tries to hang this lady from a big chandelier. We got her down, then a weird thing happened. I was looking up at the chandelier, acting my socks off, and I started a line with something like, 'A queer thing . . .' But I was concentrating so hard on the swinging chandelier, I just stopped speaking. The two people on the stage with me were going, 'Yes, yes, what next?'. But I was away. There was no audience, there was nothing, just the chandelier. They were making up lines all around me, and it seemed ages before I came out of it."

These excerpts are presented in the same order as they occurred in the discussion, so it is quite likely that the earlier stories prompted later ones of a similar kind. Nevertheless, these anecdotes raise some interesting points about the skill of acting and the factors which can disturb it. From many of the comments, it is clear that actors regard the attainment of a certain level of automatization, at least with regard to the actual lines they speak, as an essential prerequisite to a satisfactory performance. It is also evident that this automaticity, as with other skilled activities, is a precarious affair. The most common form of disruption seems to stem from what we might call a temporary loss of *attentional balance*. And, as in absent-minded errors, the fall can go either way. On some occasions, the actors report that they attended too closely to the details of what was going on around them, and so faltered in the same way that typists or pianists would if they thought too much about what their individual fingers were doing. Thus, a number of the stories suggest that something like the nosy supervisor syndrome was the culprit. At other times, the reverse happens: attention is caught by some striking but irrelevant aspect of the surroundings, like the hat in the front row or the swinging chandelier. This again causes them to go "absent" from the character momentarily, and when they return they are likely to find that they have lost their place. This attentional capture, though short-lived, can obviously be a very intense and alarming experience. One actor, it will be remembered, described it as being mesmerized or hypnotized.

Another interesting point to emerge was the analysis made of the way lines, once learnt and practiced sufficiently, serve to trigger what comes next without the need for conscious recollection. In fact, such an attempt to think deliberately about the next speech is likely to disrupt these delicate linkages. But sometimes, as we discussed earlier, similarities in the sound or meaning of the dialogue at widely differing points in the text can link inappropriately, causing the actor to jump several pages, or even into the next act, without immediately noticing the error. This echoes what we said earlier about the premature triggering of cognitive demons, lining up to take their turn in the Action System. For words, structural triggers—the sound, the number of syllables, or the general context—seem especially liable to bring about these premature exits.

By the nature of their craft, actors are a rich source of research material for cognitive psychologists, particularly when they are as articulate and insightful as those encountered here. It is surprising, therefore, that so little has been done in this regard; and we have only scratched the surface. Let us leave our actors with an excerpt taken from the final part of the discussion, in which one of them described, very eloquently, the actor's nightmare.

> "What you said reminded me of the famous actor's dream. I don't know whether you've ever had it, but my version of it goes something like this: I am actually on stage, and it always seems to be 'Henry V'. I am in full armour, and I am actually delivering a line when I suddenly realize I have not rehearsed this, I have not learnt this, in fact there haven't been any rehearsals. I am just here and I have one syllable in my mouth at the moment. I might find another syllable to follow that, but thereafter I'm lost. And it's a very long play."

To which another actor added: "Yes, and the audience always looks so evil, don't they?"

SIGNALMEN'S ERRORS

One very common problem in carrying out routine tasks is the large amount of time many of us waste in trying to track down some object or tool that we put down a short time before. This is the familiar *But-I-only-had-it-in-my-hand-a-moment-ago* experience. In view of what was said earlier about the low probability of storing correctly executed actions, this is not altogether surprising. But in certain circumstances, such as in the railway signal box, an inability to remember previous actions can have catastrophic results.

In his comprehensive account of British railway disasters, Rolt makes the following observation.

> The mistake which has probably caused more serious accidents in the last sixty years than any other is that of a signalman forgetting, especially at night, that he has a train standing near his box. It may be a train that he has halted in obedience to his danger signals, or it may be one that he has 'wrong roaded', that

is to say transferred to the wrong running line to wait there until
a fast following train has passed.[7]

A terrible example of the results of this type of error occurred at
Quintinshill, just north of Gretna Green on the Carlisle-Glasgow line
in 1915. This was Britain's worst railway disaster. Two hundred and
twenty-six people were killed, most of them soliders. The precise
details of this accident are complicated, but its main features can be
summarized as follows.

On the morning of May 22, two "lay by" loops on the up and
down sides of the line* were occupied by goods trains, and so a slow
northbound passenger train was backed on to the up-line to let the
Scottish express, bound for Glasgow, come past. This action had
been carried out by Signalman Meakin who had worked the night-
shift and was scheduled to go off duty at 6 o'clock. However, due to
an unofficial arrangement he had with the day-shift man, Signalman
Tinsley, he remained on duty until 6:30 to allow Tinsley, who lived at
Gretna Green, to hitch a ride up on the slow passenger. Meanwhile,
Meakin would write down all the train movements since 6 o'clock on
a piece of paper so that Tinsley could afterwards copy them into the
Train Register, thus making it appear that he had come on duty at the
proper time.

On this morning, Tinsley had jumped off the slow passenger
train as it was backing on to the up-line. When he came up to the box
at 6:34, there were three trains standing at Quintinshill. Just prior to
this, Meakin had accepted the Scottish express from Gretna Junction.
It was the last signal he made before handing over to Tinsley. The
two men talked for a few minutes, and while they were doing so, a
message came through from the north to say that a special troop
train, en route to Liverpool, had passed through Lockerbie at 6:32.
Then Meakin settled down to read the morning paper, and Tinsley
busied himself at the desk copying Meakin's entries into the Train
Register. At this point, the train parked on the up-line was clearly
visible in broad daylight, some 65 yards away from the signalmen.

*Lines to London are called *up*-lines; lines from London are called *down*-lines.
[7]L.T.C. Rolt, *Red for Danger* (London: Pan Books, 1978), p. 194.

Meakin had not informed Tinsley that the line was blocked, presumably because he assumed that Tinsley was aware of the fact, having just jumped off the very same train. Moreover, Meakin had also failed to place reminder collars over his signal levers, which was normal practice when a line was blocked by a standing train.

Tinsley now set about adding the final ingredients to the disaster. At 6:38, he pulled off his down signals for the Scottish express, allowing it to enter his section. At 6:42, he accepted the up troop train. At 6:46, he offered the troop train forward to Gretna Junction where it was accepted immediately. Then he pulled off all his up main line signals. Two minutes later, the troop train came in sight, traveling very fast on a falling gradient. The train smashed into the parked passenger train with great violence, and the wooden coaches of the troop train caught fire. But worse was to follow. Seconds later, the northbound Scottish express crashed into the wreckage.

Why did it happen? The main reason was that Tinsley suffered a lapse of memory. He forgot that there was a stationary train on the up-line, even though he himself had just got off it and it was in plain view just outside his box. A contributory factor was Meakin's failure to put the reminder collars on the signal levers that would have alerted him to the presence of the stationary train.

This particular sequence of events differs from other signalmen's errors of the same type in that it was not Tinsley but Meakin who had shunted the passenger train on to the up-line. But in some senses, it is even more remarkable that Tinsley could have forgotten the location of this train, having ridden on it almost to the point of its stopping. Why this happened we shall never know.

LOSING TRACK OF EVENTS: A PROBLEM OF OLD AGE

Many old people complain of increasing absent-mindedness. Though we have no direct evidence to indicate that older people are more prone to these errors in general, a number of ingenious studies carried out by Dr. Patrick Rabbitt and his co-workers at Oxford do suggest that advancing age brings with it an increased susceptibility to *specific* kinds of error; in particular, to those which stem from losing track of previous events.[8]

This was demonstrated in the laboratory using the following task: subjects sat at a keyboard and were asked to tap out two kinds of overlearned sequences of letters. The first was the straight alphabet in which items did not repeat (A,B,C,D,E,F ... etc.). In the second sequence, however, items did repeat, *e.g.* (A,B,C,B,C,E,F,G,B,A ... etc.). Both old and young subjects were practiced so that they could tap out the two kinds of sequence at the same high speed without any errors. But after they had reached this equivalent level of proficiency, they were asked to carry out the procedure again, this time with a concurrent distraction task (counting backwards in fours).

Tapping out overlearned sequences like these is comparable to running off a program of actions in everyday life, in which the order and timing of the events are governed by an action demon. Following some period of distraction, we need to know what we have just done in order to pick up the task at the right point, particularly if we are making a conscious check on our position. In sequences of the first kind, each item is unique, so that if the subject knows the single response he or she has just made, this is enough to tell him or her what to do next. But in sequences of the second kind, where items are repeated, the subject will have to track back further to establish his or her present position. Thus, for B's, he or she may have to recall at least one previous B, and for other letters the subject may have to go back to two previous responses in order to fix his or her place.

With the distracting task, sequences with repeats were slower and less accurate for both young and old subjects. But the number of errors was much greater for older than for younger subjects. The old subjects often tapped out iterative loops within the same sequence (*e.g.* B,C,E,F,G,B,C,E,F,C, ... etc.), or even switched sequences altogether, branching from one to the other in mid-run.

Rabbitt interpreted these findings as illustrating three points. First, playing off practiced sequences involves constant cross-checking between a short-term working memory (that keeps a brief record

[8]P.M.A. Rabbitt and S.M. Vyas, "Selective anticipation for events in old age." *Journal of Gerontology* 35(1980), 913–919. P.M.A. Rabbitt, "Talking to the old", *New Society*, 22 Jan, 1981, pp. 140–141.

of what has just been done) and long-term memory (that contains the program or action demon). Second, this checking process may make more or less demand on working memory, depending on how the sequence of events is structured. Third, this trackkeeping process is more vulnerable to distraction in old than in young people.

In view of this difficulty, it would seem likely that old people would be particularly disadvantaged in situations where they are required to keep track of conversations, especially when there is more than one speaker. Rabbitt tested out this notion using video-tapes of deliberately staged conversations. In a base-line condition, one speaker delivered a sequence of statements. In other conditions, the same statements were made, in various patterns of alternation, by two or three speakers. Old and young subjects watched these tapes, knowing that they would be asked to recall what was said and, sometimes, who said it.

Young subjects recalled statements equally whether they were made by 1, 2, or 3 speakers. But when, in addition, they had to say which speakers made which statements, they recalled fewer statements, as well as making some false attributions. Old subjects always recalled fewer statements when they were made by more than one speaker, and were markedly worse than young subjects when attempting to recall who said what. This is evidence that old subjects experience particular problems in keeping track of events during conversations, in the same way that they had difficulties on the letter-tapping task with concurrent distraction.

In another study, Rabbitt and his co-workers required old and young subjects to actively interact with video-taped conversations. A speaker, or a number of speakers, make taped utterances as described above. But these are interspersed with timed pauses in which the subject is invited to join in. That is, he should treat the situation as one in which the speakers are his audience, and to make comments upon what they have just said. After these pauses, the video-tape may or may not continue. When it does, the subjects are required to recall statements and attribute them to speakers as before. The studies are still in their early stages, but they have already yielded two rather striking findings. Old people have excellent recall for what they themselves said, but seem to have little or no remembrance of the events which preceded their own statement, as distinct from the events which occurred before other people's statements.

Preliminary observations by this research group also indicate differences in the nature of the conversational contributions made by old and young people. Old people's interjections tend to be less closely related to earlier comments made by others. They often indicate a loss of memory for the source of earlier comments. Old people's remarks are less modified by recent changes in the topic of conversation, and they are more often related to the speaker's own earlier utterances than to remarks made by others.

Taken as a whole, these elegant studies by the Oxford group indicate that old people may be deficient in one important type of control process by which we keep track of our progress through the routines of daily life. In particular, they appear less efficient at using recently acquired information to check their current behavior, and so are liable to lose their place. In addition, their conversational characteristics suggest that they are inclined to stick doggedly to some favorite theme, even when it is no longer relevant to the present topic of discussion. In some cases, this may be due to plain cussedness; but these experiments also provide strong grounds for believing that it may arise from a genuine confusion as to what has gone before.

These studies bring into sharp relief the failures to which all of us are liable at almost any age. The fact that old people show a rather specific deterioration in this one aspect of cognitive function provides us with a clearer understanding of the part it plays in the whole process of guiding our routine actions. Here, as elsewhere in psychology, it pays us to follow La Fontaine's advice: "En toute chose il faut considérer la fin."

POSTSCRIPT: VERBAL REPETITIONS AND OMISSIONS

Throughout this chapter we have concentrated primarily upon track-losing errors as they occur in action, rather than in speech or writing—although these are rich in such instances. Our reasons for this were twofold. In our own research we have been concerned

primarily with slips of action, and so possessed more original examples of these than slips of the tongue or pen. Second, verbal errors of
this kind have been considered in great detail elsewhere.[9] This same
bias, however, is not so evident in the chapter that follows.

[9]V.A. Fromkin, ed., *Speech Errors as Linguistic Evidence* (The Hague: Mouton,
1973). J. Aitchison, *The Articulate Mammal: An Introduction to Psycholinguistics* (London:
Hutchinson, 1976). V.A. Fromkin, ed., *Errors in Linguistic Performance: Slips of the Tongue,
Ear, and Pen* (New York: Academic Press, 1980).

chapter eight
DISMEMBERED DEMONS: BLENDS AND SPOONERISMS

In Chapter 3, we briefly mentioned that cognitive demons, in scrambling for control of the Action System, occasionally become dismembered in the struggle. When this happens, the Action System may be momentarily occupied, not by an intact demon, but by fragments of one or more that have come together in a curious, though by no means random, combination. The outward result is that our words or actions deviate from their intended path in one of two ways: as *blends*, in which parts of two different words or action sequences combine to form a novel utterance or an unintended piece of behavior; or as *spoonerisms*, in which the proper order of two segments in a planned sequence of words or actions is reversed.

This chapter is concerned with the nature and the possible causes of these characteristic errors as they appear in both word and deed. Because slips with words have been more closely studied and their origins are better understood, we shall begin with an examination of verbal blends and spoonerisms. We will then go on to look at their counterparts in action. In both domains, however, we shall be concentrating on what these slips can tell us about the hidden processes involved in the programming and execution of speech or routine action. We shall attempt to relate these inferences to the theory of action set out in Chapter 3.

VERBAL BLENDS AND SPOONERISMS

Blends

These are simplest kind of slip of the tongue, so they make a convenient starting point. They have been defined as follows: " ... a word formed from two other words (very rarely more than two) by dividing each of the two original words into two parts, and combining one part from each original word into a new word called a blend."[1] Below are some actual examples. The two likely original words are shown on the left, and the resulting blends on the right.

Drill + dig	Drig
Behavior + deportment	Behortment
Shabby + shoddy	Shaddy
Frown + scowl	Frowl
Splinters + blisters	Splisters
Tummy + stomach	Stummy
Terrible + horrible	Herrible
Grizzly + ghastly	Grastly
Striving + trying	Strying
Dealer + salesman	Dealsman
Best + most	Boast
Everybody + everyone	Everybun
Person + people	Perple

Notice that in many of these examples the two originals, if not actually synonyms, are closely related in meaning or usage. They also show a close *formal* similarity. This includes phonetic similarity (*e.g.* behavior and deportment—both have three syllables, and both are stressed on the second syllable), and grammatical similarity (*best* and *most* are both adjectives, *drill* and *dig* are both verbs, *dealer* and *salesman* are both nouns, and so on).

---

[1] Rulon Wells, in *Speech Errors as Linguistic Evidence*, ed., V.A. Fromkin (The Hague: Mouton, 1973), p. 85.

The frequent presence of both semantic and formal similarity in the two original words provides some indication as to what is going on in the speaker's brain, beyond the reaches of consciousness. In speaking, we are aware of an intention to say something; but between that often vague intention and the actual words which finally emerge, there is an impenetrable shadow. For most of the time, we quite literally have no idea of what we are going to say next. William James has provided us with an elegant description of this experience.

> And has the reader never asked himself what kind of mental fact is his intention of saying a thing before he has said it? It is an entirely definite intention, distinct from all other intentions, an absolutely distinct state of consciousness, therefore; and yet how much of it consists of definite sensorial images, either of words or of things? Hardly anything! Linger, and the words and things come into the mind; the anticipatory intention, the divination is there no more. But as the words that replace it arrive, it welcomes them successively and calls them right if they agree with it, rejects them and calls them wrong, if they do not. It has therefore a nature of its own of the most positive sort, and yet what can we say about it without using words that belong to the later mental facts that replace it?[2]

As the result of a hundred years of exhaustive investigation of slips of the tongue, we now have some idea of what is going on in this dark space between the intention and the utterance. In translating an intention into speech, we go through a number of complicated stages, building up what the psycholinguists term an *articulatory program*.[3]

The first step, obviously enough, is to settle upon the general meaning that utterance is to convey. The second stage is the selection of a syntactic outline. In effect, this specifies a succession of word slots. The third step is to select from the Word Store the nouns, verbs, adjectives, and adverbs to fit into the available slots. These are called *content* words. The next stage is to spell out the *function* words—the articles, conjunctions, and prepositions. The final step is to build up

[2] W. James, *The Principles of Psychology Vol. I* (New York: Henry Holt & Co., 1890), p. 253.
[3] For a further account, see J. Aitchison, *The Articulate Mammal: An Introduction to Psycholinguistics*, pp. 206–229.

fully specified phonetic segements, syllable by syllable. The articulatory program is now ready to be executed. But, typically, some attentional capacity is still allocated to check that what is being said corresponds with what was intended. However, this limited attentional resource can be claimed elsewhere at this point, and it is under these conditions that slips are likely to be made.

Blends make it clear that at the stage of word selection (Stage 3), speakers must have simultaneous access to several words closely related to their intended meaning. Within the terms of our action theory, we could suggest that the messenger demons (whose job it is to shriek the Intention System's general wishes to the word demons) are sometimes confronted with two equally suitable word demons, for instance *slick* and *slippery*, and, being unable to choose between them, allow both demons to scramble for the appropriate slot in the articulatory program. Since the slot has only space for one word, the result is a blend—*slickery*.

This conflict is further compounded by the phonological similarity between the two words. It is easy to imagine how the word *slick* may be the first to respond to the messenger's shrieks, but then the phonetically identical first segment *sli* causes the last two syllables of *slippery* to occupy the latter part of the available program slot. Most anticipations, perseverations and reversals of phonetic segments occur in closely similar or identical phonetic contexts. For example, in the reversal *left lemisphere* (left hemisphere), the *h* and *l* both come just before an *e* in a stressed syllable.

In these blends, we see the result of an equal competition between two strongly activated word demons. But where one demon clearly wins out over the other, the result may be a *word substitution*—and these, as we saw in Chapter 4, often take the form of strong habit intrusions. Consider the following attested examples of word substitution.

Intended to say	Actually said
in Afghan hands	in Afghan hounds
sesame seed crackers	Sesame Street crackers
in our academic ivory tower	in our academic ivory league
like wild fire	like wild flower

In all of these cases, it is clear to see that prior words, already slotted into the articulatory program, triggered off strongly associated though unintended word demons, who then leapt into the available slot in the program ahead of the correct word. On some occasions, however, the unwanted intrusion is not so much a strong associate as an antonym. Here, the shrieks of the messenger demon have obviously reached into the right part of the Word Store, but—possibly because it is more activated—the word of opposite meaning leaps out first, as in the following examples.

> My dissertation is too *short*. (intended: *long*)
> You'll have to call *earlier*. (intended: *later*)

Mistakes of this kind commonly occur in some patients suffering from *dysphasia* (a Greek word meaning "bad speech"—to be distinguished from *aphasia* which means, literally, "no speech"). Such people repeatedly confuse words like *yesterday*, *tomorrow*, and *today*. They seem able to locate names connected with the general area they are talking about, but unable to pinpoint specific words within it, so that a garden roller is likely to be called a lawn mower, a rake a hoe, and so on.

A similar type of word selection error, the so-called *malapropisms*, occurs when a person confuses a word with a similar sounding one. The term comes from Mrs. Malaprop, a character in Sheridan's play "The Rivals", who continually confused like sounding words, as in:

> "She's as headstrong as an allegory on the banks of the Nile." (She's as headstrong as an alligator on the banks of the Nile.)
> "A nice derangement of epitaphs." (A nice arrangement of epithets.)

These slips of the tongue make it evident that the semantic plan in the speaker's mind specifies only the approximate meanings of the words to be spoken, together with a rough indication of the number of word slots to be filled. The actual word selection is left to the messenger demons who ply between the Intention System and the Word Store. But these selections are subject to the same general forces influencing the activation of all cognitive demons; namely, frequency of past use, shared features, prior context, and need.

So far, we have postulated the existence of three kinds of cognitive demon: action, word, recognition demons, and a corps of functionary demons that we have called messenger demons. However, the very precise form taken by blends and other word slips suggests that we need, at least in the verbal domain, to create a second corps of functionary demons, called *syntax demons*. We can suppose that these act rather like quality controllers on a production line. They stand just before the Action System and reject word demons that do not conform to the syntactical rules of spoken English, as they line up in the articulatory program waiting for delivery by the vocal apparatus.

One of the remarkable features of blends is their lawfulness. This does not necessarily mean that if we had privileged access to a speaker's mind we could predict precisely the blends he or she will make, given a knowledge of what he or she intends to say. But we can make some fairly confident guesses about the kinds of blend he or she is *likely* to make, and also those that he or she certainly will *not* make. Rulon Wells has formulated three laws governing the formation of blends.[4]

1. A blend is practically always a phonetically possible noise (and this applies to slips of the tongue in general).
2. If the two original words are rhythmically similar, a blend of them will, with high probability, rhythmically resemble both of them.
3. If the two original words contain the same sound in the same position, a blend of them will also contain that sound in that position.

As an illustration, Wells considered the possible blends that can be formed from the two words *past* and *by*. *Past* can be split in three ways: *p-ast*, *pa-st* and *pas-t*. *By* can be broken up in only one way: *b-y*. Thus, six blends are theoretically possible: (1) *p-y*; (2) *pa-y*; (3) *pas-y*; (4) *b-ast*; (5) *b-st*; (6) *b-t*. (throughout this discussion it must be remembered that the letter *a* has the sound it has in *past*, and *y* as in *by*).

Of these six possibilities, three can be ruled out on the grounds that they disobey the first law. Possibilities (2), (5), and (6) do not make noises compatible with spoken English. Of the remaining three

[4]Rulon Wells, in *Speech Errors as Linguistic Evidence*, p. 86.

possible blends (3) is rendered highly unlikely by the second law. *Pas-y* is not rhythmically similar to the monosyllables *past* and *by*, and consequently this is not likely to be uttered as a blend of these two words. We have now narrowed the field to two possibilities (1) *py* and (4) *bast*, but the available laws do not allow us to choose between them. Each are equally likely to occur as blends.

In conclusion, it is worth pointing out that some blends are constructed quite deliberately. Lewis Carroll, in "Alice Through the Looking Glass", causes Humpty Dumpty to explain that *slithy* means "lithe" and "shiny", commenting: "You see, it's like a portmanteau—there are two meanings packed into one word." Other examples of deliberate blends are *smog* (smoke + fog) and *brunch* (breakfast + lunch).

Spoonerisms

Blends (and word substitutions) are examples of *selection failure* in which mixes of intended words or words of similar sound and meaning are incorrectly slotted into the articulatory program, but usually in the right place and in obedience to grammatical and syntactical rules. Spoonerisms, on the other hand, are better described as *program assembly failures* in which the right elements are added, but where the positions of two such elements are reversed. (Anticipations and repetitions also fall within this general class of program failures.)

The elements that switch places can be either sounds, syllables, or whole words. In the case of transposed sounds, we can reverse initial letters, as in *"with this wing I thee red"* (for: "with this ring I thee wed"), and noninitial sounds, as in *"a cop of cuffee"* (for: "a cup of coffee"). They also frequently occur between phonetically similar sounds as in *"leak wing"* (for: "weak link"), and with vowels sandwiched between consonants, *"David, food the peach"* (for: "David, feed the pooch").

Some of the best known sound transpositions are attributed to the Reverend William A. Spooner, who was Dean and Warden of New College, Oxford around the turn of the century. His reversals often resulted in preposterous sentences like *"The cat popped on its drawers"* (for: "The cat dropped on its paws"), *"You have hissed all my mystery lectures"* (for: "You have missed all my history lectures"), or

"Queer old dean" (for: "Dear old queen"). It seems more probable, however, that these were subtle jokes rather than truly inadvertent reversals. One thing that tends to give the game away is that Spooner's reversals always made sense—or, at least, deliberate non-sense—whereas, in real life, this is the exception rather than the rule. Nevertheless, the joke paid off for Spooner: his name is not likely to be forgotten.[5]

"I'd like a Vienel Schnitzer" (for: "I'd like a Viener Schnitzel") is an example of syllable reversal. The following are instances of whole word reversals: *"Don't buy a car with its tail in the engine"* (for: "Don't buy a car with its engine in the tail"), and *"I can't help the cat if it's deluded"* (for: "I can't help it if the cat's deluded."ial.).

Spoonerisms have been artificially elicited in the laboratory by Baars, Motley, and MacKay.[6] They took as their starting point a party game in which one person asks another to respond by saying "duck" whenever the first person says "busy". This is repeated rapidly several times. Then the first person suddenly switches to saying "dizzy". Quite often the victim will respond with "buck", and then express genuine surprise at having made the slip.

The technique used in the study was to get subjects to articulate a target (*e.g. bad goof*) that had been preceded by biasing items containing the initial phoneme (/g/) of the desired spoonerism (*gad boof*). Thus, they were presented sequentially with three phonological interference words (words that resembled the desired error outcomes) and then two target words. On seeing the target words, they were required to utter them as quickly as possible. A particular point of interest was the relative likelihood of meaningful and non-meaningful words appearing as spoonerisms. For example, two very similar target pairs, such as *darn bore* and *dart board* will have different outcomes in terms of the meaningfulness of their reversals. *Darn bore* spoonerizes to the meaningful *barn door*, while dart board spoonerizes to the nonmeaningful *bart doard* (*i.e.* words unlikely to be in the subject's mental lexicon).

[5]J.M. Potter, in *Errors in Linguistic Performance: Slips of the Tongue, Ear, Pen and Hand*, ed., V.A. Fromkin (New York: Academic Press, 1980), pp. 13–34.
[6]B.J. Baars, M.T. Motley and D.G. Mackay, "Output editing for lexical status in artificially elicited slips of the tongue." *Journal of Verbal Learning and Verbal Behavior* 14(1975), pp. 382–391.

The results showed that when the target words themselves were meaningful, the lexical outcomes (*e.g. barn door*) occurred more frequently as reversal errors than did nonlexical outcomes (*e.g. bart doard*). However, there was some indication that if the spoonerism was faintly salacious (as in *cool tit* from *tool kit*), or exceedingly so as with target words *fuzzy duck*, it might well be suppressed before it is uttered.

It would appear, therefore, that we edit spoken output at a number of levels, and that errors making lexical sense are more likely to evade the scrutiny of the editor. Except, that is, when they are socially unacceptable or embarrassing words. But, as we know to our cost, some blush-worthy spoonerisms do escape our lips, indicating that even at this higher level the editing is not always perfect. It seems likely that this editing function draws upon our limited attentional resources, and when these are taken up elsewhere, the editing fails and we make speech errors. We will return to this issue in Chapter 11.

BEHAVIORAL BLENDS AND SPOONERISMS

Whereas linguists and others have been assiduously collecting and analyzing slips with words for a hundred years or so, their nonverbal counterparts, the behavioral blends and spoonerisms, have only recently attracted interest among cognitive psychologists. To those of us more concerned with slips of action rather than slips of the tongue, the apparent similarity between the forms of the errors in these two domains is very seductive. But before we try to draw too many parallels with regard to the underlying mechanisms, we should be aware at the outset of some important differences between speech and action.

In the first place, actions, unlike words, are not drawn from a finite store or dictionary. The words we speak and write come from a common stock, depending upon the language we are using. Each word has an accepted form, pronunciation, and meaning. The same is not true for most actions. Of course, in highly formalized activities like ballet, fencing, sign languages for the deaf, or semaphore signalling, a vocabulary of action has been developed; but these are exceptional cases.

Second, unlike words, actions are not clearly segmented. We do not yet know what the units of action are, or indeed whether it is ever likely that actions could be meaningfully segmented into something comparable to the units of language. It is interesting to note, however, that recent studies have shown a remarkable degree of agreement in the way observers partition video-taped sequences of simple tasks.[7] But this correspondence exists in the way people *perceive* the units of someone else's actions. It is not necessarily the case that the same units are employed by the actors themselves.

Obviously, we need to be cautious about these basic differences between verbal and nonverbal behavior—but not to the extent of overlooking the many points of similarity between these two domains. Both speech and action are *planned* activities. In each case, the execution of these plans involves, we believe, the internal manipulation of cognitive demons. We have already discussed in Chapter 3 the common influences upon word and action demons; but it is also worth reminding ourselves that in order to achieve either coherent speech or appropriate action, we must first marshal the right demons in the correct order. Since both the selection and ordering process can and do go wrong, it is parsimonious to assume that they do so for similar reasons. Although it must be remembered that, with slips of action, we have neither the range of examples nor the precise analytical techniques that are available to those studying verbal slips.

Behavioral Blends

Since actions are neither segmented nor executed in the same way as speech, it would be unrealistic to expect a truly equivalent form of blending to occur in both domains. Unlike actions, words are made up of discrete pieces that can be broken apart and fitted together in novel combinations without causing the tongue to stumble, particularly if the resulting blend obeys the basic linguistic roles. Words emerge in sequence from the same set of effectors, but actions usually involve several different modes of response. Intended actions are usually tied to specific effector systems. If we want to kick a

[7]D. Newtson, "The process of behavior observation." *Journal of Human Movement Studies* 2(1976), 114–122. D. Newtson, R. Rinduer, R. Miller and K. La Cross, "The effects of feature changes in behavior segmentation." *Journal of Experimental Social Psychology* 14(1978), 379–388.

football, it is not likely that we would use our hands by mistake. Nor in making a cup of coffee are we likely to pick up the kettle in our teeth. One could imagine having the intention to scratch one's nose with a forefinger, and then actually doing it with the thumb or the back of the hand. But even if such a blend did occur, we would probably not notice it, since we would not have been conscious of formulating the plan at such a detailed level. All that we would need to be aware of is whether the itch persisted or went away.

For these reasons, behavioral blends tend to be rare, or perhaps even nonexistent in the strictly equivalent sense. In any case, they would be difficult to distinguish from strong habit intrusions. In behavior, we can find many close parallels to word substitutions (as we saw in Chapter 4), but we have collected no slips of action that are structurally similar to verbal blends. There are, however, two kinds of mistake which, though clearly different from verbal blends, appear to reflect the same kind of underlying mechanism.

The first of these involve an inappropriate combination of words and actions. We find ourselves saying something which, in the context of our current actions, is quite absurd, although what has happened is often evident to the observer. Here are some examples for our collection.

> "My office phone rang. I picked up the receiver and bellowed 'Come in' at it. It had been one of those mornings with a lot of people knocking at the door."
>
> "The train conductor approached me to collect my fare. I handed him the correct change, saying 'Six-o-seven-o-four-double-three', my phone number."
>
> "I had just finished talking on the phone when my secretary ushered in some visitors. I got up from behind the desk and walked to greet them with my hand outstretched, saying 'Smith speaking'."

These are all quite literal instances of cross talk between the Intention System and the current activity. In two of these cases, it is clear that the words spoken related to what had just gone before, and were triggered by features of the current environment.

The second class of behavioral blends involves the intermeshing of two presently active intentions. Here is an example:

"I went to make a cup of tea in the kitchen. I had emptied the teapot and had the kettle boiling when the cat came clamoring at the kitchen door to be fed. I went to the cupboard, fetched out a can of cat food and opened it. Then I took a spoon from the drawer and deposited a large chunk of evil smelling meat into the teapot which was open to receive the tea leaves."

Behavioral Spoonerisms

As with words, behavioral spoonerisms are characterized by a complete or partial reversal of the intended order of things. On some occasions, they involve the right actions being made to the wrong objects within the same task. At other times, particularly when one has the intention to carry out two separate tasks in a particular order, components from one task appear in the other, and vice-versa.

"When I leave for work in the morning, I am in the habit of throwing two dog biscuits to my pet corgi and then putting on my earrings. One morning, I threw the earrings to the dog and found myself trying to attach a dog biscuit to my ear."

"I put the butter on the draining board and two dirty plates in the fridge—instead of the other way round."

"In a hurried effort to finish the housework and have a bath, I put the plants meant for the family room in the bedroom and my underwear in the window in the family room."

"I threw my glasses in the wastebasket, and kept some dirty tissues I was holding in my other hand."

"During the Second World War after I was just married, my husband, who was stationed away from home, called me one morning just as I was going to my bath to say that the date for the regiment to go overseas had been fixed. I walked to my steaming bath, put my sponge and washcloth carefully on the chair and threw my clothes into the bath."

An important feature of these errors is the clue they offer as to the possible units of action. Of special interest is the temporal proximity of the reversed objects within the intended action sequence. As compared to verbal spoonerisms, where the reversed elements are usually separated by milliseconds only, an action sequence is usually extended over a much longer time scale, and it is presumably for this reason that partial spoonerisms are more common in action than complete reversals. It would require an unusually sustained bout of preoccupation or distraction to divert attention for a sufficient amount of time not to catch the reversal before the symmetry was complete. Although for the lady mulling over the news of her husband's imminent departure overseas, this obviously was the case.

THEORETICAL ISSUES

What does our theory of action tell us about the causes of these slips? What happens during the assembly of a planned sequence of words or actions to allow unwanted demons to claim another's slot, or for legitimate demons to end up in the wrong order?

One part of the answer is fairly obvious, and we have discussed it at length already. Demons are intensely active and competitive creatures. The more fired up they become by current intentions, frequency of use, context, need, and so on, the more likely they are to jump the queue. But there is another important factor as well: simply being highly activated does not guarantee just any demon access to the Action System. Within each line-up of intended demons there are certain local characteristics, existing over and above the demons themselves, that will admit some usurpers but not others. The evidence from both verbal and behavioral slips suggests that intruders must conform to a particular expected pattern. Only in this way can they evade the scrutiny of the syntax demons, introduced earlier in this chapter.

In the case of words, these characteristics are fairly well understood. Slips of the tongue must obey the rules of spoken English *and* be compatible with our intentions to some degree. In the case of actions, the issue is less obvious. But one thing our behavioral mistakes do tell us is that just as wrong words have to obey linguistic rules, so also do wrong actions have to conform to the basic laws of physics. They have to fit in with the natural order of things. If a right action is applied to a wrong object, then that object must be one for which that action is in some way feasible. Otherwise, these unwanted action demons would never get past the syntax demons who serve as a kind of screening device or template between the Action Store and the Action System.

The main purpose of this chapter has been to demonstrate the need to add these syntax demons to our basic theory of action. The syntax demons clearly operate within fairly broad limits that are set by the currently active plan.

chapter nine
THE FREUDIAN SLIP
REVISITED

Almost everyone has heard of the Freudian slip. Like many of Freud's penetrating insights into the human condition, it has wide currency in the everyday language of the Western world. We generally take such a slip to mean one in which the nature of the erroneous words or actions reveals something about their maker that they would prefer to have kept hidden from public or even private view. It is the gaffe, the *faux pas*, or "blooper". We have all made them—like a favorite example of Freud's in which the President of the Lower House of the Austrian Parliament opened the assembly with the words, "Gentlemen, I take notice that a full quorum of members is present and herewith declare the sitting *closed*."[1]

That such slips *can* occur is not in dispute. What we would wish to argue, in contradiction to Freud, is that most absent-minded errors have more prosaic causes—of the kind we have been discussing in previous chapters. For Freud, of course, it was the other way round. In his view, most mistakes, although not consciously intended (quite the reverse in fact), are actually in keeping with the individual's unconscious needs or wishes.

Freud was perfectly well aware of the kinds of explanation we

[1]Sigmund Freud, *Introductory Lectures on Psychoanalysis*, trans. Joan Riviere (London: George Allen & Unwin, Ltd., 1922), p. 26. Used by permission of Liveright Publishing Corporation and George Allen & Unwin (Publishers) Ltd.

have been advancing. He called them "psycho-physiological factors", a label which embraced fatigue, excitement, strong associations, distraction of attention, preoccupation, and so on. He was even willing to acknowledge (though not with any great conviction) that some errors, a trivial few, could occur for these reasons alone. He put it very plainly: "Let me once more emphasize the fact that we do not maintain—and for our purposes do not need to maintain—that every single mistake which occurs has a meaning, although I think that probable. It is enough for us to prove that such a meaning is relatively frequent in the various forms of error."[2]

The issue that faces us in this chapter, therefore, is not whether there are meaningful slips (in the Freudian sense), we will take that as read; but whether they make up the larger part of our absent-minded errors as Freud would have us believe. We are not trying to challenge the existence of the Freudian slip; only to contend that not all slips, relatively few in fact, are truly Freudian.

We will start with a summary of Freud's arguments, and since he was, by and large, a far better communicator than most of those who have since tried to interpret him, we will use his own words as much as possible. Then we will present the case for the opposition. And, in the final part of the chapter, we shall attempt to show that there is a place for the "meaningful" slip in our theory of action (Chapter 3). Any theory of human error that fails to accommodate the Freudian slip would obviously be an incomplete one. Our debate with Freud is not so much about the nature of the underlying mechanisms, but about the extent to which they operate. But that, we must accept, will never be an easy issue to resolve—Freud was a man who usually managed to have the last word. Or was he?

What Freud Actually Said
About the Freudian Slip

Let us begin with an account of Freud's interest in errors. He first became aware of the meaningfulness of certain everyday mistakes while he was writing *The Interpretation of Dreams*. The first mention of this was in a letter to his colleague Fliess, dated August 26, 1898. He

---

[2]Sigmund Freud, *Introductory Lectures on Psychoanalysis*, p. 47.

wrote that he had " ... at last grasped a little thing I had long suspected"; namely, the way in which a name sometimes escapes our search, and a wrong one is substituted for it. In this case, he had been unable to recall the last name of the poet, Joseph Mosen. "I was able to prove (i) that I had repressed the name Mosen because of certain associations; (ii) that material from my infancy played a part in the repression; and (iii) that the substitute names that occurred to me arose, just like a symptom, from both (recent and infantile) groups of material."[3]

Having determined the significance of this apparently trivial name-blocking (and therein lies his genius), he began to collect examples of many different forms of everyday error: misreadings, slips of the tongue and pen, bungled actions, and so on. Gradually, he was convinced that all of these normally inconsequential slips betrayed the presence, within the unconscious mind, of repressed impulses or intentions. Most of the time they remain suppressed, but occasionally they seize upon an opportune moment to make themselves known to the skilled observer. He started preparing *The Psychopathology of Everyday Life* in 1900, much of which appeared in two issues of a Berlin journal in 1901. In 1904, the work was issued as a separate volume for the first time. Thereafter many additions to the basic collection were made almost continuously over the next 20 years. It became one of Freud's most popular books, and ran into many editions. It is said that Freud first became aware that he was a famous person when, on his way to America to deliver his Clark University lectures in 1909, he discovered his cabin steward reading this book.

We can best capture the flavor of his arguments by citing a few of his own examples. Not surprisingly, many of these slips were seen by him as showing sexual undertones. Here are three fairly typical instances.

Freud wrote of a visit he made to a friend's home where he met a young girl who excited in him " ... a feeling of fondness which I had

[3]From *The Origins of Psychoanalysis: Letters to Wilhelm Fliess, Drafts and Notes: 1887–1902* by Sigmund Freud. Edited by Marie Bonaparte, Anna Freud, Ernst Kris. Authorized translation by Eric Mosbacher and James Strachey. Introduction by Ernst Kris. Copyright 1954 by Basic Books, Inc. By permission of Basic Books, Inc., Publishers, New York, and Hogarth Press, Ltd.

long believed extinct." While he was there, the girl's aged uncle
arrived and both she and Freud jumped up to fetch him a chair. The
girl got there first. But Freud, although pipped to the post, was
reluctant to give up his intention of providing the old man with a
seat, so he stood behind the girl and reached for the chair she was
already carrying. Instead of catching hold of the chair, however, he
grabbed the girl and, as he so decorously put it, " . . . for a moment my
hands touched her lap."[4]

In a similar vein, he tells of an incident that occurred to his
friend Stekel. On departing from a morning house call, Stekel offered
his hand to his hostess, and then discovered to his horror that his
hand was undoing the bow which held together her loosely fastened
dressing gown. Stekel remarked, "I was conscious of no dishonorable
intent, yet I executed this awkward movement with the ability of a
juggler."[5]

One of Freud's favorite slips of the tongue was committed by a
professor of anatomy who, in a lecture on the female sexual organs,
was heard to declare, "In the case of the female genitals, in spite of
many temptations (*Versuchungen*)—I beg your pardon, experiments
(*Versuche*)." This same professor, after lecturing on the nasal cavities,
once asked his audience whether they had understood their complexities. When the students indicated that they had, the professor,
who was well known for his conceit, exclaimed in surprise: "I can
hardly believe that since, even in Vienna with its millions of in-
habitants, those who understand the nasal cavities can be counted on
one finger. I mean the fingers of one hand."[6]

Without denying that such sexual undertones exist, we feel that
these examples tell us more about what thrilled old Vienna than what
causes slips of the tongue. Far more convincing, however, were his
less sexually charged explanations of blunders. These he expressed
most succinctly in the *Introductory Lectures on Psychoanalysis*, given
(one suspects to a rather suspicious and disapproving audience) at
the University of Vienna between 1915 and 1917. To ease his lis-
teners in gently, he opened with three lectures devoted largely to the

[4]Sigmund Freud, *The Psychopathology of Everyday Life* (London: Ernest Benn Ltd.,
1914), pp. 136–137.
[5]Sigmund Freud, *The Psychopathology of Everyday Life*, pg. 136–137.
[6]Quoted by F.J. Sulloway, *Freud: Biologist of the Mind*, p. 355.

meaning of fairly innocuous slips of the tongue. Along with dreams, these everyday slips enabled him to extend to the activities of daily life the discoveries he had first made in connection with the neuroses. He regularly used them as preliminary material for introducing nonmedical people to psychoanalysis. The subject matter was simple, recognizable and, on the surface at least, unobjectionable. Although we are no longer shocked by his revelations about the ubiquity of the sex drive, these lectures still remain more credible than the rather showy mental gymnastics he displayed in *The Psychopathology of Everyday Life.*

When Freud expressed a scientific opinion, he tended not to mince his words. In the fourth lecture, he asserted: "A suppression of a previous intention to say something is the indispensable condition for the occurrence of a slip of the tongue."[7] This suppression could operate at any one of three levels. At the most conscious level, the resolve to suppress a particular feeling and any verbal reference to it could be quite deliberate. At the next level, the person who has made the slip can recognize with hindsight the wish to suppress it, but was not aware of this tendency beforehand. At the deepest level, this suppressing tendency is energetically denied by the speaker when it is subsequently pointed out to him. Thus, the suppression may be recognized or not recognized, accepted or denied, conscious or unconscious; but, in all cases, the slip is the result of the conflict between two forces—the underlying, unacceptable need and the tendency to keep it hidden. To the psychoanalyst, therefore, these slips provide yet another window to the unconscious mind.

Freud, like most of his scientific contemporaries, was a committed determinist. It was his unshakable belief that all mental as well as physical events have ultimately identifiable causes. And, for him, the causal agencies in the psychic realm stemmed from the unconscious, wherein lie our basic biological drives. Among these drives, the sexual urge was dominant; though he would acknowledge that not all slips manifest these sexual needs directly. But since these forces (according to Freudian theory) play a major part in developing the personality, an indirect sexual connection could probably be unearthed in the course of lengthy analysis.

[7]Sigmund Freud, *Introductory Lectures on Psychoanalysis,* p. 52.

The Case for the Opposition

Freud's interest in slips has been curiously double-edged in its consequences. It was his genius for noting the minutiae of life that first revealed the rich pickings to be found among the debris of the mental world. Yet it was his personal and scientific need to fashion simple, powerful but largely untestable explanations that effectively closed the lid again on this fascinating psychological wastebasket. One can judge by the readiness with which we use the term *Freudian slip* in ordinary speech how enticing this theory was for the layman and psychologist alike. But such a compelling theory unfortunately conveys the mistaken impression that the origins of all these lapses are wrapped up and need no further explanation.

If one of the greatest thinkers of our time can be said to have had an undoing, it lies in the aggressive extremes to which he pushed the generality of his truly remarkable insights. One of the sadder episodes in his life was the falling out that occurred with his close friend and collaborator, Josef Breuer, over the issue of the sexual origins of hysteria. This estrangement has been discussed by many writers, but perhaps the most convincing explanation has been offered by his most recent biographer, Frank Sulloway. The following passage, although concerned with the break-up between Breuer and Freud, also communicates precisely the strengths and weaknesses of his stance toward slips of the mind.

> ... the estrangement between Breuer and Freud was, more than anything else, simply a matter of incompatible scientific styles. Where Breuer advocated an eclectic approach to understanding hysterical phenomena, Freud sought rigid incontrovertible laws that suited his more dogmatic and revolutionary self-image in science. What Breuer saw as Freud's greatest intellectual weakness—his fanatical propensity for exclusive scientific formulations—Freud valued as one of his most courageous and fruitful abilities, while sorely regretting its absence in his friend.[8]

One can never really detach the psychology from the man. In many ways, Freud was right to be passionately dogmatic. Considering the times in which he lived, and the message he had to preach, it was the

---

[8]F.J. Sulloway, *Freud: Biologist of the Mind*, pp. 98–99.

only possible style. Other men before Freud had known of the unconscious mind, but it took Freud's vision *and* his vehement articulation of it to alter the world's view of human nature. But absolute assertions invite equally total denials; and there is always the danger of the baby going out with the bathwater. The time, we feel, is now right for a compromise.

As we mentioned earlier, Freud's belief that absent-minded actions and slips of the tongue serve to fulfill some unconscious intention shares with many of his other ideas the difficulty that it is not open to any unequivocal test. We can neither prove nor disprove it. Anyone confronted with an apparently unintended action can usually provide some retrospective explanation, as Freud himself did with great ingenuity for his own slips and seeming accidents. But the fact that these views are unassailable by scientific means does not render them invalid. Our personal experience leaves us with the definite feeling that some of our slips are indeed Freudian. But the present authors would prefer to accept that most of them have a much more straightforward—and, inevitably, more boring— explanation.

This particular view has been stated most forcefully by the Italian textual critic, Sebastiano Timpanaro, in a book called, appropriately enough, *The Freudian Slip*.[9] In it, he examines in very great detail the slips that Freud presented as evidence for the psychoanalytic interpretation. Here, we will only focus upon one such example, though a pivotal one, since Freud devoted a whole chapter to it in *The Psychopathology of Everyday Life*. It is evidently one that Freud himself regarded as clear proof of his position. We will let Freud describe the incident.

> Last summer—it was once again on a holiday trip—I renewed my acquaintance with a certain young man of academic background. I soon found that he was familiar with some of my psychological publications. We had fallen into conversation— how I have now forgotten—about the social status of the race to which we both belonged; and ambitious feelings prompted him to give vent to a regret that his generation was doomed (as he

[9] S. Timpanaro, *The Freudian Slip* (London: NLB, 1976).

expressed it) to atrophy, and could not develop its talents or satisfy its needs. He ended a speech of impassioned fervor with the well-known line of Virgil's in which the unhappy Dido commits to posterity her vengeance on Aeneas: 'Exoriare ... ' Or, rather, he *wanted* to end it in this way, for he could not get hold of the quotation and tried to conceal an obvious gap in what he remembered by changing the order of the words: 'Exoriare ex nostris ossibus ultor.' At last he said irritably: 'Please don't look so scornful: you seem as if you were gloating over my embarrassment. Why not help me? There's something missing in the line; how does the whole thing really go?'

'I'll help you with pleasure,' I replied, and gave the quotation in its correct form: 'Exoriare ALIQUIS nostris ex ossibus ultor.' (Literally: 'Let someone (aliquis) arise from my bones as an avenger!')

'How stupid to forget a word like that! By the way, you claim that one never forgets a thing without some reason. I should be very curious to learn how I came to forget the indefinite pronoun *aliquis* in this case.'[10]

Freud, of course, " ... took up this challenge most readily, for I was hoping for a contribution to my collection." He persuaded the unfortunate young man to free associate around the forgotten word *aliquis*, and these associations went something like this: the idea of dividing the word into *a* and *liquis*; relics; liquefying, fluidity, fluid; saints' relics; Saint Simon, Saint Benedict, Saint Augustine, and Saint Januarius (the last two being calendar saints); Saint Januarius's miracle of blood (a phial of this saint's blood is said to liquefy once a year on a particular holy day); and, finally, he came to the crunch—the fact that he was extremely worried that his girl friend had missed her last period and might be pregnant. According to Freud, the important clues were the allusions to *calendar* saints, and the idea that *blood* flows on a certain day. Why that particular quotation? Freud had an answer for everything. Dido was crying out to her *descendants* to avenge her race. But in this case, the young man had the equally fervent hope that *no* descendants would appear as the result of his most recent sexual encounter.

Should we bow to the great man's wisdom and provide the

[10]Sigmund Freud, *The Psychopathology of Everyday Life*, p. 11.

expected round of applause? Or should we consider another possibility? Timpanaro offers us a more pedestrian but more credible alternative. Before giving it, however, we should note that two errors were made: (a) the word *aliquis* was omitted, and (b) the words *nostris* and *ex* were reversed. Now let us hear what Timparano had to say.

> What is the explanation for this double error? The most mediocre of philologists would have no difficulty in giving one. Anyone who has anything to do with the written or oral transmission of texts (including quotations learnt by heart) know that they are exposed to the danger of *banalization*. Forms which have a more archaic, more high-flown, more unusually stylistic expression, and which are therefore removed from the cultural-linguistic heritage of the person who is transcribing or reciting, *tend to be replaced by forms in more common use.* (our italics)[11]

He then goes on to demonstrate very convincingly (we will not bother with the details here), that, to a young man of his classical education, both the presence of the word *aliquis* in the sentence (which is redundant anyway), and the correct order of *ex* and *nostris* are highly unusual forms, and therefore susceptible to banalizations. Or, to use a more familiar term, liable to strong habit intrusions.

Timpanaro's case can be summarized as follows: It has long been known by those whose business it is to look for mistakes in transcriptions and quotations that errors frequently take the form of banalizations. That is, they reveal a tendency to substitute for the correct word one whose meaning or usage is more familiar. For example, many of us are inclined to misquote Shakespeare's line "All that glisters is not gold" as "All that glitters is not gold"—where, for us, *glitters* is more commonplace than *glisters*. The same process is clearly evident in many of Freud's own examples. For a slip to have any likelihood of being truly Freudian, it must take a *less familiar* form than the intended word or action. This does not happen all that often, but we cannot ignore the fact that it sometimes does. We would accept, for example, that the Viennese lady, calling the children in from the garden, who instead of saying "children" (Jungen), said "Jews" (Juden), had probably made a genuine Freudian slip.

[11]S. Timpanaro, *The Freudian Slip*, p. 30.

Reconciling the Freudian Slip
and the Cognitive Demon

In outlining the basic components of our theory of action (see Fig. 3.2 in Chapter 3), we indicated that the Need System connects directly to the Intention System, and also to the Recognition, Word, and Action Stores. By these channels, the Need System is able to energize cognitive demons in all these domains independently of the current preoccupations of the Intention System. We have already seen, in Chapter 5, how needs can shape our perceptions of ambiguous stimuli. The same possibilities exist for word and action demons as well.

That such connections exist between our knowledge structures and our needs, feelings, and emotions cannot be in doubt. Anyone who has grieved for the loss of someone they love will know how obsessively the mind dwells upon the separation or bereavement. It is in the nature of such grief that, for a time, every part of the mental world is crowded by images and memories of the lost person. To escape, we try desperately to distract ourselves with other concerns, but almost immediately we stumble upon some association which, no matter how remote, causes our feelings of loss to come flooding back with renewed force. Almost everything that reaches our senses seems to carry some painful reminder. At first, we have no defense against our grief. Then we start to construct flimsy barriers that crumble almost instantly. Gradually, our defenses become stronger, and although our protective walls continue to be breached with the same devastating consequences, they do so less often. Eventually, the flood begins to recede, but we always remain vulnerable to the occasional spring tide.

Although we are now talking more about images and feelings than words or actions (though these too are involved), it will be evident that the processes we have just been describing are not dissimilar to the mechanisms that Freud proposed for slips in general, except that they operate largely in the subjective area. In grief, we consciously strive to fill the void with neutral matters. But at first there are no neutral matters. Then, as the intensity of the need begins to wane, the Intention System gains strength. For much of the time, it succeeds in suppressing painful thoughts and recollections; but every now and again it is caught unawares. In one sense, therefore, these backslidings into despair are not unlike Freudian slips. The undercurrents may not necessarily spring from long repressed child-hood crises, as Freud would have it, but two of the basic ingredients are the same. We have strong feelings that we consciously wish to suppress, and occasionally we fail.

These experiences can be restated in the more pedestrian terms of our action theory. Loss of a loved person creates an overwhelming need for their restoration in our lives. This need is pumped furiously into all the places in which cognitive demons lurk. Any demon of whatever kind that embodies some aspect of the loved person or the shared existence will receive an enormous boost to its activation level. A vast host of demons will become heated to boiling point, and many beyond. Those that are not actually driven into their particular acts by this frenzy require only the slightest kick from the outside world or the Intention System (either directly or indirectly) to provide them with escape velocity. Since living would be insupport-able otherwise, time takes the heat out of these needs, and the boiling reduces gradually to a slow simmer. A kind of normalcy begins to return. Old priorities are restored and new ones established. Life goes on.

Now a jump from the sublime to the ridiculous: Consider the following story (it is not from our collection, but it rings true). A dinner guest is expected who has a nose of extravagant proportions. The host, anxious not to cause embarrassment, briefs himself to avoid any reference to noses in the conversation, to avoid staring at his guest's nose, and, in fact, to steer the course of the evening as far as possible from any consideration of noses whatsoever. Yet, when the guest arrives, and they sit down at the dinner table, the host, intend-ing to ask for the salt, leans toward his guest and says: "Pass the nose please."

Taken at face value, this seems an open-and-shut case of Freudian slipping. But, within our theory, there are two other possi-ble ways of explaining this gaffe. The first is that the host's concern invested this otherwise emotionally neutral word demon with addi-tional drive from the Need System (the need to avoid embarrass-ment, not to cause hurt, etc.). In other words, his worries *primed* this specific demon. This is a view similar to Freud's own, except that it does not necessarily require an interfering tendency. The slip could have happened through need priming even without the host's desire to evade all social contact with the formidable nose.

The second possibility, and the one more in line with our recurring theme of strong habit intrusions, is that the host's repeated resolutions to censor the "nose demon" brought about an increase in its activation level simply by the frequency-and-recency of use effect. By seeking to suppress a particular word, it is perhaps possible to achieve the same result—in terms of raised activation—as if we had actually practiced uttering it. Thus, we are suggesting that what could matter for demon activation is not the *mode* of its employment (*i.e.*, whether it was internally rehearsed or spoken aloud), but the number of times the particular word demon was called into play and how recently that occurred.

Again, we stress we are not insisting that the Freudian explanation of such a slip is wrong, simply that it is not the only possible one. That Freud had personal and polemical reasons for overstating his case should be his problem, not ours. For the moment, it seems more desirable to keep all the possibilities open. We do not resist Freud's arguments, only his efforts to exclude all others. We must also acknowledge that our theory does not, at present, allow us to discriminate between the various alternatives. This is a weakness of the theory, but one we are prepared to live with until better evidence comes along.

Should Freud Have the Last Word?

If we were able to show Freud what we have written so far in this book, we predict that his reactions would be a mixture of mild boredom and patient exasperation. "Look," he might say, "there is absolutely nothing new here. Don't think that these ideas weren't knocking around in my time. I know all about habits, associations and cognitive demons (or whatever you choose to call them), and dressing them up with fancy computer metaphors and references to artificial intelligence and other new-fangled technologies doesn't alter a thing. There is nothing new under the sun, and especially in psychology. Let me remind you that I have dealt with these points before." Then he would reach for a copy of his *Introductory Lectures on Psychoanalysis*, and indicate (probably with the ultimately fatal cigar) the following passage.

> Psycho-physiological factors such as excitement, absent-mindedness, distraction of attention, obviously provide very little in the way of explanation. They are mere phrases; they are screens, and we should not be deterred from looking behind them. The question is rather what has here called forth the excitement or the particular diversion of attention. The influence of sound-values, resemblances between words, and common associations connecting certain words, must also be recognized as important. They facilitate the slip by pointing out a path for it to take. But if there is a path before me does it necessarily follow that I must go along it? I also require a motive determining my choice and, further, some force to propel me forward. These sound-values and word associations are, therefore, just like the bodily conditions, the facilitating causes of slips of the tongue, and cannot provide the real explanation for them.[12]

Should we let the matter rest there? These have proved difficult arguments to refute. But we believe there are two reasons why he should not have the last word. First, the evidence assembled in this book, as well as theoretical advances in cognitive psychology, strongly suggest that absent-minded errors have multiple causes, albeit many of them quite systematic and predictable. Second, as we shall hope to demonstrate in the next chapter, it makes more sense (and is more useful) to regard the human agents of catastrophe, not as victims of some repressed death wish, but as people subject to an unhappy coincidence of normal cognitive failure (or, more frequently, a number of them) with an unforgiving environment. As we shall argue, it is more helpful to regard these disastrous lapses as being the consequence of *imperfect rationality* rather than of irrationality. But in a very important sense, Freud was right. It is quite meaningless to attempt to divorce the mechanics of cognitive psychology from the emotional forces which drive them. Too much reliance on intelligent machines as models for mental function has had a strong tendency to lead us in this direction. It is time the heart was put back into cognitive psychology, although not necessarily in the precise way that Freud indicated.

[12]Sigmund Freud, *Introductory Lectures on Psychoanalysis*, p. 36.

chapter ten
CATASTROPHIC LAPSES

In 1854, during the Battle of Balaclava, an aide-de-camp, bearing an ambiguous order to the commander of the British Cavalry Division, offered a verbal interpretation of its meaning that was largely responsible for the destruction of the Light Brigade.[1] In June, 1895, the two leading battleships of the British Mediterranean Fleet, on maneuvers off Tripoli in clear daylight, turned sharply toward one another under signalled instructions from the C-in-C's flagship and immediately collided with the loss of 356 officers and men.[2] On February 28th, 1975, a tube train entered Moorgate station on the Northern Line without reducing speed and crashed into the end wall of a short extension tunnel beyond the station; 42 passengers and the driver lost their lives, 72 passengers were injured.[3] At Santa Cruz Airport, Tenerife, on March 27th, 1977, a KLM Boeing 747 began its takeoff run along a fogbound runway before receiving clearance from air traffic control and collided with a Pan American Boeing 747 taxiing in the opposite direction; 577 people died in the crash, the

[1]Cecil Woodham-Smith, *The Reason Why* (Middlesex, England: Penguin Books, 1958). C. Hibbert, *The Destruction of Lord Raglan* (Middlesex, England: Penguin Books, 1963). N. Bentley, ed., *Russell's Despatches from the Crimea* (London: Andre Deutsch, 1966). H. Moyse-Bartlett, *Nolan of Balaclava* (London: Leo Copper, 1971).

[2]J. Watkins, in *Explanation in the Behavioral Sciences*, eds., R. Borger and F. Cioffi (Cambridge: Cambridge University Press, 1970), pp. 212–216.

[3]Report on the Accident that occurred on 28th February 1975 at Moorgate Station, Northern Line, London Transport. (London: H.M. Stationery Office, 1976).

worst in the history of aviation.[4] These are the disasters that we shall be examining closely in this chapter. What do they have in common? By what criteria were they selected? What can we learn from them?

Despite the diversity of their circumstances, all the cases to be considered share at least two important characteristics. In the first place, the means of executing the intentions, whether it be the Light Brigade, the train, the ships, or the aircraft, were all judged subsequently to be fully functional and intact prior to the incidents. No blame can therefore be attached to these effector mechanisms directly (and here it is not altogether inappropriate to regard the main body of the Light Brigade as a largely unreasoning mechanism for delivering sudden death). Second, all of these unhappy episodes clearly involved some form of human error; and, in three cases out of four, were due to lapses committed by more than one person. In some, the original blunder was later compounded by other participants; in others, a variety of mistakes were made by a number of different people. Nevertheless, most of the contributing failures are recognizable as part of the body of errors to which all of us are prone in the course of our daily lives. Our contention is that no matter how bizarre or irrational these disastrous actions may appear at first sight, they can, for the most part, be equated with familiar mental lapses, at least conjecturally. In this context, we shall be applying what the philosopher, John Watkins, has called the *principle of imperfect rationality* in order to fill in, no matter how speculatively, the gaps in our understanding regarding the psychological events leading up to these catastrophes.[5] We do this not so much to add further causal hypotheses to the many that already exist, but more to elucidate the psychological processes that could conceivably have been implicated.

The first factor determining our choice of these particular incidents was the availability of documentary evidence concerning both the circumstances of their occurrence and their possible causes. Beyond this, each catastrophe was selected to illustrate a number of specific points concerning the causes of accidents in general and the involvement of mental lapses in particular. Thus, the events

---

[4]P.A. Roitsch, G.L. Babcock, W.W. Edmunds. *Human Factors Report on the Tenerife Accident* (Air Line Pilots Association Study Group Report. Washington, D.C.: Engineering and Air Safety, 1978).

[5]J. Watkins, *Explanation in the Behavioral Sciences*, pp. 212–216.

preceding the destruction of the Light Brigade reveal some of the systematic biases to which human communication systems are prone. The collision between *HMS Camperdown* and *HMS Victoria* provides a further example of how messages, apparently clear and unambiguous to the sender, can be read in a number of different ways by the recipient. The Moorgate tube disaster is included because although, on the face of it, the failure of the driver to stop or even slow down the train before the end of the tunnel is difficult to comprehend on grounds other than some extreme form of mental disturbance, a very speculative explanation of this occurrence can be offered in terms of the more commonplace lapses familiar to us in everyday life. Finally, the Tenerife disaster reveals something of the complex relationships existing between psychological, situational, and medical factors in the production of critical mental lapses.

In presenting these selected case studies, our first aim is to provide some factual support for the argument advanced in the previous chapter that catastrophic lapses are not qualitatively distinct from the normal run of everyday mistakes. Great disasters, arising from human fallibility, do not necessarily require equally monumental blunders to create them. More often than not, they are the product of a series of minor cognitive failures that in more ordinary surroundings would go unremarked, but which in these unforgiving circumstances exact terrible penalties. In trying to understand the origins of these catastrophic lapses, therefore, we do not need to limit ourselves to searching retrospectively among the debris of some actual disaster. For those whose principal aim is to elucidate the underlying causes of mental lapses, as distinct from those who seek to apportion responsibility or to identify remediable systems failures, it is probably more profitable to inquire among the living rather than the dead, to study the frequent rather than the rare occurrence, and to look in commonplace everyday settings rather than in atypical or dangerous environments.

Nevertheless, as in other branches of psychology, the intensive study of the single case can yield valuable information. Where sufficient evidence is available regarding both the antecedent and prevailing circumstances of a particular disaster, we are able to study the interaction of the various causal factors over time thus obtaining a longitudinal perspective which is well nigh impossible to acquire for the inconsequential lapse. Although any one catastrophe may result from the chance conjunction of several causal chains of events, and hence be a truly unique happening, the precise effects of this peculiar combination of contributing factors teaches us something about the limits of human performance that could not be learned from the psychological laboratory or from naturalistic observations of everyday life. However, just as an understanding of the origins of the first World War did little to prevent the outbreak of the second, so it would be unrealistic to suppose that merely knowing what lapses contributed to a particular disaster will necessarily allow us to prevent their recurrence under similar circumstances. But by adding this knowledge to a systematic theory or set of theories concerning the occurrence of the more predictable forms of human error, we not only extend our understanding of cognitive function in general, but we can also begin to assemble a body of principles which, when applied to the operation of military or transport systems, could reasonably be expected to reduce the likelihood of future catastrophic lapses. In the absence of such a theoretical framework, however, we can only progress in a piecemeal fashion. One of the more ambitious aims of this book is to provide the foundations of such a framework by analyzing what we already know about systematic mental lapses as they occur in a variety of activities.

Although we have previously stressed the idiosyncratic nature of these selected case histories, we believe it is still possible to draw from them some tentative conclusions about the causes of disasters and accidents in general. Perhaps the most important is that none of these incidents—with the possible exception of the Moorgate crash, about which so little is known—can be attributed to a single causal factor. Nearly all of them were clearly the outcome of a number of quite distinct chains of events which only proved disastrous when they intersected at a particular time and place. By tracing these individual chains back into the past, it is possible to identify a number of critical stages at which the accident sequence could have been thwarted. One further point: although mental lapses were involved in all of these incidents, one gains the impression that in some cases at least they would not, by themselves, have been sufficient to cause the disaster. On a number of occasions, they appear to have been brought into critical prominence by the simultaneous presence of medical or environmental factors.

Now let us turn to the first of our case studies: the events leading up to the destruction of the Light Brigade.

THE CHARGE OF THE LIGHT BRIGADE

At ten minutes past eleven on the morning of October 25th, 1854, some 670 splendidly attired horsemen began to advance down a grassy, undulating valley a mile and a quarter long and just under a mile wide. Facing them at the far end were 12 Russian guns supported to the rear and on either flank by many squadrons of cavalry. Lining the hills down the left hand or northern side of the valley were four additional squadrons of enemy cavalry, eight battalions of riflemen and 14 guns. On the opposite hill, stationed among captured Turkish redoubts, were eleven battalions of Russian infantry and a further 32 guns. The greater part of the valley along which the Light Brigade were to charge was therefore covered by hostile fire from three sides. It made an ideal killing ground.

By eleven thirty-five, the last of the 195 survivors of the Charge had stumbled, crawled, or been carried back to their starting positions. Virtually none had escaped injury, and many were seriously wounded. The remainder of the Light Cavalry Brigade, acknowledged to be the finest in Europe, were dead, dying, or captured. Five hundred of their horses had been killed outright, or were then being destroyed by the farrier's pistol. Aside from the near annihilation of the Light Brigade, what had been achieved? The twelve Russian guns at the far end of the valley had ben temporarily silenced when their crews had been cut down; but no guns had been carried away. Nothing of any tactical value had been gained, and an opportunity to recover the Turkish redoubts along with their British naval guns had been lost. What was the Light Brigade's intended objective? Why did they attack the wrong target? Somebody had indeed blundered, but who and how?

To answer these questions we must go back to the preceding phase of the curiously episodic action that has come to be known as the Battle of Balaclava. But first let us briefly set the scene. During the early weeks of October, the British and French armies had entrenched themselves on the bare heights to the south of the key Russian naval base of Sebastopol, and had begun to bombard the city.

The French army's left flank was protected by the sea, but the British right flank was relatively exposed, as was their base four miles away in the tiny land-locked port of Balaclava. The bulk of the British infantry were encamped behind their trenches on the Sapouné Heights (see the map shown in Figure 10-1). The Cavalry Division, under the command of Lord Lucan, was encamped in the South Valley, just beneath the Causeway Heights. Along these Heights were six redoubts manned largely by Turkish troops, their purpose being to protect the Worontzoff Road, a vital means of communication between the camps on the plain and the siegeworks above Sebastopol.

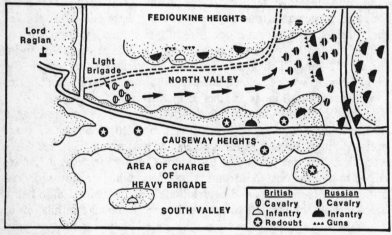

Figure 10.1

At dawn on the 25th, a Russian army of some 25,000 men moved into the eastern end of the North Valley. During the early part of the morning, they attacked and captured four of the six most easterly redoubts. In addition, a large force of Russian cavalry advanced down the North Valley. One part of it crossed the Causeway Heights and charged the position of the 93rd Highlanders defending the approaches to Balaclava. They had been repulsed, and had retired back across the Heights into the North Valley. Subsequently, the larger part of the Russian cavalry had crossed the Heights at a point just above the site of the Cavalry Division camp. There they had been charged and routed by a much smaller force of British cavalry made up of eight squadrons of the Heavy Brigade. After this action, the Russians retreated back over the Heights and reassembled at the eastern end of the North Valley.

During and immediately after the successful charge of the Heavy Brigade, the Light Brigade, under the command of Lord Cardigan, was stationed some 500 yards away. But they took no part in the action, nor did they attempt to pursue the demoralized Russians. Although Captain Morris of the 17th Lancers had begged for permission to charge the retreating enemy, Lord Cardigan refused it on the grounds that he had been " . . . ordered into a position by Lieutenant-General the Earl of Lucan, my superior officer, with orders on no account to leave, and to defend it against any attack of the Russians; they did not however approach my position." But Lord Lucan gave a different account of his orders. He claimed that he had instructed Lord Cardigan " . . . to attack anything and everything that shall come within reach of you." Whatever the truth of the matter, it is clear that a more competent commander of cavalry than Lord Cardigan would not have passed up such an opportunity to strike a crushing blow at a defeated but still effective enemy force. Although the Light Brigade's subsequent charge down the North Valley is remembered as the great blunder of the day, it is likely that their inactivity on this occasion constituted an even greater one. If they had attacked at this moment, it is unlikely that the later disaster would ever have occurred. It was the 12 guns accompanying this force of Russian cavalry when it was attacked by the Heavy Brigade that formed the mistaken objective of the Charge of the Light Brigade.

Meanwhile, Lord Raglan, commander-in-chief of the British forces, had been situated together with his staff some 600 feet above the North and South Valleys with a panoramic view, both of his own and the enemy troop movements, rarely enjoyed by commanders in the field. He had been growing increasingly uneasy at the slow progress of the two infantry divisions ordered down earlier that morning from the Sapouné Heights to support the redoubts. He was also extremely irritated at the opportunity missed by the Light Brigade. At this point he sent Lord Lucan the following order: "Cavalry to advance and take advantage of any opportunity to recover the Heights. They will be supported by infantry, which have been ordered to advance on two fronts." To Lord Raglan, high above the battlefield, it was clear that the key to victory lay in the possession of the Causeway Heights. Although four of the six Allied redoubts were still held by the Russians, the immediate threat to Balaclava posed by the Russian cavalry attacks had been removed. Further, the surprising success of the Charge of the Heavy Brigade had left the British with a moral ascendancy in that part of the field. An immediate attack upon the enemy-held redoubts by the entire Cavalry Division could well have caused panic among their defenders who had just witnessed the defeat of an apparently invincible force of cavalry at their hands. This supposition was indeed supported by Russian comments after the war. Thus, Lord Raglan's intention was that the cavalry should attack straightway without waiting for the infantry, which could be expected to arrive later to support them. Lord Lucan, however, derived entirely the opposite meaning from the order. To him, it meant that he should advance *only* when supported by infantry. His response was to move the Cavalry Division into the western end of the North Valley, with the Light Brigade drawn up facing eastward and the Heavy Brigade positioned behind them and to their right (see Figure 10.1).

Three-quarters of an hour passed and Lord Raglan became increasingly frustrated at the apparent inactivity of Lord Lucan's cavalry. Then occurred the event that triggered the critical order. Through their glasses, staff officers saw teams of Russian artillery horses approaching the redoubts carrying with them tackle for dragging away the 12-pounders, the British naval guns with which the redoubts had been armed. Captured guns were a clear token of defeat, and their removal must be prevented at all costs. So began the sequence of communications, involving five men, Lord Raglan, General Airey, Captain Nolan, Lord Lucan, and Lord Cardigan, that led to the destruction of the Light Brigade. It is in these communications that our principal psychological interest lies.

At one end of what in contemporary jargon we would call a communication channel was Lord Raglan, a diffident, courteous, rather frail old man, who had last seen active service nearly forty years earlier when he lost an arm at Waterloo, and who occasionally still referred to the enemy as "the French" to the acute embarrassment of his staff officers and French allies. He was not by any standard a great general, but he was one who in that moment had correctly gauged the buoyant mood of his troops and the sagging morale of the Russians, and who had formulated a plan of action which, although unconventional—cavalry do not usually attack artillery unsupported—had a very reasonable chance of success in those particular circumstances. At the other end of the communication channel was the Light Cavalry Brigade, an exquisitely tuned instrument of war, disciplined, courageous, finely mounted on fresh horses, and, above all, desperately impatient to get to grips with the enemy after the galling frustrations of the morning. Not much wrong with the plan, nor with the means of executing it; so what went wrong in between? Why was the action not as planned?

Lord Raglan gave instructions to his Quartermaster-General, Brigadier Airey, who scribbled an order in pencil on a scrap of paper resting on his sabretache. After having the order read back to him, Lord Raglan added some further words. The final version went as follows: "Lord Raglan wishes the cavalry to advance rapidly to the front—follow the enemy and try to prevent the enemy carrying away the guns. Troop Horse Artillery may accompany. French cavalry is on your left. Immediate. Airey." The order contained a number of ambiguities—what exactly was to be the role of the Horse Artillery, and of the French cavalry? The most crucial lapse was the failure to specify clearly what was meant by "advance rapidly to the front." Both the eastern end of the North Valley and the captured redoubts lay in that general direction relative to the present position of the British cavalry, but rises in the ground concealed the activity around these redoubts from observers on the valley floor. These local inequalities of terrain were not evident to Lord Raglan and his staff, perched 600 feet or more above the plain. The only event of obvious significance to them was the presence of the artillery teams about to remove the British naval guns. But this was obscured from Lord Lucan for whom the order was intended. To some extent at least, both Lord Raglan and General Airey can be excused for not appreciating this fatal ambiguity. Not only were they unaware of the undulations of the valley from their vantage point, but, for them, the last order was really a more urgent reiteration of the previous one, not yet acted upon, and this had clearly specified the Heights as the cavalry objective.

Instead of the order being delivered to Lord Lucan by the next aide-de-camp for duty, the honor of carrying it was claimed by Captain Lewis Nolan, an officer of the 15th Hussars attached to Lord Raglan's staff. As he started to gallop headlong down the face of the steep slopes leading to the plain, Lord Raglan called after him "Tell Lord Lucan the cavalry is to attack immediately." Aside from being a superb horseman, Nolan was rare among cavalry officers in that he was something of an intellectual and the author of two professional works, one on the training of cavalry remount horses and the other on the history and tactics of light cavalry. He was also a very excitable man who, for the past two hours, had watched tormented by frustration as the Light Brigade had stood "shamefully inactive" while the Heavy Brigade had won lasting glory. Now, as one historian put it, ". . . he swooped like an avenging angel from the heights" bearing the order that would redress the balance. By a particularly malign twist of fate, it was Nolan, the passionate advocate of light cavalry, who was to play the major part in destroying the Light Brigade.

On receiving the order, Lord Lucan read it through with irritating slowness while Nolan fumed with impatience at his side. Lord Lucan began to protest the order, but Nolan cut him short and repeated Lord Raglan's final words, that the cavalry were to attack immediately. Lord Lucan, already not in the best of temper, piqued by Nolan's evident insolence and contempt, burst out angrily "Attack, sir? Attack what? What guns, sir?" To which Nolan made his fatal reply: he flung out his arm and pointed not to the Causeway Heights but to the line of guns at the eastern end of the valley, "There, my lord, is your enemy, there are your guns." It was this outburst, delivered in a tone of voice guaranteed to anger a far more mild-mannered man than Lord Lucan, that effectively sealed the fate of the Light Brigade. Saying nothing more, Lord Lucan turned his back on Nolan and rode away. A few minutes later, he rode over to Lord Cardigan who was seated on his horse some distance in front of the Light Brigade. The two men had detested each other for thirty years, and whatever opportunity there still existed for a rational consideration of the order, it was now lost in the wall of enmity that stood between them. Nevertheless, the interchange between them was icily polite. Lord Lucan ordered Lord Cardigan to advance down the North Valley and to attack the guns at the far end. Lord Lucan himself would follow behind with the Heavy Brigade. With stiff formality, Lord Cardigan pointed out the presence of the enemy on either side of the valley. Lord Lucan shrugged his shoulders and replied, "I know it, but Lord Raglan would have it." Thereafter, Lord Cardigan gave the order to advance and the Light Brigade began to move off at a walk down the valley.

There is one strange postscript to this disastrous sequence of communications. Having delivered his interpretation of the order, Captain Nolan sought out his friend Captain Morris, stationed in the front rank ahead of the 17th Lancers, and gained permission to ride beside him in the charge. There he remained until the advance had been underway for a few minutes, then he galloped his horse diagonally across in front of Lord Cardigan who was immediately outraged at this breach of cavalry etiquette. Whatever it was Captain Nolan intended by this action will never be known since he was killed a moment later by a shell burst. When Lord Cardigan was subsequently asked what he was thinking about as he rode toward the guns, he replied that he was for the most part preoccupied with Nolan's unseemly behavior in trying to push past him in the charge.

It is evident that many people share the responsibility for the Charge of the Light Brigade. Lord Cardigan indirectly precipitated the catastrophe by failing earlier to attack a routed enemy cavalry force. Lord Raglan and General Airey between them concocted the ambiguous order. Lord Lucan, by neglecting to reconnoiter his immediate vicinity, was unaware of what was happening on the Causeway Heights. He also allowed himself to be goaded into ordering an action which he knew to be unwise in the extreme. But if we isolate one crucial factor then it must be the intervention of Captain Nolan. What could possibly have prompted him to indicate the eastern end of the North Valley as the target of the attack? Particularly when, as a staff officer, he too had enjoyed a panoramic view of the battlefield, and he could hardly have been unaware of the activity of the Causeway Heights. Or could he?

The short answer, of course, is that we shall never know for certain. But we can offer a theory which, although unverifiable, is derived from an appreciation of psychological processes that are known to distort both perception and judgment in a fairly predictable way.

The essence of the theory is that Captain Nolan was a man obsessed. His obsession was light cavalry; not cavalry in general, but light cavalry in particular. His whole professional life had been dedicated to understanding its function, to improving its effectiveness and to extending its roles so that it should "govern the issue of battles." Initially at least, the Crimean campaign presented a splendid opportunity to put these principles into practice against the first European adversary since Napoleon's armies. But since landing with the Cavalry Division at the aptly named Calamita Bay in early September, he had known only professional and personal disappointments. In all the actions prior to Balaclava, he believed, and not without justification, that the cavalry had been ineptly led and, on several occasions, had been held in check when a timely attack would have demonstrated its worth as an effective and versatile military arm. Furthermore, as General Airey's aide-de-camp, he had been forced to adopt the role of observer rather than participant. It is not difficult, therefore, to imagine his anguish on the morning of Balaclava as he witnessed the inglorious immobility of the Light Brigade after the dramatic success of the Heavy Brigade.

Our thesis is simply this: that Captain Nolan's perception of the battlefield was biased at the best of times, but from the occasion of the Light Brigade's failure to exploit the triumph of the Heavy Brigade, it became increasingly blinkered. He could only see events as they related to the Light Brigade. He was possessed by a fervent desire to obliterate the shame and anger he had felt at Lord Cardigan's refusal to unleash the Light Brigade when the moment was right. His perception and judgment were selectively tuned to one thing only: the present state of the Light Brigade and the opportunity for its future vindication. All the information reaching him from the battlefield was evaluated against the single frame of reference. Anyone who has been in love will recognize the experience. Captain Nolan was like a man in love, not with a single person, but with a whole brigade of light cavalry.

Assuming that we have assessed Nolan's state of mind correctly, it is then not a large step to suggest that, upon receiving the order, he misread or misheard its contents in a way that conformed with his passionate desire to see the honor of the Light Brigade restored. Considering the extremely vague terms in which it was worded, this would not have been difficult to do. An hour before he had watched them stand idly by while a demoralized and disorganized force of Russian cavalry had retreated back over the Heights toward the far end of the North Valley, where they had since regrouped behind the 12 guns they had brought with them. Given his narrow view of the morning's action, it is not unreasonable to suppose that it was this force that he regarded as the Light Brigade's legitimate prize. The removal of the British naval guns, which in any case had already been captured, would have seemed a very secondary objective in comparison with this chance to recover lost opportunities and to restore the tarnished reputation of the Light Brigade.

The first words of the order, "Lord Raglan wishes the cavalry to advance rapidly to the front . . .," could, to his tormented mind, have only one meaning: that Lord Raglan was finally seeing things his way and urging an immediate attack upon the previously shattered cavalry force at the far end of the valley. This reading of the order would have been confirmed by the current disposition of Lord Cardigan's squadrons, facing as they now were in that direction. Similarly, the remainder of the instruction, " . . . follow the enemy and try to prevent the enemy carrying away the guns," could also be interpreted in the same light. The battery of enemy guns at the far end of the valley were indeed the rightful trophies of the Light Brigade. They had been carried away, now was the opportunity to secure them before they were removed from the field completely. That these guns were fully serviceable and capable of annihilating any force advancing on them from down the valley would have seemed less important to Nolan than the fact that they were manned and supported by troops who, but a short while previously, had been charged and scattered by a very much smaller force of British cavalry. If they had been routed earlier by the inferior "Heavies," imagine how they would panic at the sight of the Light Brigade bearing down upon them in all their fearsome splendor. Moreover, the Russians were clearly expecting an attack. They had begun the day by taking the offensive, they had been repulsed, now they seemed to be taking up a defensive posture to cover their withdrawal across the Tchernaya River. Or so it may have appeared to Nolan.

These are, of course, only speculations. But they have some psychological substance, and they accord, in part at least, with Nolan's curious behavior on delivering the order of Lord Lucan. Captains, even staff captains, did not usually address lieutenant-generals in such an insolent fashion, even if they did hold them in contempt. Eye-witnesses recorded that Nolan behaved as a man in the grip of tremendous passion. Indeed, this was evident earlier in the day. A short while before, the adjutant of the Grenadier Guards, riding down from the plateau to the plain, had met Nolan coming up, and was struck by the strangeness of his manner: " . . . he gave (the impression) during the short conversation we had together, that under the stress of some great excitement he had lost self-command."[6] There is in addition the point made by Cecil Woodham-Smith, the historian and author of *The Reason Why* who in part subscribes to the theory set out above. She observed that after Nolan had received permission from his friend, Captain Morris, to ride beside him, there followed an interval of several minutes before the charge began. She writes: " . . . it is almost impossible to believe that Nolan sitting beside his friend, did not disclose the objective of the charge. If Nolan had believed the attack was to be on the Causeway Heights and the redoubts, he must surely have told Captain Morris. Morris, however, who survived the charge though desperately wounded, believed the attack was to be on the guns at the far end of the North Valley."[7] It should also be emphasized that Nolan did not carry the previous order to Lord Lucan, specifying the Heights as the target of the cavalry attack, and so he would not necessarily be in possession of the knowledge to resolve the ambiguity as to the direction of the attack contained in the final order.

But if Nolan truly believed the far end of the valley to be the intended objective, why did he ride out across Lord Cardigan's path in the last seconds of his life, giving every indication of a man who wished to halt or divert the course of the charge? Again, we shall never know. We can only suppose that from his new vantage point on the valley floor he became aware, for the first time, of the dreadful odds facing them as they rode into the three-sided trap. Or it may

---

[6]Cecil Woodham-Smith, *The Reason Why*, p. 235.
[7]Cecil Woodham-Smith, *The Reason Why*, p. 235.

have been that this realization came with the release of pent-up tension that, in his case, must have followed the knowledge that he had finally succeeded in putting the Light Brigade on its path to glory. Whatever it was though, he had only one course open to him if he was to avert the disaster and that was to attract Lord Cardigan's attention and to confess his terrible blunder. But the Russian shell denied him this last opportunity.

To conclude this examination of the reason why the Light Brigade made its catastrophic charge, let us consider what the events leading up to it can reveal about the systematic error to which human links in a communication system are prone.[8] We have already discussed at length one such pervasive bias, namely the tendency for messages to become distorted in the direction of expected rather than actual inputs to the communication system. Where "noise" reduces the discriminability of the signal (as General Airey's shaky handwriting might well have done on this occasion), then we are likely to pass on a message that more closely fits our preconceptions than the original contents would justify. And where, as in this instance, the expected input conforms very closely to the transmitter's own attitudes or desires, this bias is likely to be even further enhanced. Thus, whenever a message is sufficiently vague to encourage confabulatory reconstruction or filling in on the part of the human link, the resulting distortions will be predictably in the direction of that individual's own expectations or attitudes. This was apparent in Captain Nolan's contribution to the message chain. But, irrespective of his part in this tragic affair, the communication channel as a whole manifested yet another even more widespread bias that predictably results in abbreviation, simplification, condensation, and loss of detail. The output of a human communication system, if imperfect, will on average be shorter, simpler, and less detailed than the input. By the time the order reached Lord Cardigan it had become reduced to a simple instruction to advance down the North Valley. This was then passed on to Lord George Paget, his second-in-command as "Lord George, we are ordered to make an attack to the front. You will take command of the second line, and I expect your best support—mind, your best support." No mention was made of the French

[8]D.T. Campbell, "Systematic error on the part of human links in communication systems." *Information and Control* 1(1958), 334–369.

cavalry (who subsequently successfully charged the guns on the hills to the north of the valley), nor, as far as we know, was any reference made to the involvement of the Troop Horse Artillery, referred to in the original version of the order. The message by the time it had reached the men who were to execute its intentions had been pared down to a single erroneous instruction: "make an attack to the front." Anyone who wishes to know more than the brief account given here of the origins of this most fascinating of military disasters should consult Cecil Woodham-Smith's *The Reason Why*.

THE SINKING OF H.M.S. VICTORIA

In the early afternoon of June 22, 1893, the British Mediterranean Fleet, comprising 13 ships, was approaching the shallow waters off Tripoli, having left Beirut that morning. The ships were formed into two columns, or divisions, streaming parallel to one another. The starboard column was led by *H.M.S. Victoria*, the flagship of the C-in-C, Vice Admiral Tryon. The Second Division, assembled in the port column, were commanded by Rear-Admiral Markham in the *H.M.S. Camperdown*. The *Camperdown* was located some 1200 yards on the *Victoria's* port beam.

At 3:25 P.M., Tryon hoisted a signal ordering the two divisions to turn inward 180° in succession. Since the turning circles of the two flagships were both about 800 yards, requiring well in excess of 1600 yards to clear each other safely on an inward turn, this signal caused great alarm aboard the *Camperdown*. Markham sent back that he had read but not understood Tryon's signal, and ordered it to be queried by semaphore. But before the query could be transmitted, Tryon signalled back: "What are you waiting for?", and hoisted the *Camperdown's* identifying pendants as a further rebuke for her tardiness. The chastened Markham then indicated that he had understood the order, where upon both ships swung sharply toward one another and collided. Since both battleships were equipped with powerful rams, the effects were devastating. The *Camperdown*, having made a tighter turn, sliced through the *Victoria's* hull causing it to sink almost immediately with the loss of 356 lives. Admiral Tryon also perished. His last words were reported to have been "It was all my fault."

Before trying to piece together the decisions that could have led to this apparently lunatic maneuver, it would be helpful to introduce the imperfect rationality principle, advanced by the philosopher John Watkins to explain, among others, this particular catastrophe.[9] Watkins takes as his starting point the view presented by the historian Collingwood that only successful actions can ever be fully understood. Collingwood's assertion is based on the argument that "every action is an attempt to solve a definite problem that has arisen in a specific situation." The historian, he maintained, can only explain a past action if he knows what problem it was intended to solve, and he can only arrive at this explanation " ... by arguing back from the solution." It follows from this that where an action failed to yield a solution for the problem it was intended to solve, the historian cannot identify the problem, and, as a consequence, cannot explain the action. But Watkins disagrees with the supposition that the only way to gain an understanding of the problem is by way of its solution. Such an assertion, he argues, ignores the possibility that we can obtain independent evidence concerning the nature of the problem.

Since both historians and psychologists are at liberty to seek an explanation for *any* action, successful or not, Watkins suggested the imperfect rationality principle as a means of bridging the gap between what a person intended and what actually occurred. As applied to actions like those of Admiral Tryon, it enjoins us not to dismiss or dehumanize him as a man who had taken leave of his senses, but to seek new evidence, or reinterpret the existing evidence, so as to explain the behavior in rational rather than irrational terms, no matter how imperfect that rationality may have been. In short, we must begin with the assumption that Admiral Tryon was neither drunk nor insane that afternoon, and ask what it was he sought to achieve by his curious order, and why it went wrong.

Shortly after the collision, a letter appeared in *The Times* which offered just such a rational reconstruction of Tryon's intended maneuver. This letter, written by Sir William Clowes, a naval historian who had known Tryon personally, was largely ignored until another naval historian, Richard Hough, expanded the idea into a book entitled *Admirals in Collision*.[10] The key to this reconstruction is a fact

[9]J. Watkins, *Explanation in the Behavioral Sciences*, pp. 212–216.
[10]R. Hough, *Admirals in Collision* (London, 1959).

that seems to have been largely overlooked at the time, namely, that Tyron's signal did not simply instruct the two columns to turn inward in succession, it also added that "the order of the fleet was to be preserved." In other words, at the end of the maneuver, the *Camperdown* was still to be on the *Victoria's* port beam, as it was prior to the turns. Now even supposing that two ships, each with 800 yard turning circles, could turn inward upon each other simultaneously without colliding when they were initially separated by only 1200 yards, the outcome of such a maneuver would *reverse* the order of the fleet. That is, the *Camperdown* and its following ships would now be steaming on the *starboard* side of Tryon's division. Clearly, therefore, to obey that final instruction, one division would have to wheel round on the *outside* of the other. But who was to go around whom?

To answer this, we need to refer to two rules governing the passing of ships at sea. The general rule of the sea is that approaching ships should pass port side to port side. But there was also a Queen's Regulation in force at that time, applicable to the handling of Royal Navy vessels, which would override the rule of the sea stated earlier. This went as follows: "If two ships under steam are crossing so as to involve risk of collision, the ship which has the other on her starboard side shall keep out of the way of the other." By this Regulation, therefore, it was for the *Camperdown*, with the *Victoria* on her starboard beam, to keep out of the way by turning *outside* Tryon's division.

With these facts in mind, we can attempt to reconstruct Tryon's ill-fated plan in these terms: "The Fleet's course will have to be reversed as it approaches the shallow water off Tripoli. I will do this with one of those daring maneuvers which help to keep my captains on their toes. I will bring the two divisions fairly close together in line ahead, after which they will wheel round, the Camperdown leading the port column outside the starboard column. That one column is to pass outside the other will be made clear by adding 'order of the fleet to be preserved' to the signal. It will be unnecessary to include in the signal that it is the *Camperdown* who is to pass outside since that is implied by a Standing Regulation. Moreover, when Markham sees that my helm is hard-a-port he will be left in no doubt that it is I who am turning inside and that he must go outside me." In addition, there was the question of the separation between the two leading ships.

When the maneuver had been outlined some hours earlier to his Flag-Captain and Staff-Commander, the latter had remarked: "It will require at least eight cables (1600 yards) for that, sir." In the event, Tryon had reduced the distance to six cables (1200 yards), presumably on the assumption that this even smaller separation would make it absolutely clear to Markham that there was to be no question of the columns turning inward on each other.

We are assuming, then, that something like this was going on in Tryon's mind when he planned and began to execute the maneuver. This is not to defend Tryon, nor to suggest that it was a good plan. Subsequent events clearly showed that he had grossly underestimated the extent to which the order could be misread. But, whatever its merits as a decision-scheme, it was based upon rational rather than irrational considerations. So how did it go wrong?

Markham's first response on seeing Tryon's signal was to remark "It's impossible." But Markham had considerable respect for his commander, so he struggled to find some sensible interpretation. His first hypothesis was that the two columns were to execute the order separately; the First Division turning in succession to port followed by the Second Division turning to starboard. His second idea was that the turns were to be executed simultaneously, and that it was Tryon's intention to turn the *Victoria* slowly on a wide turning circle, allowing her to pass outside the *Camperdown's* hard-a-starboard turning circle. This would obey the general rule of the sea that ships were to pass "port to port." He appeared to be unaware at that moment of the overriding Queen's Regulation that directed quite the opposite manner of passing. By this time he had received Tryon's rebuke, and thinking that he had at last made sense of the original signal, he acknowledged that he understood the instruction and ordered the *Camperdown's* helm to be put hard-a-starboard. Then to his horror he saw that the *Victoria's* rudder signals were indicating that her helm was hard-a-port. This clearly refuted his second idea that the *Victoria* intended to make her turn on the outside of the *Camperdown's* turn. But instead of slackening off his own turn so that he could pass around the *Victoria*, he responded to this new information by ordering the starboard engine full steam astern so as to make the *Camperdown's* turning circle still smaller. When collision was imminent, he ordered both engines full astern.

With the benefit of hindsight, we can suggest that whereas Tryon's over-ambitious plan and laconic signal set the stage for the disaster, Markham's reactions to the signal interchange and what he saw of the *Victoria's* subsequent handling, particularly his apparent unwillingness to reject the idea that it was Tryon's ship which was to make the wider turn, made it inevitable. This reluctance to reject hypotheses in the face of contradictory evidence is one of the common biases leading to lapses of thought and judgment that we touched upon in Chapter 4.

THE MOORGATE TUBE DISASTER

Moorgate station, located just within the City of London, is a major London Transport interchange with 10 platforms. Platforms 9 and 10 form the southern terminal of a short tube branch line, 2 miles in length, that runs through Old Street, Essex Road, Highbury and Islington, to Drayton Park, the northern terminal. Between February 15th and 28th, 1975, platform 10 was out of use due to engineering works, and trains were terminating on platform 9 beyond which there was an overrun tunnel some 67 feet in length ending in a solid wall. A single central hydraulic buffer was mounted 12 feet from the end wall, and a sand-drag, heaped to about 2 feet above rail level, extended from 17 feet within the overrun tunnel to 19 feet outside it. At 8:46 A.M. on Friday, February 28, 1975, a six-car tube train, driven by Motorman L.B. Newson, ran through platform 9 at between 30 and 40 mph and crashed into the end wall of the overrun tunnel. The first and second cars of the train and the front portion of the third car were crushed into approximately half their normal length. Forty-two passengers and the driver were killed, and a further 72 passengers required hospital treatment. The last survivor was not freed until 13 hours after the accident, and the driver's body was not removed until the evening of the following Tuesday.

The Moorgate crash was not only London Transport's worst train accident, its cause remains among the most mysterious of any in the history of British railway disasters. Close examination of the wreckage revealed that the train was under power until two or three seconds before hitting the tunnel wall, and even then power was probably cut off automatically when the train ran into the sand drag. No defect was found in the train's braking system, and forensic experts failed to find any evidence at the post-mortem of sudden illness, use of drugs, or any other cause of incapacity on the part of the driver. Witnesses on the platform reported that they had seen Motorman Newson seated upright with hands on the controls, looking perfectly normal, only moments before the crash. Moreover, the position of the body indicated that his hands were still on the controls at the moment of impact.

Colonel McNaughton, the Chief Inspecting Officer, who conducted an extremely detailed and painstaking examination of the available evidence, concluded his report as follows: " . . . the cause of this accident lay entirely in the behavior of Motorman Newson during the final minute before the accident occurred. Whether his behavior was deliberate or whether it was the result of a suddenly arising physical condition was not revealed as a result of post-mortem examination, and there is not sufficient evidence to establish, but I am satisfied that no part of the responsibility for the accident rests with any other person and that there was no fault or condition of the train, track, or signalling that in any way contributed to it."

Thus, the only psychological explanation of Motorman Newson's behavior offered was " . . . that the collision was the outcome of a deliberate suicidal act . . . although there is no positive evidence to support it."[11] Are there no psychological factors that could account for his failure to slow down on approaching Moorgate and his inactivity prior to the crash other than that he chose to commit suicide by driving a train with some 300 passengers aboard into a blind tunnel on his third trip into the station that morning? Reports from his road training instructor and from other colleagues suggest that he was a conscientious, even cautious driver; if he had a fault, it was that he tended to be too careful, approaching stations rather more slowly than conditions demanded. Another colleague described him as a "cheerful chap one could have a joke with," and when he saw him earlier that morning, the same colleague stated that "he seemed absolutely normal and fit." If we know anything of what

[11]Report on the accident that occurred on 28th February 1975 at Moorgate Station, p. 16.

was on his mind that morning it was that he intended to buy his daughter a second-hand car after he finished his duty in the afternoon, for which purpose he was carrying with him a sum of cash. These are not, on the face of it, the preoccupations of a man contemplating suicide. To kill one's self under such circumstances must be regarded as an irrational act. Can we not again apply the principle of imperfect rationality, no matter how speculatively, to try to account for these apparently bizarre actions?

In applying this notion to Admiral Tryon earlier, we attempted to reconstruct the plan that governed his ill-fated signals, and to show that although it was not a particularly wise plan, it was nevertheless based upon rational considerations. In the case of Motorman Newson, however, we must assume that he had no plan other than to operate his train punctually and safely, and try to demonstrate that his failure to execute this plan successfully was due to a mental lapse that is known to afflict otherwise ration minds. In other words, we shall begin by presuming that he had no suicidal intent and then go on to inquire whether there are any known cognitive failures that could have caused him to act in the way he did. These conjectures can never be verified, but at least we may succeed in presenting a theory that is intrinsically more probable than a deliberate act of suicide in such circumstances.

Before proceeding with these alternative hypotheses, however, we need to present some additional information that will allow us to separate the questions we are asking about Motorman Newson's behavior. According to witnesses at Old Street station, the train accelerated away quite normally on its final journey into Moorgate. From what is known of Newson's driving technique, it would be expected that having reached a speed of 30 mph after travelling about 250 yards, he would shut off power and coast for some 15 seconds before braking to around 15 mph prior to arriving at platform 9. However, all the evidence suggests that on this occasion, the train continued to accelerate on full-power and would have reached a speed of 35 mph prior to the Moorgate platform. Thus, we are faced with two questions. First, why did Newson not reduce speed at his usual spot? Second, why did he continue to maintain a speed of 30 to 40 mph until the sand drag at the end of platform 9 automatically shut off the power?

One suggestion that would provide an answer to the first question was made by an electrical engineer working for the New York subway system.[12] This was that Motorman Newson believed that he was between Essex Road and Old Street when he was actually between Old Street and Moorgate. If this was the case, then he would have had no cause to shut off power some 30 seconds after leaving the station since the distance between Essex Road and Old Street is over a mile, in contrast to the rest of the stations on this branch line that are about half a mile apart. But why should a moderately experienced driver who had taken trains into Moorgate on 228 occasions in the preceding two weeks make such an error? Aside from the fact that single bore tunnels tend to look alike, there was one feature of the Old Street to Moorgate line which differed significantly on this third and fatal trip from the two previous trips that morning. On the first two runs into Moorgate, the lights in the tunnel between Old Street and Moorgate had been switched on; but at some time between the second and third trip they had been turned off. On this last trip, therefore, the short stretch of tunnel into Moorgate would be dark, as were all the other tunnels along the line. It is possible that Newson had, perhaps subconsciously, come to place an undue reliance on this powerful visual cue to mark the tunnel leading to Moorgate. If he had been engaged in some kind of reverie or daydream on leaving Old Street, he may have made a low level check on his location (of the kind that we employ when we are engaged in some highly routine activity), noted the absence of tunnel lights, and formed the false hypothesis that he was between Essex Road and Old Street. That being so, he would have had no need to reduce speed almost immediately (because of the wider separation between Essex Road and Old Street), and could continue to remain in a condition of reduced vigilance for several seconds further.

This brings us to the second and much more difficult question to answer. Assuming that Newson had mistaken his location between Old Street and Moorgate and as a consequence had not reduced speed at his normal spot 30 seconds along the line, why did he remain inactive when faced with the barrage of cues indicating his imminent arrival at platform 9, Moorgate? Just consider for a moment

[12]G. Ruggiero, personal communication, 1978.

what these cues were: (a) the Moorgate outer home signal with a repeater signal 166 feet in the rear giving an effective sighting distance of 610 feet, plus the inner home signal with a sighting distance of 690 feet (this displayed a junction aspect which was a specific cue for the Moorgate approach); (b) the latter signal was located at a point where the line makes a right-handed curve which, at the speed the train was travelling, would have imposed perceptible lateral accelerations on the driver; (c) just after the bend, there was an illuminated crossover where the rails forked left into platform 10 and straight on into platform 9; (d) aside from the visual information provided by this illuminated crossover, there would also have been a marked auditory cue as the wheels of the train rattled over the points; (e) once round the bend, a driver would have full view of platform 9 and, at the far end, marking the sand drag at the entrance to the overrun tunnel, there was a fixed red light on a post. To quote once more from Colonel McNaughton's report: "The signalling and track layout on the approach to Moorgate are such that it is quite impossible to mistake it for any other location on the Highbury Branch and it is possible to stop a train well short of the sand drag, even if it is still travelling at the maximum attainable speed when the red lamp at the end of the platform comes into view."[13]

To stop the train in an emergency, it was only necessary for the driver to release the pressure on the main controller handle by a mere 3½ lbs. to activate the "deadman's handle" automatic braking system. But the evidence clearly shows that the main controller handle remained in the running position and depressed until the moment of impact. Nor was there any indication that the brake lever, held in the driver's left hand, had been moved out of the release and running position. In other words, from the moment of rounding the curve until the train hit the wall of the overrun tunnel, a period of about 10–11 seconds, Motorman Newson appears to have remained fully upright with his eyes to the front, and without making any attempt to move the controls from their full running position. How could this be possible?

The Railway Inspectorate placed great emphasis, as we have done, upon the number and variety of cues indicating the approaches

[13]Report on the accident that occurred in 28th February 1975 at Moorgate Station, p. 15.

to Moorgate station, and, on this basis, have strongly suggested that no man in his right mind could have mistaken this station for any other along the line. And indeed this is an inescapable conclusion. But there is another way of looking at this wealth of identifying cues; namely, that for a man whom we have assumed was, a few seconds earlier, under the mistaken impression that he was in the long tunnel between Essex Road and Old Street, the sheer quantity and diversity of these signs, following upon each other so rapidly, may have proved too great a shock for his automatic nervous system to cope with. Rather than triggering the necessary actions to stop the train before the sand drag, this barrage of unambiguous cues that he was approaching Moorgate at twice his normal speed might have delivered such a sudden and terrifying jolt to his reputedly cautious mind that he remained frozen into inactivity for the ten seconds that elapsed before crashing into the tunnel wall. Such an extreme case of involuntary immobility is in accord with him not raising his hands from the controls to protect his face as he saw the tunnel wall approaching. One feels that even a man intent on suicide would automatically have made this protective gesture.

Of course, we have no direct evidence to support this highly speculative hypothesis. But there is no lack of medical and psychological evidence to indicate that such a condition of freezing can be induced by sudden and intense fright. Gellhorn, for example, has argued that bodily responses to fearful stimuli reflect the activity of the two major divisions of the autonomic system, the sympathetic and the parasympathetic nervous system.[14] With a rise in the activity of the sympathetic nervous system, there is an increased cortical excitation (indicated by EEG desynchronization), together with increased activity and tone of the voluntary or striated muscles. Conversely, increased parasympathetic reactivity is associated with reduced muscle tone and the presence of sleep-like waveforms in the EEG record. Under normal conditions, the two systems operate reciprocally so that a stimulus which excites one system depresses the other. But when emotional excitement is great, Gellhorn maintains that reciprocity between the two systems breaks down. At moderate levels of fear, reversals occur such that stimuli which

[14]E. Gellhorn, "The emotions and the ergotropic and trophotropic systems." *Psychologisch Forschung* 34(1970), 48–94.

ordinarily excite one system now excite the other. At very high fear levels, there is increased simultaneous activity of both systems. Gellhorn cites instances where terror is associated with a massive parasympathetic reaction which can manifest itself as fainting, retching, and a form of temporary paralysis. What we are suggesting, therefore, is that Newson's horrifying realization that he was actually approaching Moorgate's dead-end platform 9 well in excess of his usual speed provoked such a sudden and intense parasympathetic reaction that he was temporarily rendered incapable of corrective action. Such a state would not have been revealed at post-mortem examination, particularly after the body had spent over four days in an excessively warm stretch of tunnel.

We have rejected the suicide notion as intrinsically improbable, considering what is known of Newson's personality and the circumstances of his death. As alternatives, we offer two related hypotheses: first that Newson suffered a mental lapse in which he "lost his place" along the track, and second, that he was made aware of his error by such a sudden onrush of cues that he was shocked into a state of parasympathetically induced inactivity. Our critics might well point out that the cues to the approach of Moorgate were not necessarily sudden; the outer home signal was visible very soon after leaving Old Street, and even if that had been missed the inner home was evident well in advance of the crossover and its associated bombardment of cues. In reply, we can only point out, as Rolt and others have done, that drivers are particularly prone to missing or misreading signals when they are working under a "false hypothesis" into which the true information is not readily assimilated. But whether or not these particular hypotheses are correct, they cannot dehumanize Motorman Newson nor damage his reputation more than the suggestion that the catastrophe resulted from a deliberate suicidal act.

THE TENERIFE RUNWAY COLLISION

On March 27th, 1977, two Boeing 747's en route for Las Palmas on the holiday island of Gran Canaria were diverted to Santa Cruz airport on the nearby island of Tenerife. The cause of the diversion was a terrorist's bomb explosion in the passenger terminal at Las Palmas.

The first to land at Santa Cruz was KLM flight 4805 on charter from Amsterdam with 234 passengers and a crew of 14 commanded by Captain "Jaap" van Zanten. On landing at 1:44 P.M. it was ordered to park in a holding zone at the far end of the runway. Ninety minutes later, the second jumbo jet landed and was directed to park next to the KLM aircraft. This was Pan Am 1736, a charter flight from Los Angeles and New York, carrying 373 passengers and a crew of 16 commanded by Captain Victor Grubbs. At this point, there were 11 aircraft on the ground, and the apron serving the airport terminal was heavily congested. Santa Cruz has a single runway, more than two miles long, and at this time of the year was prone to fog. At 3 P.M., visibility at the airport was more than six miles, but by 4 P.M. it was less than one mile and worsening.

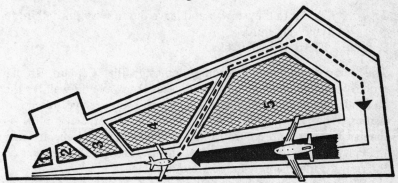

Figure 10.2

While he was waiting, Captan van Zanten decided to refuel. He was concerned that when Las Palmas reopened, the large number of aircraft attempting to land in quick succession might cause him to remain stacked for some time before receiving landing permission. This decision further delayed the departure of the Pan Am aircraft since their way to the runway was blocked by the Dutch aircraft. On completing their refueling, KLM 4805 called for start clearance at 4:51 P.M., Pan Am 1736 requested start clearance some 20 seconds later. By this time, runway visibility was down to about 1000 feet and in certain patches was a good deal worse.

At 4:58 P.M. KLM 4805 was cleared onto the runway, and after some initial confusion regarding the taxi route, received an amended clearance to backtrack to the far end of the runway and then to make a 180° turn to be lined up in the right direction for takeoff on Runway 30. There, Captain van Zanten was required to hold for further instructions.

The Pan Am plane received its clearance instructions some four minutes later. Like KLM 4805, they were directed to taxi down the runway, but then to leave it by the third slipway on the left—which would take them onto the taxiway and then to the holding point for Runway 30. It should also have had them off the runway by the time KLM 4805 was ready for takeoff. But due to poor transmission and Spanish accents, this message was not at first understood by the American copilot. After it had been repeated, he still heard it as "the first intersection on the left." Then, the following exchange took place:

Tower: Taxi into the runway and leave the runway third, third to your left, third.
Pan Am: Third to the left, okay.

The intracockpit voice recordings indicated that Captain Grubbs would have preferred to hold short of the runway and wait for the KLM aircraft to take off. But the tower did not receive this information. When they changed radio frequency to approach control (as distinct from ground control), their instructions were repeated and the Pan Am aircraft taxied onto the runway. As soon as they were on the runway, the visibility fell to around 300 feet.

When the approach controller asked KLM 4805 for their position on the runway, the copilot replied that he thought they had just passed junction 4. The controller, who could not actually see them because of the fog, acknowledged this position report and asked them to make a 180° turn at the end of the runway and to call him when they were ready to receive their airways clearance (this states the air route by which to depart and is given before takeoff clearance).

Soon after this, the Pan American copilot again called to confirm that they were to turn off at the third taxiway. From the timing of this request, it appears to have been made before they had yet reached the first intersection. The tower's reply ("The third one, sir, one, two, three, third, third one.") seems finally to have cleared up his confusion. Although the Pan Am crew do not recall using the airport layout chart to help them as they taxied down the runway, they felt certain about their point of departure. The intracockpit recordings show that they counted at least two slipways as they passed them, but there is no mention of passing a third one.

The KLM aircraft completed its 180° turn in relatively clear weather and lined up on Runway 30. Their visibility down the runway was about 3000 feet. Earlier interchanges with the tower had already estimated that the center lights on the runway were not working at that time. At this point, Captain van Zanten began to advance the throttles as if to take off, but was reminded by his copilot that they did not yet have their airways clearance; nor, of course, their takeoff clearance, although this was not actually mentioned. The captain then closed the throttles and told the copilot to call for clearance. At about 6 minutes past 5, KLM 4805 was given the following ATC clearance: "KLM eight seven zero five (an incorrect designation) you are cleared to the papa beacon, climb to and maintain flight level niner zero. Right turn after takeoff, proceed with heading zero four zero until intercepting the three two five radial from Las Palmas VOR." Toward the end of this transmission from the tower, the cockpit recording shows that the captain made the exclamation "ja" (yes). Some five seconds later, while the first officer was still reading back the ATC clearance, the captain said "We go—check thrust." This was followed by the sound of the engine spin up.

The cockpit voice recording showed that the last portion of the copilot's readback was noticeably more hurried and less clear than the initial part. He ended his transmission with the words, "We are now—uh—taking off." The tower replied: "Okay (pause), Stand by for takeoff, I will call you." On hearing this interchange (both aircraft were on the same radio frequency), the Pan American copilot transmitted: "We're still taxiing down the runway—the clipper one seven three six." But this was largely blocked out by the controller's transmission to KLM. Only the words "Clipper one seven three six" were heard in the tower. The controller then said: "Papa alpha one seven three six, report runway clear." To which the Pan American copilot replied, "Okay, we'll report when we're clear." During these transmissions, the KLM aircraft was continuing to accelerate toward them down the runway.

Robert Bragg, the Pan American copilot, recalled what happened next. "We saw lights ahead of us in the fog. At first we thought it was KLM standing at the end of the runway. Then we realized they were coming toward us." In the remaining seconds, the Pan Am crew boosted the engines and turned the plane's nose left toward the grass. Captain Grubbs called the tower: "We're still on the runway," while the cockpit recordings show Bragg as shouting "Get off, get off."

But the KLM aircraft was already approaching 150 knots. It could neither stop or swerve. Three seconds before impact, the Dutch crew saw the Pan Am plane directly in front of them, turning to the KLM's right in a desperate effort to clear the runway. Captain van Zanten pulled the control column all the way back, and the aircraft pitched up striking its aft fuselage on the runway. It left the ground just before hitting the American jumbo jet at a point about 4000 feet down the runway and near the intersection of slipway C4. The Pan American had overshot C3. The Dutch aircraft struck the American plane amidships, ripping the top off. It then crashed to the ground some 450 feet further on. Within minutes, it had exploded, killing everyone on board. In all, 577 people died in the crash, the worst in the history of aviation.

The causes of this accident are multiple and complex. They include such factors as the terrorist's bomb at Las Palmas, the congested state of Santa Cruz airport, the additional stresses this imposed on the three air traffic controllers on duty, the weather, the fact that two of the airport's three radio frequencies had been out of action for six months, the lack of ground radar enabling controllers to plot the course of taxiing aircraft, the impromptu taxi routes devised by the controllers for the two jumbo jets, and the strains imposed upon the flight crews by long hours of duty, irksome delays, and, in the case of the KLM crew, the additional uncertainty caused by the fact that they were approaching the legal time limits on their duty periods. But our primary interest in mental lapses directs us to consider two crucial questions. Why did the Pan Am flight crew not exit the runway at C3 as directed by the tower? If they had made the turn, the aircraft would have been clear of the runway at least half a minute before KLM 4805 started its takeoff run. Secondly, and perhaps most importantly, why did Captain van Zanten not wait for the final clearance before taking off?

We can deal with the first question fairly briefly. There appear to be at least two plausible reasons why the Pan American was heading for the fourth rather than the third slipway. In the first place, the transition to C3 and then a resumption of direction on the taxiway parallel to the runway would have required a 148° turn to the left followed by an equal turn to the right. But the taxiways were not wide enough to allow an aircraft the size of a Boeing 747 to make these turns without going on to the grass. Thus, it is possible that the Pan Am crew was convinced the controller was mistaken, and actually meant them to leave at the fourth intersection whose configuration was much more suitable for the turn. Rather than disputing the matter with a foreign air traffic controller whom they probably did not greatly trust, and adding further transmissions to an already overcrowded radio frequency, they may have decided simply to get on with it. Another possibility suggested by a study group of the American Air Line Pilots Association is that the airways clearance was given to the KLM plane at precisely the moment the Pan American was passing C3. In the Pan Am cockpit, someone started to speak but fell silent when KLM asked for their clearance. "Since they were unfamiliar with Tenerife Airport, and since they knew they could expect the same departure as that given KLM, the Pan Am crew was probably concentrating deeply on the clearance being given. The silence and the Pan Am captain's almost verbatim recollection of the clearance attest to this. This concentration on the aural channel rather than the visual channel, along with the very low visibility may have prevented their seeing taxiway C3 as they passed."

But if there was one action more responsible than any other for this disaster, then it must be Captain van Zanten's attempt to take off before receiving takeoff clearance from the tower. It would appear that the reason for this action was the KLM captain's false hypothesis that the runway ahead of him was clear. A number of factors could have contributed to this mental lapse. The short-term factors include: (1) As KLM was nearing the end of the runway, the Dutch crew must have heard the Pan Am copilot asking for additional confirmation that they (the Pan American aircraft) were to turn left at the third intersection. This query and the subsequent affirmative response from the tower may have led Captain van Zanten to believe that Pan Am was looking at C3 taxiway and wanted one more confirmation before using it. (2) Captain van Zanten may have taken the tower's positive response to the copilot's request for ATC clearance as an assent to two clearance requests: the airways clearance and the takeoff clearance. In delivering the ATC clearance, the controller gave them a ... right turn after takeoff ... ." The use of the word *takeoff* may have reinforced the assumption that takeoff as well as airways clearance had been given in a single transmission. This was not standard procedure, but then it had not been a day for following standard procedure. (3) It is likely that the last reinforcement of the erroneous takeoff decision occurred when the copilot told the controller, "We are now—uh—taking off." The controller responded with "Okay (pause)" followed by a high-pitched squeal which obscured the rest of his statement.

In addition to these more immediate factors, the study group from the ALPA placed considerable emphasis on a long-term factor they called the "training syndrome." This refers to the fact that Captain van Zanten's principal job within KLM was head of the Flight Training Department. The breakdown of his flying time for the previous six years showed that he had spent the majority of his time conducting training, some 1545 hours on the 747 since January 1971. Significantly, this was his first line flight in 12 weeks. The study group argued that, to some extent, Captain van Zanten's lapses at Tenerife were conditioned by his extensive experience as KLM's chief training instructor. The study group describe these duties as follows: "The task of a training instructor is to compress the maximum amount of training into the available simulator or airplane time. In order to accomplish this, he may delete normally realistic ATC procedures and delays when training and checking a crew. There are no ATC constraints in the simulator and only minimal constraints to the operation of the training aircraft. In the simulator, the instructor acts as the controller, always responding affirmatively to the trainee pilot's requests for expedited handling during emergencies. The instructor generally issues ATC and takeoff clearance to the crew just prior to the final items of the pre-takeoff checklist. There is never a need for the crew to hold the simulator in position awaiting takeoff clearance."[15]

[15]P.A. Roitsch, G.L. Babcock, W. W. Edmunds. *Human Factors report on the Tenerife Accident* (Air Line Pilots Association Study Group Report. Washington, D.C.: Engineering and Air Safety, 1978).

The study group suggested that the considerable stresses upon the KLM captain blurred the distinction among the unreal and standardized training world and the variable environment encountered in the actual line flying, and contributed to his erroneous impression that he had been cleared for takeoff. In short, he may have reverted to an habitual or preprogrammed mode of behavior derived from the predictable world of the simulator, where ATC and takeoff clearances are given *at the same time*. Once again, therefore, we see the pervasive influence of frequently and recently used action sequences in bringing about mental lapses. We have dealt with this bias as it shows itself in our more commonplace daily actions in Chapters 3 and 4.

chapter eleven
ATTENTION
AND CONTROL

In the early chapters of this book, we likened the trivial slips and lapses of everyday life to the contents of some mental waste-basket. But perhaps a better image is that they resemble the incomplete scraps from some enormous torn-up photograph. If we could manage to fit even these few small pieces into a partial semblance of order, we might then be able to make some guesses at what the total picture portrayed. The picture in this case is of the mind, and the part we are especially concerned with is that which controls—or occasionally fails to control—our largely automatic actions.

In the preceding chapters, we have tried to group together those scraps which appear to share some common feature. In this final chapter, our aim is more ambitious: we want to put these fragment groups together, and to speculate upon what they reveal of the picture as a whole. Particularly, we want to examine the part which deals with the hidden mechanisms that *control* our words, thoughts, and deeds. No matter how presumptuous this aim might be, we feel that we have an edge over the more conventional psychological investigation. Whereas most studies concentrate deliberately upon some very small portion of the total picture, possibly in the domains of perception, memory, language, motor action or whatever, we have collected our scraps from all aspects of mental life. So even if we put the pieces together in the wrong order, as we surely will, we can and must permit ourselves the indulgence of a panoramic view. Although such a grandiose enterprise is unlikely to yield much in the way of specific predictions that science demands of its theories, it may serve some useful purpose in trying to organize and simplify—and inevitably oversimplify—what now exists as a disorderly scattering of psychological oddities.

One of the consequences of venturing beyond the laboratory door into the undisciplined flesh-and-blood world of everyday life is that we are forced to abandon the artificial and often misleading compartments into which tidy-minded experimentalists like to assign their research topics, or that academics find convenient to organize their courses and textbook chapters. These subject boundaries have their uses; but not in the present endeavor. As William James knew very well, the tangled complexities of mental life do not lie easily on such procrustean beds. Unlike his Leipzig-trained contemporaries who generally abhorred loose ends, he was committed to the view that unkempt, dishevelled but holistic conceptions of the mental world do greater justice to its ragged edges and ephemeral nature than neat, unit-based constructions. He had the courage to be incomplete, and we would like to follow his example. There is yet another reason why this should be the case. It is not just that he gave elegant expression to a wide range of cognitive experiences (we would not presume to match that), but rather that he addressed himself to the immediate, ordinary, and recognizable aspects of mental life. This stands in sharp contrast to the relentless pursuit of the recondite and counter-intuitive that dominated much of psychology in the bleak years that followed him. In short, he did not mind stating the obvious when he found it among the commonplace, and nor shall we.

As the title indicates, this chapter focuses upon the nature of attention and its role in the control of mental processes. Attention, as such, was given no specific place in the theory of action described in Chapter 3. Our purpose here is not to provide attention with such a position, but to outline what slips and lapses tell us about its *function*—which, as we shall argue, transcends the confines of any single location.

THE NATURE OF ATTENTION

"Everyone knows what attention is." So wrote William James, and in the everyday sense of the term, he was probably right.[1] But subsequent debates in the psychological literature show that the professionals are still far from agreed about the precise nature of attention. This is not the place to discuss these disputes. Others have done this well enough already. What we wish to do here is to present our view of what absent-minded errors tell us about the function of attention. But let us first return briefly to William James.

Attention, he stated, " . . . is the taking possession of the mind in clear and vivid form, of one of what seems several simultaneously possible objects or trains of thought. Focalization, or concentration, of consciousness are of its essence. It implies withdrawal from some things in order to deal more effectively with others."[2]

His first point is that attention is *selective*. We choose, or are compelled, to consider a certain object, think about a particular topic, try to recall a specific item, or carry out some action. The second point is that *consciousness*—"the taking possession of the mind"—is intimately involved in attending. But from what has been said earlier about automatization and skill, we also know that this conscious component is not the whole story. Much of our perception, mental activity, and the fine control of action is conducted at some level beyond the easy reach of consciousness. In the final sentence, he makes it clear that attention is a *limited commodity*. If we give it to one thing, we must necessarily take it away from another. Little, if anything, has happened in the subsequent ninety years of psychological research to challenge any of these assertions; so we will accept them as given.

Elsewhere, James commented upon the reciprocity that exists between attention and interest. Novel and exciting objects grab our attention involuntarily but those less naturally engrossing demand an effort of will for us to focus attention upon them. One of the most conspicuous features of this voluntary and often laborious mode of attention is that it cannot be sustained. "When we are studying an

---

[1]W. James, *The Principles of Psychology Vol. I* (New York: Henry Holt & Co., 1890), p. 403.
[2]W. James, *The Principles of Psychology Vol. I*, pp. 403–404.

uninteresting subject, if our mind tends to wander, we have to bring back our attention every now and then by using distinct pulses of effort, which revivify the topic for a moment, the mind then running for a certain number of seconds or minutes with spontaneous interest, until again some intercurrent idea captures it and takes it off."[3] So now we have another characteristic of attention: its *continual redeployment*. The switching mechanism that governs these changes is something over which the Intention System exercises only a limited sway, and then often at the expense of considerable effort.

So far, we have listed the principal characteristics of attention, but these tell us little about its function. What does attention actually do? We know that a substantial portion of this limited commodity is bound up with consciousness. This part we can term *focal attention*, or *conscious attention*, and is accessible to introspection. It evidently has something to do with keeping our minds and actions on an intended track, or with alerting us to unexpected or interesting events in the outside world. Since we are only capable of performing a very restricted number of activities, either mental or physical, at any one moment, some agency is required to facilitate the time-sharing of our limited effectors between the various possibilities that the Intention System has devised. But what about the nonconscious portion of attention, the part that has been labelled the "fringe of consciousness," "diffuse attention," or "tacit knowledge?"[4] It is in regard to this hidden aspect that slips of the mind can provide some clues.

The time has come to present our own ideas about what attention does, and the simplest way is to begin with a list of assertions that we will later attempt to support with evidence drawn from the preceding chapters and elsewhere. We do not claim much novelty for these views, merely that they seem to accord with our absent-minded error data and with certain aspects of the experimental literature.

1. Attention is a limited control resource of which we are only partially conscious.
2. Conscious concerns, whether internally or externally generated, consume the major part of this resource during waking hours.

[3]W. James, *Talks to Teachers on Psychology: and to Students on some of Life's Ideals* (London: Longmans, Green & Co., 1908), p. 101.
[4]M. Polanyi, *Personal Knowledge* (London: Routledge and Kegan Paul, 1958).

3. In addition to continual moment-to-moment variations in the total amount of this resource, the quantity that is drained off by these conscious concerns varies according to their nature and intensity.

4. All mental and physical activities, no matter how apparently automatic, make some demands on the total resource. The more habitual the activity, and the more invariant the environment in which it takes place, the smaller is this demand.

5. For every routine or habitual activity, there is an optimum amount of attention necessary for successful performance. Both too little and too much of this resource can prove disruptive, depending on the stage of the activity.

6. Since cognitive demons (in all domains) are capable of being energized independently of the Intention System—by needs, context, associations with other demons, and the frequency and recency of past use—some part of this limited resource is always being consumed in restraining those active demons not required for our current plans. The more active these unwanted demons are, the more of this resource is consumed in holding them in check.

Stating that attention is a control resource, we must admit, does not really *explain* anything, since it leaves wide open the question of what is meant by the term *control*. This is not a question we can answer. What we can say, however, is that it appears to take a variety of forms; it illuminates the mental arena and, in that sense, is the very stuff of waking consciousness; it suppresses active but unwanted demons that are clamoring to get their hands on the controls, and thus enables intended demons to occupy the Action System; and, in some way, it facilitates the passage of control from one intended demon to the next. These, on the face of it, seem to be quite different processes that defy a single unifying description. But perhaps the most important thing about them is that irrespective of what these various control functions are, the one factor that binds them all together is that concentration of attention in one quarter reduces the amount available elsewhere. In other words, the crucial point of our initial assertion is not so much the issue of what is meant by control, but the fact that, however it operates, it is a *limited* resource.

One undisputed feature of absent-minded errors, as the very term suggests, is that most of them occur when a large part of this limited resource is directed toward something other than the task in hand. Now, if our highly routinized activities depart from intention because this limited attentional commodity was being employed elsewhere, the obvious conclusion is that a greater degree of attentional involvement was necessary on those occasions to ensure the desired outcome. It is on this basis we argue that some measure of attention is essential for all physical and mental activities, even the most apparently automatic ones. We are not suggesting that a fixed quantity is needed throughout. Our slips and lapses indicate that the amount required varies according to the particular phase that has been reached. Some points in a sequence, as we discussed in Chapters 6 and 7, actually suffer from too much attention. But there are other periods—particularly those *nodal* points where a familiar sequence branches into a variety of well-established paths—when a larger attentional investment is clearly demanded.

We are not maintaining, however, that this attentional resource necessarily contributes to the level of activation of any particular cognitive demon. Demon activation is derived in large part from the Intention System and also from the general energizing factors of need, context, frequency, and the like. Nor are we suggesting that attention is essential to permit individual demons to carry out their localized control functions. They are largely autonomous entities that can perform perfectly adequately under environmental guidance alone, if need be. Three examples from our collection illustrate this independence quite nicely.

"In the course of making a cup of tea, I picked up the coffee jar instead of the tea caddy. To open the former requires an unscrewing of the lid, while the latter simply requires the lid being lifted off. My hand (apparently recognizing what it was holding, though my mind did not) unscrewed the lid of the coffee jar, and I deposited three spoonfuls of coffee into the teapot. It was only when I poured my boiling water in, and smelled the coffee that I realized my mistake."

"I went to feed the goldfish. Beside the tank were the fish food and a lump of sticky plastic used for attaching pictures to the wall. I picked up the plastic instead of the fish food, pulled off a piece, and was just about to drop it in the tank when I noticed what I was doing. The interesting thing was that handling a lump of plastic required quite a different action of the hand than sprinkling the fish food. Yet my hand seemed to know what it was doing."

"I was thirsty and went to pour a glass of orange juice. I saw a
dirty glass by the sink, so I filled it with water from the tap to
rinse it and poured the water away. Having now an empty glass
in my hand I filled it with water again, emptied it, filled it again
and so on, three or four times, until eventually I remembered the
juice. While this was happening, it seemed to me that each time
the glass was empty I was filling it because I was thirsty, and that
each time it was full I was emptying it in order to rinse it for some
reason. I knew something was wrong, because I knew I was
caught in a loop, but as long as I forgot the juice, I couldn't see
why."

Each of these instances suggest that, at some level in the control
system, the wrong objects were correctly perceived and responded
to, even though these actions were not those called for by the current
intention. In the first two examples, at least, it was as if the hand, once
in contact with the wrong object, came under the influence of its
specific control demands. Thus, like slips of the tongue, these erroneous actions obeyed the local rules; although they were out of
step with the prevailing intention. This implies that familiar objects
possess what we might call an *immediate controlling region*. Once in
touch with them, our actions conform to the structural needs of the
object. In other words, some kind of input-output interaction can go
on between the Action System (albeit occupied by the wrong
demon) and the item in question that has nothing to do with the
Intention System, or even perhaps with the limited attentional
resource.

The third of these examples is more complicated, but it bears
the same stamp of environmental control. In this case, the actions of
filling and washing the glass continued to recycle—presumably reflecting a rather bizarre interchange between two demons in whom
the actions governed by the one triggered off the actions dictated by
the other. The important one, however, is that for the short period in
which this curious recycling took place, the attentional resource was
evidently taken up in other direction.

Why, then, if cognitive demons are quite capable of managing
their particular affairs by themselves, does the execution of some
routine activity make demands upon the attentional resource? The
answer, we suggest, comes in two parts, both of which are closely
interrelated. The first is that the execution of any activity requires the

correct sequencing of several necessary demons, and since each of these transitions could potentially lead in many directions, some attentional supervision is needed to keep them on the desired course. The second part of the answer concerns the attentional effort required to restrain those active demons struggling to grab a piece of the action. To keep a series of words or movements on the right track, it is necessary not only to *select* the next appropriate demon, but also to *suppress* those that seek to usurp this position.[5] If demons were merely passive creatures who only acted on orders from above, this problem would not arise. But, as we have argued throughout, they can be both energetic and highly competitive, and continually strive to display their expertise, just like children vying with one another for adult approval.

Because words provide the possibility of a much finer-grained analysis than actions, it is among the slips of the tongue that we can see the failure of this attentional suppression most clearly. As we mentioned in Chapter 8, blends are nearly always phonetically possible words, and spoonerisms are more likely to occur if the outcome is lexically acceptable. Yet salacious spoonerisms are much rarer events. In discussing these findings, we suggested the operation of varying degrees of attentional editing, occurring at a stage just prior to speech production. It was also argued that a sifting over of the potential utterance drew upon the limited attentional resource. When just a small part of this necessary amount of attention is diverted elsewhere, then only the best camouflaged wrong words manage to evade the slightly relaxed vigilance of the editor. These are the phonetically and lexically possible slips. But the editor needs to be a good deal more distracted to permit a hurtful or socially embarrassing slip to emerge in speech. This indicates that there are different levels at which the attentional resource can operate, and, although not so evident, it seems reasonable to assume that these variations in the degree of attentional supervision could be found in slips of action as well. In these, perhaps the best index of the extent to which the necessary attentional resource is lacking is the time it takes for the individual to notice that his or her actions are no longer

[5]See also D.A. Norman and T. Shallice, *Attention to Action: Willed and Automatic Control of Behavior* (La Jolla, California: Center for Human Information Processing, CHIP 99, 1980).

running to plan. These detection delays can vary from an instantaneous "caught in the act" to an awareness that only comes many minutes later. Those that we discover after some hours—like finding the wrong papers in a briefcase—can hardly be taken as indicators of sustained states of abstraction; they are more often a matter of circumstance.

We do not need to confine ourselves to slips of the tongue in order to find other examples of the failure of attentional suppression. As we mentioned in Chapter 9, everyday life has a nasty way of providing all too many of these instances. In states of worry, anxiety, grief, or being in love, the Need System fires up a particular set of demons, related to the object of our strong emotion, such that they continually propel their associated images into consciousness. Where these images are painful or unpleasant, we try to occupy our minds with other things. But even if successful, the respite is only temporary. Soon our efforts to divert attention fail, and these obsessive thoughts, memories, and images come crowding back on to the mental stage, screeching at us like an unrehearsed chorus in some third-rate opera company. When, as is mostly the case, the music is not to our taste, we expend further amounts of the dwindling attentional supply in trying to blot it out. But we still hear it. In such moments, we feel that our limited resources are running very low indeed. When people talk to us, or external events demand notice, our minds positively groan with the labor of paying attention, and even then we do so only intermittently.

Of course, these drains upon the attentional reservoir can come from the outside world as well. External stress is a major consumer of this limited commodity. Those who have done jury duty will know how frequently witnesses fluff their lines during the relatively simple task of being sworn in. It is not so much the reading of the oath that bothers them, as the fact that they are unaccustomed (as they say) to public speaking; to hearing their voices holding forth to an alien audience in a daunting place. Surprisingly, as we noted in Chapter 2, external stressors are not, in themselves, often regarded as the primary cause of an absent-minded slip. But on some occasions, they are clearly implicated. In December 1939, for example, the Royal Air Force launched an ill-advised and abortive attack upon German naval vessels at Wilhelmshaven.[6] The raid was carried out by a relatively small force of Wellington bombers with regular service crews (in other words, they were not lacking in flying competence) who had mostly never been in combat before. As they approached the target area, they came under furious attack by German fighters. In one aircraft, the second pilot reached down to open the bomb doors. On a Wellington, this control is located beside the flap lever. He inadvertently pulled the wrong lever and put on full flap. The Wellington soared abruptly upwards, stalled, and then plunged earthwards. Fortunately, the pilot of the attacking Messerschmitt was so taken aback by the strange maneuver that he lost contact. The English pilot eventually recovered control, and they limped homewards at sea level. The history of warfare is undoubtedly filled with such incidents, which raises the interesting question of how closely such qualities as courage and endurance are related to the available extent of this attentional resource.

So far, we have outlined some of the grounds for our earlier assertions concerning the function of attention. Although conjectural, these arguments relate quite closely to the evidence provided by our collection of slips and lapses. In the next section, we move into a far more speculative region and consider why it is that some people are consistently more prone to absent-minded errors than others, and why this tendency should apparently render them more susceptible to the adverse effects of stress.

INDIVIDUAL DIFFERENCES IN ATTENTIONAL RESOURCE

On the basis of the preceding arguments, we would suggest that people vary characteristically in their proneness to minor cognitive failures (as Broadbent's data and our own indicate—see Chapter 2) because they differ in the amount of attentional resource that is available to monitor and control largely routine mental and physical processes at critical moments. In particular, it seems likely that they

[6]M. Hastings, *Bomber Command* (London: Pan Books, 1981), p. 31.

vary in the spare attentional capacity necessary to keep unsought demons in their proper place.

Such a view is quite in accord with the fact that, for error-prone individuals, mistakes are not limited to one particular aspect of cognitive function but show themselves across the mental board. The limited attentional resource is not something which is confined to a specific cognitive location, but is a fluid quantity that is constantly flowing in and out of all parts of the mental machinery, both within and outside the reaches of consciousness. If, as is often the case in patients with brain damage or in certain old people, the errors occurred primarily in a particular cognitive domain such as language, perception or memory, one would suspect a far more localized, structural basis for the observed dysfunctions. But in the healthy individuals tested by the Oxford group and by ourselves, this was not the case; so we are compelled to look for our underlying causes in a far more generalized process. Our conception of attention as a universal but finite control resource fits this bill.

The next question is why do some people have less of this spare, or nonfocal, attentional resource than others? On logical grounds, there are a number of answers, and the following list is by no means exhaustive.

1. It could be said that some individuals are simply endowed with a smaller *total* quantity than others, and hence have less of it to spread around to all the cognitive demons at any one time. While such a suggestion cannot be ruled out, since we know that almost every human characteristic, mental or physical, varies widely between individuals, it does not seem to be a very satisfactory answer. For one thing, if attention is a generalized mental resource, one would expect that those people possessing a smaller total amount would show fairly marked deficits in a wide range of activities. But the available data do not support this. Broadbent's group, for instance, found virtually no relationship between liability to minor cognitive failures (as measured by the Cognitive Failures Questionnaire) and test intelligence or educational attainment.[7] These are areas in which one

---

[7] D.E. Broadbent, P.F. Cooper, P. Fitzgerald, and K.R. Parkes, "The Cognitive Failures Questionnaire (CFQ) and its correlates." To be published in *British Journal of Clinical Psychology*.

would expect a chronically small amount of this resource to manifest itself. Similarly, we have found wide differences in proneness to absent-minded errors in samples drawn primarily from a university population, where the variation in intelligence (as compared to the potential range of such differences) is relatively small. This possibility cannot be dismissed altogether, but it does not seem very promising.

2. A more attractive proposition is that, in some individuals, fairly long-standing additional demands are made upon the limited resource, leaving only a reduced amount free to cope with non-conscious control activities. The possible sources of these persistent attentional claimants are legion; but a few spring to mind immediately. There is, for instance, the traditional figure of the absent-minded professor, so preoccupied with intellectual matters that there is little attention left to cope adequately with the banal routines of everyday life. Clearly, these people do exist, as the quotation from Sir William Hamilton showed in Chapter 4; but one suspects that such consistently abstracted individuals are comparatively rare birds. Nevertheless, chronic abstractedness must remain as one possible breach in the attentional reservoir through which this limited resource could be continually leaking.

But for most of us, it seems more likely that the major source of this extra attentional demand comes from the emotional rather than the intellectual sphere. Here we are inexorably tugged back into Freudian concerns, and that is no bad thing. The time has clearly come for the heart to be put back into cognitive psychology. Information-processing models of human cognitive function, and parallel work in the area of artificial intelligence have proved immensely useful in elucidating the mechanics of memory, recognition, problem-solving, and the like. But no matter how well these models simulate mental processes, as investigated in the laboratory, we must not lose sight of one fundamental difference between intelligent machines like computers and human beings, which is that the former receive their driving force from an electric socket in the wall while we get ours from the explosive and capricious mixture of biological drives, emotions, and passions that we have subsumed in our theory under the pallid heading of the Need System.

While Freud was preoccupied with the primal, underlying emotional currents and their origins, we must content ourselves here with more easily demarcated surface features. What kind of emotional factors could make a continuing drain upon our attentional resources? One obvious candidate is a chronically high level of anxiety. Another is neuroticism. Both of these possibilities receive some support from Broadbent's data. He found positive and significant correlations (although not all of a high order) between the total score on the Cognitive Failure Questionnaire and the Spielberger Trait Anxiety Test, and the neuroticism scale of the Eysenck Personality Questionnaire. In addition, all three of these measures were positively and significantly correlated with the score obtained from Rotter's measure of the perceived locus of control (either internal or external to the person). Those people who reported a comparatively large number of minor cognitive failures, and who also tended to be somewhat anxious and neurotic, were inclined to see their actions as being more governed by external agencies than by self-determined ones.[8]

At present, findings like these can do little more than give us valuable pointers as to the various ways in which relatively enduring states within the Need System can lead to a steady seepage of the limited attentional resource. There are obviously other possibilities that need to be considered. For the moment, though, it is sufficient to indicate that both intellectual and emotional characteristics can, through a variety of means, make persistent demands upon this stock, and thus reduce the amount remaining to deal with lower-level control activities.

3. Another alternative is that liability to minor cognitive failures may not necessarily depend primarily upon the *quantity* of the spare attentional resource, but upon the facility with which individuals *dispose* of this commodity from moment to moment. In other words, people may vary in the effectiveness with which they *deploy* their attentional reserve in response to the current demands of the situation. It may be simply a question of good generalship. Victory does not always go to the big battalions. The Army of Northern Virginia,

---

[8]D.E. Broadbent, P.F. Cooper, P. Fitzgerald, and K.R. Parkes, "The Cognitive Failures Questionnaire (CFQ) and its correlates."

under the leadership of Lee and Jackson in the first two years of the American Civil War, showed how effectively underfed, underequipped but determined veterans could be used against the much larger armies of the North, despite the fact that the latter had greater access to almost all the necessary resources; except, of course, good generals. More recently, the same qualities have been demonstrated by the Israelis and by the North Vietnamese.

A useful consequence of this idea is that it offers a means of accommodating something we mentioned earlier, but have so far neglected; which is that too much of this attentional resource can, at certain levels and at particular times, be as disruptive of performance as too little. To restrict ourselves only to the notion that it is the localized scarcity of the attentional supply that causes slips is to ignore the conclusions drawn in Chapters 6 and 7; namely, that an excess, particularly of focal attention, can also provoke errors. There appear to be at least two possible reasons for this: either that too much attention given to a particular subroutine gums up the works in some fashion, or that too great a disposition of this resource at a tactical level withdraws it from essential higher-level strategic concerns. Whatever the precise causes, however, it is clear that for every level of the control system there is an optimum quantity of attention needed at any particular moment, and that this amount changes constantly with both the nature and the state of the ongoing activities. In view of the critical complexities of these attentional requirements, it is remarkable not so much that we make slips, but that we make them so comparatively rarely.

There are, as we indicated earlier, other possible answers to why some individuals are consistently more prone to errors than others; but, for now, we wish to focus on the latter two—the idea of reduced spare capacity and the notion of attentional deployment— and to consider how they might contribute, as Broadbent has suggested (see Chapter 2), to a general vulnerability to stress.[9] It will be recalled from our discussion of his findings that student nurses emerged from a six-week initial spell on high-stress wards with varying degrees of minor psychiatric symptoms, and that the extent

[9]D.E. Broadbent, P.F. Cooper, P. Fitzgerald, and K.R. Parkes, "The Cognitive Failures Questionnaire (CFQ) and its correlates."

of these little cracks in the fabric was positively correlated with the general liability to everyday slips and lapses. Thus, those nurses whose Cognitive Failure Questionnaire scores indicated a consistently high rate of small blunders (in the six-month period prior to the ward duty) bore more scars as the result of their stressful experiences than did those with lower scores. Why should this be so?

The kind of stresses that a student nurse is likely to encounter in her first period of ward duty are many and various. They include feelings of professional inadequacy, autocratic head nurses, demanding and querulous patients, menial and distasteful jobs, the sight of suffering and first confrontations with death; to say nothing of fatigue, constant time pressure, unfamiliar sleep routines, and the usual round of emotional worries about family, social life, and the like. All of these, coming together, can add up to a sudden and fearsome burden for a person of eighteen or so. What strategies can he or she use to cope with such strains?

There are many possibilities, but an obvious one is to say: "I want to be a nurse, so I've got to get through these few weeks the best way I can, no matter how tired I feel, or how awful the head nurse is, or how disgusted I am by cleaning dirty bedpans . . . " But in the face of daily assaults upon his or her feelings, self-regard, sensibilities, and the sheer physical labor of the job, such resolves take a considerable effort to maintain. This effort is likely to make large claims upon his or her limited attentional reserves. In those student nurses in whom these resources are already partially depleted through some persistent leakage—as a high rate of slips might indicate—the pressure upon this attention-demanding coping strategy may prove too much. Also, as others have pointed out, psychiatric symptoms begin to appear as cognitive coping devices start to crumble. The same outcome would also be expected if the nurse was unable to sustain his or her coping strategy by an appropriate deployment of attention, regardless of its available quantity. We have no evidence at present to choose between these two notions, and, indeed, both may apply in some or even all cases.

These ideas are extremely speculative and difficult to test, neither of which attributes is likely to commend them to the research psychologist. Nevertheless, although much of what we are suggesting lies beyond anyone's ability to tell us directly, there is still a lot that can be learned from careful and sympathetic questioning of people such as these, and others in comparable stress situations, about the nature of their cognitive coping strategies and the extent to which they are vulnerable to the various attacks upon them. Nor is it beyond the bounds of possibility that we could devise some independent measure of the degree of spare attentional capacity, or the relative efficiency of its deployment. Indeed, such techniques have already been tried with moderate success, although the particular questions being asked were not quite the same as our own. One of the problems about taking people into the laboratory and asking them to perform two or more tasks concurrently is that the nature of the experiment places false limits on the extent of the attentional deployment. In the laboratory, the experimenter largely defines the available choices; but in real life we ourselves are compelled first to identify and then to make these choices, and the range of possible options is infinitely greater. It may well be, therefore, that the main distinguishing feature between individuals (that appears to be reflected indirectly in their general propensity to absent-minded errors) is their characteristic style in disposing of this limited commodity, whatever its available amount, when confronted with the constantly changing demands of daily life. As has turned out to be the case for memory ability, laboratory tests do not always prove to be good predictors of a person's performance in the outside world. The attempt to bridge this gulf between the highly specific and easily manipulable laboratory task and the uncontrollable and myriad concerns of actual day-to-day living remains one of psychology's most difficult challenges. Both modes of inquiry are necessary and important; but reconciling their findings is not easy.

MEDITATION AND HYPNOSIS

While still in the further realms of speculation, it seems worthwhile to cast a brief sideways glance at two phenomena which, on the face of it, seem to be far removed from our central concern with absent-minded errors. Nonetheless, they do have a close bearing on the present issue of attention as a limited controlling resource. Our treatment of them will be scanty in the extreme, but sufficient we hope to indicate their relevance.

Meditation

There are an enormous variety of meditational techniques that are practiced in an equally diverse range of cultural and religious settings. Our concern here is neither with the details of any specific technique nor with the ends that it seeks to achieve, but with the fact that most, if not all of them share one interesting characteristic: they require of the meditator an unusually sustained and narrow focus of attention upon some physical or mental target.

Achieving some command over these restive and often perverse attentional forces is regarded by most instructors of meditation as something akin to a skill. At first it demands a great deal of effort, but through daily practice under the right physical and mental conditions, the student is thought to acquire a larger measure of true control. The meditational literature abounds with instructions on how this should be done, but for our purpose a single example will suffice. Writing in 1905, the Yogi Ramacharaka (who was well versed in the works of William James and other contemporary psychologists) outlines the goal of Raja Yoga.

> The second step in *Raja Yoga* is what is known as *Dharana*, or Concentration. This is the most wonderful idea in the direction of cultivating the mental forces, and may be cultivated to an almost incredible degree, but all this requires work, time, and patience. But the student will be well repaid for it. Concentration consists in the mind focusing upon a certain subject or object, and being held there for a time. This, at first thought, seems very easy but a little practice will show how difficult it is to firmly fix the attention and hold it there. It will have a tendency to waver, and move to some other object or subject, and much practice will be needed to hold it at the desired point. But practice will accomplish wonders, as one may see by observing people who have acquired this faculty, and who use it in their everyday life. But the following point should be remembered. Many persons have acquired the faculty of concentrating their attention, but have allowed it to become almost involuntary, and they become a slave to it, forgetting themselves and everything else, and often neglecting necessary affairs. This is the ignorant way of concentrating, and those addicted to it become slaves to their habits, instead of masters of their minds. They become daydreamers and absent-minded people, instead of Masters. They are to be pitied as much as those who cannot concentrate at all. The secret is in a mastery of the mind. The Yogis can concentrate at will, and

completely bury themselves in the subject before them, and extract it from every item of interest, and can pass the mind from the thing at will, the same control being used in both cases. They do not allow fits of abstraction, or 'absent-mindedness' to come upon them, nor are they daydreamers. On the contrary, they are very wide-awake individuals, close observers, clear thinkers, correct reasoners. They are masters of their minds, not slaves to their moods.[10]

In a second passage, he describes one of the early steps along this difficult path.

Concentrate the attention upon some familiar object—a pencil, for instance. Hold the mind there, and consider the pencil to the exclusion of any other object. Consider its size, color, shape, kind of wood. Consider its uses and purposes, its materials, the process of its manufacture, etc., etc. In short, think as many things about the pencil as possible, allowing the mind to pursue any associated paths, such as a consideration of the graphite of which the 'lead' is made, the forest from which came the wood ... etc.[11]

Although, like other masters, the Yogi Ramacharaka views this attainment of voluntary concentration as merely a preliminary step toward a much higher spiritual purpose, his very down-to-earth instructions imply a notion of attention that is very close to our own. He was talking primarily about the means by which we can achieve a useful mastery over the direction of focal attention; we, on the other hand, are more interested in the other part of this limited resource which is not so readily accessible to consciousness: that marginal quantity necessary to keep our largely automatic actions on track. But, as he and his kind well understood, the ability to direct focal consciousness in a sustained fashion necessarily involves some reduction in the amount needed to keep active demons in check. Since most meditational procedures involve some form of physical inactivity (or else a highly rhythmical one), we would not expect this lower-level deficit to show up in slips of action. However, since these cognitive demons

---

[10]Yogi Ramacharaka, *A Series of Lessons in Raja Yoga* (London: L.N. Fowler, 1905), pp. 81–82.

[11]Yogi Ramacharaka, *A Series of Lessons in Raja Yoga* (London: L.N. Fowler, 1905), pp. 81–82.

are independently energized by the Need System, and the frequency and recency of past use, we would predict that meditators are likely to have their efforts at concentration undermined by the most active of these now partially liberated demons. Thus, we would expect their minds to be assailed by the recent residues of the day's events, by recurring snatches of thought, and by emotionally charged images. These would hardly constitute adequate tests of our view of attention; we are only describing what all of us experience (whether we meditate or not) on the threshold of sleep as we try to compose the mind. But it is of some interest that many novice meditators— particularly during the 1960s and 1970s when a number of these techniques became more commonplace in the western world—are occasionally subject to fits of emotion, involving tears or states of joy, that arrive unexpectedly and without any apparent cause. The jargon used to describe these turns differs from group to group, but, although not well documented in the psychological literature, their occurrence is not in doubt. Such phenomena suggest intriguing (though by no means novel) connections between the deployment of attention and psychotherapeutic techniques, which leads us on to the not altogether unrelated topic of hypnosis.

Hypnosis

Deeply rooted in both the popular and scientific view of hypnosis is the notion that it involves a state of trance which is quite distinct from our normal waking consciousness. Implicit in this is the idea that both the hypnotist and his subject require special qualities, the one to induce and the other to achieve this altered state of consciousness. A contrary view, and one that fits more readily with the recent experimental evidence, is that hypnosis is not a distinct state at all, merely a condition of heightened suggestibility in which the subject (up to a point, at least), and at some level quite voluntarily, consents to carry out certain instructions. To put it another way, the hypnotic subject agrees for a period of time and within certain bounds to hand over part of his or her Intention System's planning functions to someone else. Assuming a certain degree of competence on the part of the hypnotist and a sufficient compliance on the part of the subject, such a conception of hypnosis does not demand any special powers of either person. Of course, there are hypnotic virtuosos who, through a natural disposition, or by virtue of much exposure, can achieve deep levels of hypnosis very readily. Similarly, there are some people who have either a natural or an acquired talent for inducing so-called hypnotic behaviors. But, aside from these particular individuals, it seems reasonable to assume that most of us can achieve varying degrees of success in either role.

It is not within the scope of this book to enter into this debate. For our part, we are happier to accept the latter alternative, but also willing to acknowledge the kind of bimodality in hypnotic susceptibility that has been shown by Hilgard and his colleagues (see Fig. 11.1).[12] That is, hypnotic virtuosos form a smallish hump at the extreme end of an otherwise normal distribution of hypnotizability. People in this larger category vary simply in the level of hypnosis (as measured by a graded scale) that can be induced under reasonably controlled conditions.

Figure 11.1 Biomodality in Hypnotic Susceptibility Scores

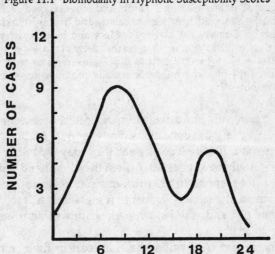

HYPNOTIC SUSCEPTIBILITY SCORE

[12]E.R. Hilgard, *Divided Consciousness: Multiple Controls in Human Thought and Action* (New York: John Wiley & Sons, 1977), pp. 156–162.

What does hypnotizing someone involve? The short answer, assuming the willingness of the subject, is that, first, some claim is made upon his or her focal attention, and, second, he or she is gradually persuaded to accept a series of control statements from the hypnotist. These usually begin with something simple like eye-closure and advance to more complex demands. Let Barber fill in some of the details.

> Typically, one person (the hypnotist) administers a hypnotic induction procedure to another person (the subject). For example, the hypnotist may ask the subject to stare at a blinking light and then may give repeated suggestions for eye-heaviness and eye-closure: 'Your eyes are becoming tired and heavy . . . heavier and heavier . . . Your lids are as heavy as lead . . . so heavy . . . The strain on your eyes is becoming greater and greater . . . .' If the subject has not closed his eyes by this time, the hypnotist may state directly: 'Close your eyes now.' The hypnotist then continues with repeated suggestions of relaxation, drowsiness, sleep and suggestions that the subject is entering a hypnotic state: 'Your muscles are relaxing . . . more and more relaxed . . . Comfortable and relaxed, breathing regularly and deeply, thinking of nothing . . . Drowsy and sleepy . . . More and more drowsy and sleepy . . . a deep, comfortable, restful sleep . . . in a deep hypnotic state . . . ' When hypnotism is being used for experimental purposes, the hypnotic induction usually continues for about 10 to 15 minutes.[13]

In this condition, subjects usually demonstrate a heightened responsiveness to a variety of suggestions. For example, on being told that their arm is rigid, like a piece of steel, they may try to bend the arm but fail. Or it might be suggested to them that their hand is numb, and it then does not respond to the prick of a pin . . . and so on. It is also possible to make the subject appear to regress in age. If told that he is now six years old, and asked to write, the handwriting resembles that of a young child.

Hypnosis and meditation share, at least in their initial stages, the voluntary capture of focal attention, aided in each case by physical relaxation. In other words, both make demands upon the limited resource. But, thereafter, our view of attention as a finite controlling

---

[13]T.X. Barber, N.P. Spanos, and J.F. Chaves, *Hypnosis: Imagination and Human Potentialities* (New York: Pergamon Press Inc., 1974), p. 3.

force suggests that there are some interesting differences between the two procedures. Whereas meditation appears to result, in part, in the removal of its more *suppressive* aspects, thus allowing active demons to come bubbling to the surface of consciousness (at least in those who have not yet achieved the kind of mastery described by Yogi Ramacharaka), the case in hypnosis, while not precisely the opposite, seems to go some way in that direction. Here it is the *selective* rather than the suppressive component of nonconscious attention that seems to be crucial. Having partially abdicated his or her position as the master of his or her Intention System, the hypnotized subject *permits* the hypnotist to gain control of specific cognitive demons that were hitherto largely under the influence of his freely deployed intentional and attentional resources. Whatever the nature of the hypnotic state, it does appear that the normal ability to dispose of at least part of this controlling quantity at will is in some way curtailed. The manner in which the remainder is allocated is, to a certain extent, in the control of the hypnotist. Thus, by suggesting that the subject has a cat sitting on his or her lap, the subject is able to energize the cat-recognizing demons to such a degree that the subject actually reports seeing the fictitious cat. By suggesting that the subject's arm is levitating, the hypnotist gains some control over the demon that normally carries out this upward movement voluntarily. The age-regression phenomenon also indicates that the hypnotist can manipulate even deeply buried demons associated with the subject's childhood. The actions dictated by post-hypnotic suggestions show that this control can extend beyond the session in which the actual hypnotizing procedures were carried out.

The interesting and still unanswered question is to what extent is the subject supplementing these external control instructions by the voluntary activity of his or her own Intention System? How far is the subject providing the intentional direction necessary to activate the cognitive demons? In the case of the initial exercises like eye-closure and arm-raising, the subject is probably contributing most of the intentional component. But for the reawakening of the more remote, slumbering demons, such as those related to particular early years, the subject's contribution is likely to be very small indeed. It would seem, therefore, that the technique of hypnosis offers an exciting avenue toward a more detailed exploration of these attentional resources.

WHAT CONTROLS ATTENTION?

If attention is a controlling resource, what controls the controller? To a large extent, we have already touched upon the obvious answers. Some of this attentional resource can be captured involuntarily by novel and engaging events in the outside world. Other claims upon it are made by highly activated demons, particularly those charged up by strong emotion or other powerful states of the Need System. We usually have to take notice of these demands, even if the Intention System says otherwise. The nearest we approximate to any direct control over attention is via the dictates of the Intention System, and that, as we have seen, can only be achieved intermittently. By exerting an effort of will, or by adopting the recommendations of people like the Yogi Ramacharaka, we can, up to a point, extend the measure of control we normally exercise over this attentional resource. This brings us face to face with the knotty issue of what is meant by terms like *will* or *volition*, and their close relation, the idea of *effort*.

Before we attempt to unravel these things, two points need to be made. First, we do not intend to get tied up with the question of free will. This is a metaphysical problem, not a psychological one. As human beings, we must resolve this issue one way or the other; but it is an area to which psychologists have brought much confusion and very little expertise. James put it well: "The fact is that the question of free will is insoluble on strictly psychological grounds." Freud and James, for instance, each came to opposing conclusions: Freud in favor of determinism ("What is thus left free from the one side receives its motive from the other side, the unconscious, and the determinism in the psychic realm is thus carried out uninterruptedly."), and James electing somewhat reluctantly, for the side of free will. But these decisions were made on personal grounds, not scientific ones.

The second point is that contemporary psychologists know very little about volition. This is a consequence of psychology's history more than anything else. In the 1920s, a revolutionary group calling themselves behaviorists ousted the then mentalist establishment, and while strong pockets of mentalist resistance continued to hold out, the behaviorist's word was law for nearly four decades until the early 1960s. During this period, there were many purges, and one of the first victims was the concept of volition or will. Other proscribed notions included consciousness, mind, intention and purpose, mental imagery—and much else that most would regard as the proper subject matter of psychology. So effective was the suppression of these mentalistic terms that the word *volition* largely vanished from the psychological literature until quite recently. Meanwhile, in the real world, the idea of will continued to play a useful, and in the case of the law, a fundamental role, as the following passage from a distinguished writer on jurisprudence will show.

> All civilized penal systems make liability to punishment for at any rate serious crime dependent not merely on the fact that the person to be punished has done the outward act of a crime, but on his having done it in a certain frame of mind or will. These mental and intellectual elements are many and various and are collected together in the terminology of English jurists under the simple sounding description of *mens rea*, a guilty mind. But in many ways the most prominent is a man's intention . . .[14]

If we now choose, as many psychologists do, to disagree with a radical behaviorist's claim that "A scientific analysis of behavior dispossesses autonomous man and turns the control he has been said to exert over to the environment," then we are thrown back to early ideas.[15] Not surprisingly, the best of these was advanced by William James. His basic notion was that actions are triggered by "ideas of movement", or by images of what the movement feels and looks like during its execution.[16] In other words, actions (and presumably switches of attention also) are initiated as an almost automatic result of imagining their sensory consequences. We start with a limited repertoire of reflex or "hard-wired" movements which produce sensory feedback. Eventually, the mental image of a movement's perceived efforts come to have the same power to initiate it as did the external stimulus which provoked the original reflex response.

Within James's theory, one of the principal characteristics of the voluntary act is that it can be withheld. This restraint is achieved by

[14]H.L.A. Hart, *Punishment and Responsibility: Essays in the Philosophy of Law* (Oxford: Clarendon Press, 1968), p. 114.
[15]B.F. Skinner, *Beyond Freedom and Dignity* (London: Jonathan Cape, 1972), p. 205.
[16]W. James, *The Principles of Psychology Vol. I* (New York: Henry Holt & Co., 1890), pp. 486–592.

"... an antagonistic representation present simultaneously to the mind." On occasions, these contrary images overcome our best intentions, as when we struggle to get out of bed on a cold morning. It is under these circumstances that an *act of will* is necessary to defeat, in this particular case, the powerful and seductive images of warm immobility. However, there is nothing especially mysterious about this mental effort, as James pointed out with characteristic clarity. "The essential achievement of the will ... is to attend to a difficult object and hold it fast before the mind." If this difficult focusing of attention is sustained for long enough then, James argued, the necessary actions will follow more or less as a matter of course.

Today, when many psychologists have come to acknowledge once again that their discipline is centrally concerned with the phenomena of mental life, this deceptively simple view of volition has been restored to a place of major importance. Although these ideas are more than ninety years old, their full impact has only lately been felt. This is, to some extent, due to the convergence of a number of previously unrelated lines of research, as indicated, for example, by Konorski's recent comments upon James's theory: "It is most encouraging to know that we have come to exactly the same concept by quite different considerations—namely, through the physiological analysis of (voluntary) movements."[17]

In trying to fix attention upon a particular object, we would suggest that the "contrary images" to which James referred were those generated by highly charged cognitive demons. It is partly their conscious fragments that drag the attentional beam away from its intended object. And it is to these images and thoughts that it every now and again involuntarily redirects itself, or, of course, to exciting events that crop up around us. We must accept that there will always be a continual tug of war going on between the voluntary and involuntary controllers of attention. Perhaps the Yogi Ramacharaka is right, and we can learn to master the direction of the attentional spotlight more effectively; but for most of us this is likely to be a vain hope. In this sense, therefore, both the behaviorists and the mentalists are correct. Whether we like it or not, many of our actions are directly controlled by immediate events in the outside world; but

[17] J. Konorski, *Integrative Activity of the Brain* (Chicago: University of Chicago Press, 1967), p. 194.

even if the behaviorists are reluctant to acknowledge it, the bulk of this controlling power lies within us, though not in a form that we can easily govern.

It will probably not have escaped notice that the preceding arguments were almost entirely circular. What controls the voluntary component of attentional control? The effort required to hold it before the mind. What form does this act of will take? The ability to sustain attention upon some intended outcome. Round and round it goes; but the alternatives are none too satisfactory either. We could, for example, get into the messy business of infinite regress: what (or who) controls the controller that controls the controller ... and so on? Faced with the unpleasant alternatives of circular arguments or infinitely regressive ones, we reluctantly plump for the former. Mystical truths are often presented in the form of paradoxes; perhaps psychological verities must inevitably appear in the guise of circular arguments. Either way, the available evidence does not help us too much. In the final analysis, it comes down to a matter of belief.

EPILOGUE

Those single-minded readers whose efforts of will have carried them this far will no doubt be feeling peeved, not to say cheated, that we have given no prescriptions of how to avoid absent-minded errors. But there are no simple remedies. These mistakes are the price we pay for being able to carry out so many complex activities with only a small investment of conscious attention. They are the inevitable penalty of the necessary process of automatization. Total "present-mindedness" would make life insupportable. We must therefore accept the usually trivial consequences. All we can usefully do is to indicate the kind of circumstances, both mental and physical, where such slips are most likely to occur, and this we have done in the preceding chapte   This is the best we can offer. As Freud understood very well, the most interesting feature of absent-minded slips is not how to avoid them, but what they reveal about the secretive workings of the mind. Only on the basis of a better understanding of mental control functions can we hope to minimize the human contributions to such potentially catastrophic events as Three Mile Island.

THE ERROR PRONENESS QUESTIONNAIRE

ERROR PRONENESS
QUESTIONNAIRE

Occupation:_____ Age:_____ Sex:_____

General Instructions

This questionnaire is concerned with finding out how frequently people make various kinds of everyday slips and lapses.

There are 30 questions. Each one asks how often you make a particular type of mistake. For most of the questions, actual examples are given to help you appreciate the kind of mistake to which the particular question is referring. When reading through these examples, do not concern yourself too much with their specific details. We are interested in roughly how often you commit that *general class* of error.

Please read through the question first. Then consult the list of possible response categories that follow, select the appropriate frequency, and enter the corresponding letter in the space provided below each question. Repeat this procedure for all the items in the Error Proneness Questionnaire. When you have finished check through to see whether you have answered all the questions.

Possible Response Categories

Having read through the question and the examples (where given) use the following list of frequencies and select one that best reflects how often you make that particular kind of mistake. Having decided upon the appropriate frequency statement, write the corresponding letter (A–K) in the space marked "response category" beneath the relevant question. Don't spend too long trying to answer each question: It is your first reactions we are most interested in.

A — NEVER.
B — ABOUT ONCE IN MY LIFE.
C — MORE THAN ONCE IN MY LIFE, BUT LESS THAN ONCE A YEAR.
D — ABOUT ONCE A YEAR.
E — MORE THAN ONCE A YEAR, BUT LESS THAN ONCE A MONTH.
F — ABOUT ONCE A MONTH.
G — MORE THAN ONCE A MONTH, BUT LESS THAN ONCE A WEEK.
H — ABOUT ONCE A WEEK.
 I — MORE THAN ONCE A WEEK, BUT LESS THAN ONCE A DAY.
 J — ABOUT ONCE A DAY.
K — MORE THAN ONCE A DAY.

1. How often do you find yourself carrying out a familiar sequence of actions that you had not intended?

For example:

"I went up to my bedroom to change into something more comfortable for the evening, and the next thing I knew I was getting into my pajamas."

"I have two mirrors on my dressing table. One I use for making up and brushing my hair, the other for putting in and taking out my contact lenses. I intended to brush my hair, but sat down in front of the wrong mirror and took off my contact lenses."

"I meant to take off only my shoes, but took off my socks as well."

Response Category: _____

2. How often do you have the "What am I here for?" feeling when you find you have forgotten what it was you intended to do?

For example:

"I went upstairs to the bedroom and stopped—not remembering what I had gone there for."

"I opened the fridge and stood there looking at its contents unable to remember what I wanted."

"I stopped halfway down the stairs, unable to remember what I was going for."

Response Category: _____

3. How often do you make mistakes where essentially the right actions are carried out, but the objects (or persons) for which they were intended get reversed?

For example:

"In a hurried effort to finish the housework and have a bath I put the plants meant for the lounge in the bedroom and my underwear in the window in the lounge."

"I unwrapped a sweet, put the paper in my mouth and threw the sweet into the waste-paper basket."

"I threw my glasses in the bin and kept some dirty tissues I was holding in my other hand."

Response Category: _____

4. How often do you leave some necessary step out of a sequence of intended actions?

For example:

"I put milk, sugar, and boiling water into my cup omitting the tea bag."

"I wrote a check and put the checkbook back into my bag without tearing the check out."

"I intended to put the key in the lock and open the door. I put the key in but did not turn it, and tried unsuccessfully to open the door."

Response Category: _____

5. How often in the course of carrying out some fairly habitual activity do you find that you have reversed the direction of your actions?

For example:

"I intended to take off my shoes and put on my slippers. I took my shoes off and then noticed that a coat had fallen off the hanger. I hung the coat up and then instead of putting on my slippers, I put my shoes back on again."

"I ladled soup into the soup bowl, and then started to ladle it back into the pan again."

"I got the correct fare out of my purse to give to the conductor. A few moments later I put the money back into my purse before the conductor had come to collect it."

Response Category: _____

6. How often do you find yourself *not* having done something you intended *after* having dealt with some unexpected interruption?

For example:

"I picked up my coat to go out when the phone rang. I answered it and then went out of the front door without my coat."

"The kettle was just about to boil when I noticed the tea caddy was empty. I fetched a fresh packet of tea from the cupboard and filled the caddy. Then I poured the water into the teapot and only when I came to pour it into the cup did I notice I hadn't put any tea in."

"I walked to my bookcase to find the dictionary. In the process of taking it off the shelf, other books fell onto the floor. I put them all back, together with the dictionary, and went back to my desk not having looked up the word I wanted."

Response Category: _____

7. How often do you make mistakes in which you reach out for a particular object and then find that you have picked up something that looks similar, or does the same kind of job, but is not the item you intended?

For example:

"I intended to pick up the deodorant, but picked up the air freshener instead."

"I intended to pick up the milk bottle but actually reached out for the orange squash bottle."

"I meant to open a tin of Kit-E-Kat, but opened a tin of rice pudding instead."

Response Category: _____

8. How often does it happen that during the course of some routine activity, something happens that requires a modification of your usual actions, you note the need for the change, but go on doing the same thing automatically?

   For example:

   "I was putting the silver away in the drawer when my wife asked me to leave it out as she wanted to use it. I heard her, agreed, and yet continued to put the silver away."

   "My son asked me to drop him off at his friend's house on the way home from school. I said I would, but then drove right past the house."

   "I was peeling potatoes for our evening meal. My husband told me he was eating out that evening. I heard him, but still peeled the usual amount for the whole family."

   Response Category: _____

9. How often do you make mistakes in which you omit something because you have switched to some other activity prematurely?

   For example:

   "I was just about to step into the bath when I discovered I still had my socks on."

   "While running the water into a bucket from the kitchen tap, I put the lid back on before turning off the tap."

   "I walked out of a shop without waiting for my change."

   Response Category: _____

10. How often in the course of driving a car, taking a walk, or some routine activity, do you "wake up" to discover that, for the moment at least, you have no recollection of the places you have just passed through or the things you have just done?

For example:

"I noticed that we were approaching the Watford Gap service area on M1. I had no idea we had come so far. The previous stretch of highway was almost a complete blank to me."

"I came out of the bathroom, and then had to feel my chin to check whether or not I had shaved."

"I found myself at the end of Union Street without any recollection of the previous few minutes of the walk. I knew the way I must have come but had no clear 'mental pictures' of having done so."

Response Category: _____

11. How often do you find yourself carrying out unnecessary actions?

For example:

"I flicked the light on as I left the room in daylight."

"I went to switch my radio off, but it wasn't on in the first place."

"I reached up to take off my glasses, but my fingers snapped together rather abruptly because I wasn't wearing them at the time."

Response Category: _____

12. How often do you find yourself saying or doing something that recognizably belongs to some other activity or situation, but which is inappropriate for the present circumstances?

For example:

"The conductor approached me to collect my fare. I handed him the money saying: six-o-seven, o-four-double-three—my telephone number."

"I picked up the phone and bellowed 'come in' at it."

"I went to the library, got the book I wanted, and then took out my wallet to pay for it."

Response Category: _____

13. How often does your mind go blank when you try to recall some piece of information that you were certain you knew?

For example:

"When I got to the ticket window, I suddenly couldn't recall the name of the station I wanted to go to."

"I thought I knew a friend's phone number by heart, but when I lifted the receiver to dial it, I discovered that it had escaped my mind completely."

"Halfway to a party, I realized I had forgotten the host's address, though I had looked it up to remind myself earlier that evening."

Response Category: _____

14. How often do you frame an intention to do something and then find yourself doing something quite different?

For example:

"I went into my room intending to fetch a book. I took off my rings, looked in the mirror and came out again—without the book."

"I went to the bathroom to clean my teeth. When I got there I picked up a towel and walked out again, without brushing my teeth."

"I meant to get my wallet from the bedroom. Instead I wound the bedside clock, and came down again without the wallet."

Response Category: _____

15. How often are you made aware of something you must have done, but have no recollection of having done it?

For example:

"I asked my husband to put the trash outside the front gate for collection. He came back and told me it was already there. I must have put it out myself, but I couldn't recall doing so."

"I found the kitchen scissors in the bathroom. I must have put them there but couldn't remember doing it."

"I went up to make the bed, but found that I had already done it."

Response Category: _____

16. How often do you formulate an intention to do something and then carry out the right action(s), but in relation to the wrong object(s) or person(s)?

For example:

"I intended to place my hairbrush in its usual place by the bookcase. I put my boyfriend's lighter there instead."

"I had an appointment at the dentist's, but went to the doctors's instead."

"I intended to close the window as it was cold. I closed the cupboard instead."

Response Category: _____

17. How often do you find that you have forgotten to carry out some planned action?

For example:

"I intended to buy orange juice, biscuits, and cheese, and forgot to buy the cheese."

"I intended to go to the shoe repairers, the post office, the supermarket, and the dry cleaners. When I got home I realized that the letter I had intended to mail was still in my pocket."

"When making pancakes, I forgot to put the egg in the mixture."

Response Category: _____

18. How often have you poured something or placed something into a receptacle for which it was not intended?

For example:

"I put the coffee jar into the refrigerator instead of the cupboard."

"I put a piece of dried toast on the cat's dish instead of in the trash."

"I began to pour tea into the sugar bowl instead of the cups."

Response Category: _____

252   The Error Proneness Questionnaire

19. How often do you find yourself still carrying something that you had intended to put down or dispose of at some earlier point?

For example:

"I left the bedroom carrying yesterday's underwear which I had intended to dispose of in a container in the bathroom before going downstairs for breakfast. However, on this occasion, I reached the kitchen before realizing I was still carrying the cast-off clothes."

"I went upstairs to put the new toothpaste in the bathroom, but I was still carrying it when I came down again."

"After having a quick cup of coffee in the Staff Room, I went to the sink and washed the cup but, instead of putting it in the cupboard where it belongs, I kept it in my hand and walked back to my classroom with it."

Response Category: _____

20. How often do you find that you cannot immediately recall the name of a familiar person, place, or object?

For example:

"I couldn't remember the name of the University Art Gallery. I came up with 'Worthington', but I knew it wasn't right. Not until much later did the correct name—'Whitworth'—pop into my head."

"I bought some cheeses. When I got home, I was asked to say what they were. I could name the two more exotic varieties, but I couldn't immediately name the Stilton, even though it was the one I liked best, and I had asked for it by name in the shop."

"I saw an actor in a TV movie. His face was familiar and I was certain that I knew his name, but I couldn't get it for ages even though it was 'on the tip of my tongue'."

Response Category: _____

21. How often do you find yourself apparently attending to something but not actually taking anything in?

For example:

"When I got to the bottom of the page, I realized that I had no idea of what I'd just been reading."

"My daughter asked me what had been happening in a TV play I was watching. I'd been thinking about something quite different with my eyes glued to the screen, and found I wasn't able to tell her."

"My husband asked me a question. I had to ask him to repeat it. I'd heard him talking but hadn't taken in the sense."

Response Category: _____

22. How often do you make a plan to do something, find that you have to modify it for some reason, and then discover subsequently that you are carrying out the original plan rather than the changed one?

    For example:

    "I walked into the bathroom intending to have a bath. One of my roommates was in the bathtub, so I returned to my room and decided to go shopping. I put my coat on, picked up my towel and went back to the bathroom."

    "I was making shortbread and decided to double the amounts shown in the recipe. I doubled the first ingredient—butter—and forgot to double anything else."

    "I decided to make pancakes for breakfast. Then I remembered we didn't have any milk, so I decided not to bother. Five minutes later I started getting together the ingredients for pancakes, completely forgetting my change of mind."

    Response Category: _____

23. How often do you find yourself searching for something that you are actually carrying around with you?

    For example:

    "I went looking for my glasses. Then I realized I had them on."

    "I went to look for my keys, then discovered I had them in my hand all along."

    "I took out my pen and continued to search for it in my case."

    Response Category: _____

24. How often do you make mistakes in which some actions are repeated unnecessarily?

For example:

"I watered my begonia twice on the same day. I usually water it about twice a week."

"I combed my hair in front of the hall mirror, got my coat and then went to the mirror again to comb my hair although I had just done it."

"I was cleaning the car windows. I started with the windshield and then went round the car cleaning the other windows. When I got back to the front I started cleaning the windshield again quite unnecessarily."

Response Category: _____

25. How often do you "lose your place" in the course of carrying out some fairly routine activity?

For example:

"I was spooning coffee into my cup, and realized I had no idea of how many spoonfuls I'd put in."

"In the shower this morning, I 'came to' to find that I didn't know whether or not I had washed my hair. It was wet and there was no easy way of telling. I certainly couldn't remember."

"I didn't know whether I had put the water into the kettle. I had to lift the lid to check."

Response Category: _____

26. How often do you find yourself doing something which you have done many times before, but which is no longer appropriate because of changed circumstances?

For example:

"I wrote my parents' old address on the envelope in spite of the fact they had been at their new address for over three months."

"I had decided to cut down my sugar consumption and wanted to have my cornflakes without it. However, I sprinkled sugar on my cereal just as I had always done."

"We now have two refrigerators in our kitchen and yesterday we moved our food from one to the other. This morning I repeatedly opened the one that we used to have our food in."

Response Category: _____

No examples are given for the following items, but they are to be answered in exactly the same way as the previous ones

27. How often, in the course of a conversation, do you intend to say something and then forget what it was when the opportunity to speak arises?

    Response Category: _____

28. How often do you write down a reminder to yourself to do something, and then forget to consult it so that you fail to carry out the intended activity?

    Response Category: _____

29. How often are you struck by the feeling that you should be doing something, either at the present or in the near future, but you can't remember what it is?

    Response Category: _____

30. How often do you find, on returning to some familiar place, that your memory of it was quite inaccurate in certain respects?

    Response Category: _____

appendix ii
TABULATED RESULTS FROM THE EXTENDED DIARY STUDY

Table A. Nature of the Intended Actions

1. How *often* have you *successfully* carried out actions identical or very similar to those you *intended* on this occasion?

	1	2	3	4	5	6	7†	
HARDLY EVER	0.5*	1.6	2.1	3.1	8.3	14.6	69.8	VERY OFTEN

2. How *recently* did you *successfully* perform actions identical or very similar to those you intended on this occasion?

	1	2	3	4	5	6	7	
NOT FOR A LONG TIME	0*	1.5	4.2	3.7	10.4	17.7	62.5	VERY RECENTLY

3. To what extent were the *intended* actions ones that would *normally* be carried out in an *automatic* way without demanding close attention?

	1	2	3	4	5	6	7	
REQUIRED CONSTANT ATTENTION	1.0*	0.5	3.1	9.9	17.7	26.0	41.8	VERY AUTOMATIC

† Scale values:
*Percent errors associated with scale values (1–7) N = 192 errors.

Table B. Nature of the Erroneous Actions

1. Were the *wrong* actions on this occasion recognizable as being appropriate to some *other* task or activity?

YES: 40%   NO: 60%

2. (If 'Yes') To what *extent* were these wrong actions recognizable as belonging to this other activity?

	1	2	3	4	5	6	7	
ONLY JUST RECOGNIZABLE	1.3*	0	5.2	6.5	5.2	13.0	68.8	VERY CLEARLY RECOGNIZABLE

3. How *often* do you engage in this other activity?

	1	2	3	4	5	6	7	
HARDLY AT ALL	0*	1.3	3.9	1.3	13.0	22.1	58.4	VERY OFTEN

4. How *recently* have you engaged in this other activity?

	1	2	3	4	5	6	7	
NOT FOR A LONG TIME	1.3*	1.3	1.2	5.2	9.1	24.7	57.1	VERY RECENTLY

*Percent errors associated with scale values (1–7) N = 77 errors.

Table C. The Relationship Between Intended Actions and Other Activity

	1	2	3	4	5	6	7
Locations	6.5*	3.9	5.2	2.6	7.8	7.8	66.2
Movements	10.4	5.2	2.6	5.2	3.9	15.6	57.1
Objects	15.6	7.8	2.6	5.2	1.3	16.9	50.7
Timing	16.9	10.4	1.3	11.7	5.2	10.4	44.2
Purpose	23.4	7.8	3.9	7.8	10.4	7.8	38.9

Scale Values: 1—NOT AT ALL SIMILAR
                7—VERY SIMILAR
*Percent errors associated with scale values (1–7) N = 77 errors

Table D. Mental and Physical State at the Time of the Slip

	1	2	3	4	5	6	7
Preoccupied	6.4*	10.1	9.5	12.6	20.1	27.0	14.3
Upset/Worried	52.9	21.9	6.9	5.8	7.9	3.7	1.1
Emotional/ Excited	42.3	22.2	5.3	10.1	11.1	5.8	3.2
Tired/Sleepy	15.3	20.1	9.5	16.4	15.9	13.8	9.0
Unwell	50.0	22.9	6.4	5.8	9.6	3.7	1.6
Rushed	30.7	16.4	8.5	7.4	13.8	16.4	6.8

Scale Values: 1—NOT AT ALL
7—FEELING VERY . . . .
*Percent errors associated with scale values (1–7) N = 192 errors.

Table E. Circumstances Prevailing at the Time of the Slip

1. How *familiar* to you were the surroundings in which the slip occurred?

	1	2	3	4	5	6	7	
NOT AT ALL	1.1*	0	2.6	1.6	3.1	11.5	80.1	VERY FAMILIAR

2. How *bothersome* were your surroundings at the time that the slip was made (*e.g.* too noisy, cold, hot, bright, dark, etc., etc.)?

	1	2	3	4	5	6	7	
NOT AT ALL	48.2*	26.7	7.3	8.9	3.1	4.7	1.1	VERY BOTHERSOME

3. To what extent did something other than your own thoughts *distract* your attention?

	1	2	3	4	5	6	7	
NOT AT ALL	2.6*	10.0	15.2	6.7	7.9	20.9	36.7	I WAS VERY DISTRACTED

*Percent errors associated with scale values (1– 7) N = 192 errors.